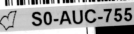

Springtime in Italy

Springtime in Italy:
A READER
ON NEO-REALISM

Edited and translated
by David Overbey

"Realism in itself is not art, but there must be harmony
between the genuineness of feelings and the genuineness of things."
Carl-Theodor Dreyer

Archon Books
Hamden, Connecticut

First published in 1978 in Great Britain by
Talisman Books, London WC2H 0HR
and in the United States in 1979 as an
Archon Book, an imprint of
The Shoe String Press, Inc.
995 Sherman Avenue, Hamden, Conn. 06514

This translation and introduction
© David Overbey 1978
All rights reserved.
Cover and typography by Stephen Lubell

Library of Congress Cataloging in Publication Data
Main entry under title:

Springtime in Italy

  Bibliography: p.
  1. Realism in moving-pictures—Addresses, essays,
lectures. 2. Moving-pictures—Political aspects
—Addresses, essays, lectures. 3. Moving-pictures—
Italy—Addresses, essays, lectures. I. Overbey,
David.
PN1995.9.R3S6 1979   791.43'0909'12   79-11858
ISBN 0-208-01824-7

Printed in Great Britain

For
two incredibly fine ladies I am lucky enough
to have as friends
Lily Latté Lang
and
Kathy Bristow

Contents

Acknowledgements

The Italians say *"traduttore-traditore"* ("translator-traitor") and they are usually right. The Italians have a somewhat more robust sense of rhetoric than the Anglo-Saxons. Often faced with full-flowing and labyrinthine sentences, it seemed I was never going to get out alive. In such cases I cut my way through, hoping to make up in clarity what I lost in style, although I tried at least to keep some of the flavour of the originals. I hope that none of the original authors have been betrayed by any of the translations in this collection. If they have, I am, of course, to blame. If they have not, credit must go to several people who helped me in getting the Italian and French into English: Martine Nicolas (Paris), Maurine Bergeaud (Paris), and David Pierce (Paris).

I also owe a good deal to Francesco Rosi (Rome) for discussing both his own films and his working days with Luchino Visconti with me; to the late and sorely missed Roberto Rossellini, to Gian-Luigi Rondi (Rome), to Lotte Eisner (Paris) for talking with me about neo-realism. I must also thank Eugene Rizzo of Rome's *Variety* office for his research assistance, and Lino Miccichè (Rome) for making it possible for me to see about one hundred films of the neo-realist period at the *Mostra Internazionale del Cinema* (Pesaro).

My publisher Kevin Gough-Yates must also be singled out for his boundless patience which I tried excessively.

If I have already thanked him for his help with the translations, I must thank him again. David Pierce helped with this book in a hundred ways. It certainly would not exist without him.

ix

1. Introduction
by David Overbey

When asked if he were a neo-realist, Roberto Rossellini replied

> ... neo-realism,[1] but what does that mean? You know, there was a Congress in Parma on neo-realism, and they discussed the term for a long time, but it remained undefined. Most of the time it is only a label. For me, it is above all, a moral position from which to look at the world. It then became an aesthetic position, but at the beginning it was moral.[2]

If Rossellini is ultimately right in suggesting that "neo-realism" is impossible to define, or is a label of journalistic convenience, like "New Wave", one can still delimit the term in several ways. Neo-realism did, after all, exist: a large number of films were made in Italy, from the early Forties to the mid Fifties, which shared at least, a certain appearance, manner, and area of subject. They were made by directors and writers, who, allowing for individual differences in sensibility, style and motivation, shared a number of theoretical assumptions about the nature of cinema and the world it presented. Nonetheless, it might be more useful to relinquish the term itself, for the moment, as well as the problems raised by a "movement" which was discussed by a large number of people, but to which no one, except Cesare Zavattini, would finally admit belonging, in order first to understand Rossellini's statement that neo-realism was a moral and ethical position before it was an aesthetic. To do that, and to understand the social, political and economic circumstances from which the movement sprang, it is necessary to review, as briefly as possible, the history of Italy from the beginning of the Fascist period, through the war, to the "restoration of normality"[3], although this essay, to a certain extent, assumes that the reader has some knowledge of the period.

Numerous critics, scholars and directors have linked the ethical and moral aspects of neo-realism to a "cultural renewal", carried out through and beyond a "second *Risorgimento*" and the "war of liberation". The age-old problems of Italy — chronic poverty in the South, unemployment, social alienation in the industrial cities, illiteracy, the unequal distribution of land, and a vast gulf between social classes, matched only by the void existing between creative intellectuals and a popular audience — were still very much present during the early Twenties when Mussolini came to power. In spite of the hopes that the Fascists might solve these problems — and for a few years, at least, some of them were ameliorated, Mussolini attracting support from surprising sources, none too soon it became clear that the "Fascist revolution" was hopelessly bourgeois and ineffective. The early hostility of the urban working class and the farmer towards Fascism was allayed for a time when industrial and agricultural production increased and wages remained high. The new government was given the *imprimatur*; the "Conciliation" between the Holy See and the Fascists was accomplished, according to terms under which the Fascists were officially recognized by the Vatican in return for the ratification of the Lateran Treaty; this was then incorporated into the constitution. The terms of the treaty were that: the Italian government accepted the papal sovereignty over Vatican City (which had been an irritant for centuries); Catholicism became the official state religion and would be taught in all state schools; the religious marriage ceremony had civil effect.

Mussolini's government was further legitimated and strengthened by statements by foreign politicians like that of the British Chancellor of the Exchequer, Winston Churchill, on June 20 1927, that if he had been Italian he would have been a Fascist from the start, a sentiment promptly seconded by the British Prime Minister, Stanley Baldwin. Described as "the man sent by Providence" by Pius XI, it was not surprising, given the single-list voting system which meant that there was no choice between parties, that in the 1929 elections, the affirmations of Mussolini totalled 8,506,576. Only 131,198 negative votes were cast.

As Giuliano Procacci has pointed out,[4] and as had been true for centuries, there was an unsettling discrepancy between official rhetoric and reality in Italy. Although the rhetoric portrayed the Fascist movement, in near rapturous terms, as a "glorious revolution in progress", in reality, it was far more a crystallised self-restoration of a

2

reactionary class structure permeating all sectors of society. The vulgarly ostentatious apartment buildings newly constructed in the centre of Rome, like more official structures, served aptly as a symbol of the verbal and moral rhetoric of the state. They had no effect in solving the misery of inadequate housing on the outskirts of Rome, nor, for that matter, in the rest of Italy, and were hardly constructed to promote human happiness, although people proudly pointed to their façades. How indeed, those grotesque buildings functioned to control behaviour is, in part, the subject of Ettore Scola's filmed reconstruction of the period: *Una giornata particolare* (1977).

Behind the rhetoric there was nothing — or at least, very little. Alberto Moravia's first novel *Gli indifferenti* (1929), portrayed the cynical void in the middle-class intellect; it is hardly by accident that Pirandello (who proved himself not entirely unsympathetic to Fascism) wrote many of his, mostly unpopular, plays about the nature of illusion and reality during this period.

As the international recession of the late Twenties and early Thirties began to damage it economically, the Italian state attempted to apply a number of solutions. It nationalised several industries; it supported others through subsidies; it manipulated import tariffs. Nonetheless, production dwindled, wages dropped, the standard of living fell, and unemployment rose. Working-class protest was quickly suppressed by a government which possessed controlling interest in most major corporations. The wave of rhetoric increased to accompany rising discontent and to disguise totalitarian Fascist policies. Through censorship and government control of publishing, radio broadcasting, and the film industry — Cinecittà, the gigantic film studio complex on the outskirts of Rome was built by the government — artistic expression and public communication were formulated to fit official rhetoric. If books were published which appeared critical, they were quickly suppressed, as happened to works by Moravia, Vittorini and others. The "white telephone" films of the period reflected the official view of prosperity and well-being, even in the glistening surface of the images themselves. Middle class fantasies romantically extolled the joys of country living and emphasised a mystic connection with the land, even as labourers were aggravating the unemployment problem by leaving the farms to look for work in the cities. In no sector of Italian life was reality permitted to express itself. To make doubly sure that uncomfortable questions would not be raised, even among the privileged, and to reinforce the tradition of class-conscious education in the humanities, Giovanni Gentile was appointed Minister of Education. Under the guise of educational reform, university professors were required to sign an oath of loyalty to the state. Only eleven refused.

It is customary for states with apparently insoluble domestic difficulties to turn to foreign policy to bolster their sagging prestige. Italy went to war with Ethiopia: visions of rich farmland and vast mineral deposits tempted bourgeois and peasant alike. Industrial production took a swing upward as the demand for war supplies grew. The short war was politically costly: Italy's diplomatic relationships with England and France degenerated, and its image abroad began to tarnish, especially as the League of Nations was unable to introduce effective sanctions. Italy, along with Hitler's Germany, entered the Spanish Civil War in support of the Falangists. The fear of Communism, so prevalent in the bastions of capitalistic conservatism, meant that England, France, and the United States, were not totally opposed to such intervention. They had decided on a pragmatic policy of non intervention themselves. Italy and Germany, therefore, were brought closer in an alliance which led to a "Pact of Steel". Although the action in Spain had not been widely popular in Italy, in spite of the open resistance among many of Mussolini's own ministers and the country's lack of preparation for war, Italy was drawn inexorably into the Second World War. Mussolini increased the level of rhetoric as if words were both fact and action. He dramaticaly pictured eight million Italian bayonets (at the beginning of the war, only one million Italians were soldiers), impregnable tanks (Italy had four hundred small ones) and a gallant air force (consisting of just over one thousand well-used airplanes incapable of making long-distance flights), all ever-ready and anxious to conquer any and every enemy (the Italian population was unenthusiastic for the war, and, for once, was vocal about it). The old inability to confront reality came full circle as Hitler tried to compel Mussolini to deliver all that his rhetoric had promised. There is a possibility, of course, that Mussolini *was* aware of his situation and, seeing how easily France had fallen, had concluded that the war would be over quickly and that he would not have to deliver the goods. As it was, he could not.

4

The resistance to Fascism in Italy, if not total, was multivarious. Benedetto Croce, the leading intellectual, had been equivocal, even approving of certain of its aspects, but in 1925, with the murder of Matteotti (the Socialist member of parliament who was outspokenly opposed to Mussolini) Croce edited a manifesto criticising the government, signed by forty leading personalities. He then loftily and ambiguously retired to his study in Naples, where he wrote a *History of Italy* and a *History of Europe*, both of which were only anti-Fascist in the narrow sense of being "histories of liberty". Croce's review *La Critica* was also élitist in its anti-Fascism — intellectual and dignified. It is clear that Croce never really grappled with Fascism in his work, neither to analyse the causes, nor to reflect upon its results. Instead, it appeared that his solution was to outwait it in the hope of re-establishing the Italy of the century's first decade. The self removal of Croce to an only semi-public ivory tower left many Italian intellectuals without a respectable rallying flag and achieved little.

Croce's attitudes were more practically felt by numerous liberal and left-wing Italians exiled in Paris (Treves, Modigliani, Turati and others) who founded an anti-Fascist newspaper, *La Libertà*. Others, (Parri, Gobetti, and Rosselli, among the rest) believed that the Fascists had played on the weaknesses and lack of unity of pre-Fascist liberals. They argued that post-Fascist Italy would have to be ideologically different and have to be founded on the basis of Libertarian Socialism. They organised the "Justice and Liberty Party" the purpose of which was to engage in "subversive" activities, including sabotage and the dropping of anti-Fascist leaflets over Milan.

The most unified and active of anti-Fascist groups were Communists who viewed the other factions as naive and ineffective. Effective anti-Fascist action, they argued, had to be mounted within Italy, as a movement of the people — workers, peasants, and leftist intellectuals united in a common aim. They managed to publish their newspaper *L'Unità* with regularity, to organise workers in the factories, and, in general, to keep their organization intact, in spite of it being banned and of consequent harassment by the Government's Special Tribunal — a court devoted specifically to dealing with anti-Fascist activities.

The most significant intellectual leader to arise among the Communists was Antonio Gramsci. His thought continues to inform and provide a basis for the Italian Communist Party which he helped to found. Of more importance and relevance here, however, is his work as a social and cultural critic, which cannot be over-estimated. It was necessary, he argued, to analyse the objective aspects of Italian society in order to understand what had occurred and therefore to see what might be done. The analysis must be kept free of dogma and preconceptions which would pre-determine any answers. Fascism was, for him, merely the most brutal and most current expression of the industrial/agrarian/bourgeois complex which had always occupied the top level of Italy's class structure, and which influenced every level of Italian life, including — perhaps especially — education and culture. In some ways, indeed, Croce's thought was a form of that expression, particularly in his insistence that art exists external to time and social reality. The racism of the industrial North against "*gli africani*" of the rural South was, according to Gramsci, one more way in which the ruling class reinforced disunion amongst the working class. Gramsci proposed an organized link between the industrial workers of the North and the peasants of the South in order to oppose their mutual oppression. Further, he maintained that any Marxist state which might evolve in Italy would, of necessity, have to grow naturally out of particularly Italian problems and from the Italian temperament and situation. It would also have to remain open to diversity, constant questioning, and change. If he embraced Lenin's idea of an alliance between workers and peasants, he rejected the developments in the Soviet Union towards strict systemizations of ideology and its hardening into a bureaucracy as oppressive as that which it sought to replace. Gramsci's ideas exerted a profound influence on Italian progressive thought. Their power is reflected in the answer of a Communist intellectual and artist like Elio Vittorini to problems of politics and culture proposed by Palmiro Togliatti. His essay is essential reading in so far as it provides a rich and multi-faceted backdrop against which most of the events and arguments in the neo-realist movement took place.

Togliatti, who, with Gramsci, had co-founded the Italian Communist Party, tended, for pragmatic reasons, to hew closer to the line of strict class solidarity and loyalty to the Soviet Union, although he too was much affected by Gramsci's thought — he too believed in a uniquely Italian path for Communism and was certainly prepared to make various compromises in the light of Italian historical reality. Gramsci's ideas, today more than ever, are operating as a motive force in Italian political and cultural life.

The war never went well for Italy. Mussolini attempted to explain to Hitler, privately, and to the Italian people, publically, (in theatrical speeches from his balcony overlooking the Piazza Venezia), why the facts failed to match the rhetoric, but did not disclose that the "parallel war" was an illusion and that Italy had become merely the lackey of Nazi Germany. The best that could be hoped for Italy was to save enough face and to have a share in whatever divisions of territory might be made after the war. The Italian people, aware of the failure of Fascism at all levels had real reason to put an end to it and, by hopeful extension, the war. Conditions at home were chaotic. Privation was the order of the day for everyone, except Fascist leaders; they corrupted the little remaining system and then resorted to the ever-expanding black market. When news reached Italy from the Russian front that as many Italian soldiers had died from the cold, (because their German "allies" had refused to give them transportation), as had died from Russian bullets, they decided to put an end to it. With military defeats reported on every front, the anti-Fascists finally united and moved into the open. In Turin, in December 1942, socialists, Communists, liberals, and two recently organized parties, the Action Party (composed largely of members of the old "Justice and Liberty" group) and the Christian Democrats, formed a joint committee. The workers of Fiat and other large industries went on strike, first in Turin and then in Milan.

On 25 July 1943, members of the ruling class, of the Fascist Party itself, and of the military who wanted to withdraw from the war by first separating Italy from Germany, and then sueing for peace with the Allies, managed, with the King's assistance, to remove Mussolini from power and arrest him. Events then became complex and confused, and led to the "war of liberation", the circumstances of which gave birth to neo-realism proper. Marshal Pietro Badoglio was appointed by the King to head the new government, which then attempted simultaneously to keep the Germans at bay with rather transparent lies, and to manipulate the Allies into giving the easiest surrender terms possible, with ominous threats of the fear of "Communist takeover". Unconditional surrender was nevertheless the result; the King, Badoglio, and most government and military officials fled by boat to Pescara and the safety of Allied occupation in the South and left Italy without a government. Mussolini was rescued by the Germans who sent him to Lake Garda to set up his puppet Salò Republic. The Allies and the King held the South; the Germans invaded. No one ruled, save by direct force of arms.

The Badoglio government then declared war on Germany. The Vatican — ever alert to changes in the political wind — gave its full support to the new government and the King. The Communists, the Action Party, and numerous other anti-Fascist organizations united with the Italian Army to repel the German invasion. Although progressive groups had called for the eradication of the monarchy as the first step toward Italian post-war renewal, pressure was applied by Croce, by the British Prime Minister, Winston Churchill, and the Allied Front in general, to retain at least the figure of the king. This ideological division split the anti-Fascist/anti-Nazi front, at which point, Togliatti, aware of Stalin's policy regarding "spheres of influence" after the war, agreed with Croce's compromise: the King would turn his powers over to his son, the title would be held in abeyance, until a referendum could be held after the war on the form that Italian government was to take. A new government was formed by Badoglio, which included all the anti-Fascist groups except the Action Party.

Resistance to Fascism grew stronger and more widespread, to be met with Nazi brutality on one hand and Allied Command mistrust and hostility to partisans, especially to Communist partisans, on the other. When the Allies entered Rome in 1944, Badoglio handed over the government to a new cabinet headed by Bonomi and including representatives of all the anti-Fascist groups, which declared itself a manifestation of the Committee of National Liberation. This move particularly upset Churchill who, with the other Allies, was worried over the political implications, for it was becoming clear that in a large number of areas, including the heavily industralised Po Valley, "liberated" by the Allies, the Resistance had taken control. The National Committee of Liberation had also fostered an insurrection in the North and had captured and executed Mussolini; they would have to be dealt with as equals when the Allies finally arrived in Milan.

8

At this point the "involution" or degeneration so often referred to in discussions of Italian neo-realism and Italian culture in relationship to political and social life occurred. The "War of Liberation" had been fought by men with articulate ideas about the future of society. Although ideas differed according to the group to which they belonged, they held in common that a regression to the society out of which Fascism in Italy first evolved was not what they were fighting for. Clear as they were about this, they misread the mood of the people and underestimated the cunning and power of conservative forces, not only in Italy, but outside as well.

The miseries undergone by the Italians, represented in films like *Roma città aperta* were real. It was, indeed, the brute force of that reality which made most people want to move rapidly through it and to forget. It became unspoken, but official policy to refuse to examine the operative causal factors of what had happened in order to prevent a similar occurrence. In the South, the American military came to terms with the Mafia, which was, it could be said, not only anti-Fascist (they had been hounded by a Fascist government jealous of its power in the South) but, better still, anti-Communist, (the Communist Party had maintained an organization among the peasants and was a threat to Mafia power in the region). This involvement was a matter of naiveté, as much as of corruption, both of which are illustrated by Francesco Rosi in his film *Lucky Luciano* (1973).

The Christian Democrat Party, the stronghold of which was in the North, soon spread throughout the country. Led by Alcide de Gasperi, who had been a librarian at the Vatican during the Fascist period, the Christian Democrats now became the rallying point for the conservative elements in Italy (especially the Vatican, with its broadly based hold over the rural population) as well as the centre liberals. Well nourished anti-Communist paranoia, fed by propaganda from the United States, the Vatican, and other conservative elements within Italy, brought the Christian Democrats to power in an uneasy coalition with the Communists and socialists. It did not take long for the Communists to be manipulated out of government, by the manoeuvering of de Gasperi, assisted by the left's own disunity and lack of clear-cut policy. The Constitution was rewritten, but retained several Fascist codes — including Article Seven, the Lateran Treaty of "Conciliation" — and Italy joined the North Atlantic Treaty Organization. The country had been truly "restored to normality".

II

The ethical and moral position of neo-realism was, in part, born in the "War of Liberation" and was dedicated to exploring and exposing the rhetorical lies of the Fascist period and to confronting the social reality of the present. Lies and equivocations had caused Italy's calamities and it was thought that the "truth" would save her, but, of course, the people had to be confronted to understand the totality of the truth. As a product of a "War of Liberation", of a kind of revolution, its artistic expression might continue the battle to success where politics had failed. This seems to have been the stance of many creators of, and commentators on, neo-realism, whose reasoning grew more and more desperate as it became clear that the long awaited revolution was not to come. The very expression of it through cinema, was atrophying because of its *own* "involution" and because applied pressure from the newly "restored" establishment co-existed with the growing hostility (or worse, indifference) of the very audiences film-makers were trying to educate. Film makers might well have heeded Orlindo Guerrini's words about the parallel situation in Italy concerning realist literature in 1878: "Art never modified the aspirations of a people or a society, but the opposite. Art does not make revolutions, but follows and supports them."[5]

The moral position of "seeing things as they are" accompanied by a corresponding analysis in order that the whole of reality might be understood, existed, in fact, more in the theory and criticism of neo-realism than it did in the films themselves, which failed to analyse the lies of Fascism. Although social problems form the basis of content in many neo-realist films, few are dealt with in any depth; many of them end with either desperate resignation or a sentimental mysticism at odds with the means of expression itself.[6] One of the supposed masterpieces of the movement, for example, De Sica's *Ladri di biciclette*, has the problem of unemployment in the city as its pivot (few films dealt with the problems of urban workers employed or not), yet, instead of treating the "total reality" of the problem the film degenerates into a sentimental, albeit often effective, tale of grace lost and restored, constantly reinforcing bourgeois notions about the sacredness of property.[7] Although a large number of directors and scriptwriters were leftist in sentiment, few of them were either Marxists or Communists. The attacks on neo-realism as being "Communist inspired", and the emphasis by many critics on Soviet cinematic "realism" as an influence on the movement were wide of the point. Neo-realist films never really approached Marxist solutions to social problems. In *Il cammino della speranza* for example (putting aside its turgid melodrama) the unemployed and dispossessed mine workers survive, to a degree, by sticking together. At the end of the film, they are still dispossessed but led toward hope by a "strong leader" across the border into Switzerland in the search for work, a road which more and more Italian labourers were later to take. Even Vergano's *Il sole sorge ancora* cannot be seen in socialist terms; the equivocal "unification of the people" comes during a communal prayer led by a priest before his execution with a partisan.

Only Rossellini and Visconti, of the original neo-realists, managed to maintain their original moral vision throughout their careers, but they were obliged to shift their terms of expression and widen their areas of examination to a point where most leftist critics and theorists disowned them both, with accusations of "involution" and "betrayal". The very term "betrayal" which is frequently used in critical essays, is, in itself, something of an indication of the critical problems involved: these had more to do with politics than aesthetics and were based on narrow definitions of the "reality" proper for neo-realist representation. With the exception of Zavattini, most neo-realist directors and writers chose to make their ethical and aesthetic statements in their films rather than in theoretical essays. The theory that was created by critics to support and define neo-realism was developed after the fact. Few contemporary critics attempted to follow and understand what the film makers were attempting when they shifted away from the theoretical constructs which the critics themselves had devised. Rossellini is an important case in point, particularly as he was almost universally attacked in both contemporary and later essays by critics of the left, right and centre. He is discussed at greater length below.

The moral position of neo-realism was also expressed in terms different from social ones, although one was never far from "social reality" in discussing it. According to Cesare Zavattini: neo-realism consisted of the principles of love and understanding of others, as those others actually exist, "with their own real first name and their

11

real family name". To represent man as he is, however, requires the elimination of invented story and character entirely, in order that "real and ordinary" men can themselves tell their own stories to the audience. This, in turn, requires a director to follow and to observe ordinary men engaged in ordinary activities. The goal is to establish a common understanding and recognition between audience and film. Although Zavattini is often called "the father of neo-realism", being the movement's most famous theorist and the author of scripts for many of the major films, there is no single neo-realistic film which fulfills his ideas; the possible exception is a sequence only in *Umberto D* in which the camera merely observes a maid getting out of bed, getting dressed, and preparing breakfast.

Yet another aspect of the moral position was what Gramsci called "popular-national" art: that which would grow organically from the particular environment, problems, character, emotions, and mentality of the Italian people, almost as an expression of a popular soul, and which would, at the same time, be truly national in origin. Such art should then flow back and nourish its original source. Here, too, however, the neo-realist situation is ambiguous. It was clear that the majority of Italian film-goers had very little use for the purer forms of neo-realism. It is a myth that *none* of the films were successful at the Italian box office, but not that neo-realist directors had to depend to a large degree on foreign receipts to show a small profit. In Ettore Scola's *C'eravamo tanto amati* (1974), Nicola is a teacher in a small Italian town. He attends a screening of *Ladri di biciclette* in 1948, after which a fight breaks out when he defends the film against the mostly political hostility of his fellow townsfolk. He is accused of being a dangerous leftist, is fired, and ends up alone in Rome scratching out a meagre living as a film critic. The individual case, as Scola presents it, is doubtless rather extreme, but the strong reactions of film-goers against neo-realist films, in favour of American cinema, in particular, is all too accurate. There were ways of dealing with the problem, of course, while continuing to make films which mirrored the reality of the Italian audience and attempting to motivate it towards change. In the opinion of critics and theorists, one tended to see films which led further and further away from the original moral position of neo-realism. Their neo-realist manner merely disguised melodramas which attracted and entertained popular audiences.

12

Riso amaro, in which De Santis ostensibly treated the problems of agricultural workers in the rice fields of the Po Valley, was an enormous financial success of this kind. The film treats its social content as a side issue and concentrates on the not inconsiderable physical attractions of Silvana Mangano, her tribulations over a false diamond bracelet, and a robbery plan during her lusty affair with a young thief.

Indeed, very few of the supposed basic tenets of neo-realism were actually observed in practice. Real people from the streets, for example, were supposed to replace professional actors in the playing of characters much like themselves, and thus to "liberate" the screen from the artificiality of acting. Aside from the basic absurdity of the idea, springing as it does from a confused notion of "reality" and an over-reaction to the falsity of "stars" as opposed to actors, it was rarely applied, except in secondary roles. To portray a down-at-the-heels retired functionary, De Sica hired an aging professor who had little other than advanced age in common with the character of *Umberto D*. The professsor was very effective in the convincing *performance* he gave, but not because "he was the character". Anna Magnani, herself a well-known actress, played in film after film, as did a great number of other professional actors from the stage, radio, and film. The illusion of "non-acting" was a matter of a style and appearance, different from that prevalent in the artificial "white telephone" films of Fascist Italy (and most glamorous Hollywood products). A matter of style, however, is not quite the same thing as a matter of "absolute reality". Only Visconti used non-professionals for the *entire* cast of a neo-realistic film, and then only once, in *La terra trema*. Again, however, it was a matter of Visconti, a great director of actors, drawing great *performances* from his village fishermen.

What was actually *new* in neo-realism *was* its style — a new set of conventions to be shared by film makers and audiences which were accepted as "being more real" than those of earlier films. Of course, even the *new* in *neo*-realism depends upon one's perspective. If there was a "new" realism, it presupposes an "old". Critics, looking outside Italy, have pointed to various possible influences on and origins of the movement — that is to the "old" realism. France and *"réalisme poétique"* is the most often cited, with Renoir generally conceded to be the major foreign influence. Certainly there is a good deal to be said for resemblances between the best of neo-realism and the films of Renoir: an open, seemingly loosely-knit narrative, a focus on the environment and its organic relationship to the characters and their actions, a refusal to make facile judgements about human action, and, almost always, a level of performance which belies the fact of acting. It is also clear that French cinema also exerted a less fortunate influence through the films of Carné, Clair, and Duvivier, whose poetic veneer of semi-sweet cynicism and sentimental resignation mar the work of the lesser French realists as much as the lesser Italian neo-realists.

Another "realism" cited as influential from outside Italy was that of the American cinema — which one critic traces back to Tom Mix — but which most are satisfied to centre about a discussion of the films of King Vidor. The degree of such influence of neo-realist directors (as opposed to critics) depends upon how many such films were available to them, in the light of the suspension just before the war of the importation of American films. Some directors have commented on their own film-going; Rosi remembers best Jean Harlow and Franchot Tone, while Antonioni speaks glowingly of American documentaries like Pare Lorenz's *The river*. Certain individual films, like Vidor's *The crowd*, were widely seen, but would seem only natural footnotes to neo-realist theory and practice. (It would be more to the point to consider the American influence on Italian film production and distribution towards the very end of neo-realism, which was considerable and not always healthy). American literature, on the other hand, played an important and more direct part in forming the neo-realist sensibility. Although many authors are cited, the most important writer must remain, at least on the practical level, James M. Cain, whose novel *The postman always rings twice* was adapted by Visconti for his first film, *Ossessione*, which, in turn, played a major role in determining the "look" of neo-realist films, even if its attitude towards character was rather too strong for most directors to imitate undiluted.

Within Italy, however, a genuine heritage of indigenous realism already existed; it is mentioned again and again to demonstrate that neo-realism was not only *the* long-awaited "popular-national" art form, but also the legitimate direction which Italian film should take. There is a division of theory here. Zavattini and the "purists" maintained that, even if a narrative is allowed in neo-realist cinema, it must "come directly from the people" and must never be derived from novels and plays — a rule which no one, not even Zavattini himself, followed. Others claimed that to follow the narrative methods of Giovanni Verga would both further and insure the purity of Italian neo-realism.

When speaking of realism and Italy, even more than when speaking about realism and the cinema, it is wise to be cautious. The plays of Pirandello indicate the problems involved, but it might be remembered that any number of opera composers and librettists have been accused in their own time of an excess of realism, Verdi included. *Nabucco*, after all, was chosen to reopen La Scala after the war in 1946 because of its "realistic" political content.

It is often pointed out by historians of the Italian cinema that there was a brief period during the second decade of the century, particularly around Naples, when "realistic" cinema flourished: Martoglio's *Sperduti nel buio* (1914) is the most often cited example. When I once suggested to Francesco Rosi that his *C'era una volta* seemed an odd film for him to have made in the light of his other films which are "social" and "realistic", he laughed:

> Well it's not as bizarre as all that! Actually ... I wanted to make a fairy story, but one which had a rather realistic colouration. Do you know Basile, the great Sicilian writer of fairy stories who wrote *Lo cunto dei cunti*? Those have a Neopolitan flavour. You know there is a very strong stream of realism in Neopolitans, so that the fairy stories too are rather realistic: the dream is to be able to eat a lot and to wear clothes like a princess. In *C'era una volta* I tried for something of that realism, so that there is the hero's relationship with his mother (he is a bit weak in that area like many men), and there is a focus on pasta and cooking.[8]

For the most part, however, the Italian cinema followed the example of a film like Pastrone's *Cabiria* (1914) and plunged into the making of historical epics, the kind of film that first brought Italian cinema to the attention of international audiences and influenced even D.W. Griffith with its length, and the scope of its content. Italian cinema repeatedly returns to such films when other streams of national production dry up. The Hercules films of the Fifties and Sixties are in direct descent from the Maciste series (which are, even now, still made from time to time) and *Cabiria*.

III

The pointing, by various critics, to a realistic tradition in Italian literature is even more apposite here. Indeed, the entire series of arguments about realism, culture, moral position, and all the rest, in many ways had already been rehearsed during the final half of the Nineteenth Century, over *verismo, realismo,* and *naturalismo*. Such discussions do not, of course, take place in a social and cultural vacuum, and in order to trace the tradition of realism and the arguments over it, the state of the cultural environment needs to be clarified.

Alberto Moravia asked, in 1944: "For whom do we write?" His description of the great gulf between the serious artist and the public can apply just as aptly to the Nineteenth Century, when the upper and middle classes comprised the majority of the reading public. In the latter half of the Nineteenth Century, the prime subject of the novel was the bourgeoisie, described usually in much the same romantic and rhetorical manner as in the "white telephone" period of Italian film. Literature was written in Tuscan, the standard Italian used for cultural and legal purposes and taught in schools, but seldom used by ordinary people in their daily lives. It was an intellectual language divorced from the masses who spoke some forty different dialects. Thus the supposed national cultural unity represented by the *Risorgimento* was a literary concept which left the masses largely indifferent.[9]

As a *symbol* of national unity, however, the preservation of Tuscan remained all-important. Even those artists who believed in the necessity of social and cultural evolution (if not revolution) remained steadfastly traditional when it came to modifying it. Many writers on neo-realism came to believe that neo-realism, which had been seen as the expression of potential change in society, might in itself institute change, just as many writers and literary critics of the Nineteenth century had come to regard Tuscan as the *means* to unity,

16

generally ignoring the fact that ordinary people continued to speak their local language and that literature written in Tuscan was read only by a very small percentage of the "Italian nation". The situation was still far removed from Gramsci's ideal of "popular-national" culture. Ironically, those writers who wished to treat the "whole of Italian reality" to touch and unite Italians, achieved exactly the opposite effect in their use of Tuscan; they spoke only to those of their own social class and further widened the gap between classes. As G.M. Carsaniga observed:

> The real scandal was that a bourgeois pastime was masquerading as the national literature, that a ruling-class culture pretended to be the national culture, when three quarters of the population were not merely uneducated but illiterate, while only a minority of the remaining quarter ever read books. What was unrealistic was to shut one's eyes to the absurdity of such a pretension, to refuse to see it for what it was — one symptom among others of the same social injustice and class exploitation that *veristi* writers were all too ready to denounce.[10]

It is probably not really necessary here to distinguish too finely between "verism" and "realism", save to remark that the first term is immediately associated with those realistic Italian writers of the Nineteenth Century who were concerned primarily with working class people and their problems (particularly in the South) and what they maintained was "objectivity". In doing so, the verists opened the door to the use of dialect as a legitimate means of literary expression. For most people, however, the use of dialect in novels and stories was another means of "objective observation" and, like most of the problems and situations described, was regarded by middle-class readers as exotic and removed from their own "reality".

Contributing to this was the influence of French naturalism, the effect of which was that for many Italian writers of the time there was no longer a place for judgement nor a push for social reform, since the characters described were usually subject to immutable "natural law" and the description of their plight in "detached, scientific, and objective" terms was something of an end in itself. Shaw's distinction between realism and naturalism as a matter of social and moral arbitration is useful here.

One of the stated goals of the verists was the social education of their readers, but, aside from the fact that very few bourgeois were deeply radicalized by their work, the work itself did not reach the class which might have drawn from it a sustaining core of shared indignity and oppression upon which to build a unified and effective protest. Instead (like neo-realism) in order to reach a more popular audience, the novels and stories assumed the *manner* of realism, re-telling standard shop-girl fantasies that gained added spice by the introduction of biologically and socially "rude" material. The added sensationalism was, of course, excused on the respectable moral basis of "reflecting reality" for the social edification of the reader. A few titles will indicate easily enough what popular verism had become: Tronconi's *Passione maledetta* (Accursed passion, 1875), *Madri ... per ridere* (Make-believe mothers, 1871), or Mariani's *Gli amori di una kellerina* (The loves of a barmaid, 1888). Had film makers half a century later, been writers instead, doubtless Lattuada, Comencini, and De Santis could easily have joined them with their *Il mulino del Po, Pane, amore e fantasia,* and *Riso amaro.*

Nevertheless, there did exist another mode of realistic novels and stories on the highest level of achievement, and, as Giuseppe De Santis continually pointed out when he was a critic, Giovanni Verga provided the richest vein here. The latter's position as a theorist, however, is vague, with equivocation and ambiguity marking the spaces between his espoused intentions and what he actually does. In his prefaces, he speaks of removing the artist's personality from a novel in order to present a "human document" through almost scientific analysis. This sounds, of course, very much like Zavattini on the cinema, but Verga was too much the poet to be able, finally, to remove himself, his understanding and sympathy for men too great to treat them as mere objects of study. He also embraced a larger view of realism — derived evidently from Edmond de Goncourt — in which he affirmed the duty of realism to investigate every level of society, a stand which the defenders of Antonioni, Visconti, and even Rossellini properly took later when the directors were accused of "betraying" neo-realism. While Verga never completed his cycle, *I vinti,* to include the upper classes, his masterpiece, *I malavoglia,* the first section of the planned cycle, demonstrates that he was not content solely to observe, nor solely to treat the characters as mere puppets in a pre-determined biological or social system; both however, exist as facets of the struggle of his Sicilian fishermen for survival and dignity. To be victorious in the struggle demands human solidarity, which is still a possibility for those who are not yet the prisoners of the many illusions of the middle classes as in *Maestro Don Gesualdo*. This theme is also to be found in those supposedly "involuted betrayers" of neo-realism, Visconti, Antonioni, and Rossellini, who were among the very few to perceive the possibility of man's redemption from oppressive illusions and unbearable reality. It is not inherent in realism that the characters be defeated — an idea closer to the usual pessimism of naturalism — yet this is often the result both in literary verism and in neo-realism. One explanation of this is suggested by Carsaniga: "to be 'defeated by life' is a natural subject for bourgeois *verisimo* . . . unable to free himself from his class ideology and to understand and express reality, the *verista* can achieve nothing more significant than to celebrate consciously and conscientiously his own defeat by chronicling the defeat of his characters."[11] Those who were able to free themselves, however, were able to create works in which the surface expression of reality reflected a "higher reality" far more vividly than a careful observation of atmosphere and detail alone could provide, an achievement illustrated by Verga himself, as well as by films like *Viaggio in Italia, Stromboli, Ossessione, La terra trema,* and *Rocco e i suoi fratelli* (in the last three of which, the immediate seeming defeat of major characters differs considerably from the ultimately and deeply sentimental defeated resignation displayed in the films of De Sica, De Santis, and Lattuada).

IV

If, then, there are a number of "old" realisms to consider when discussing neo-realism, one is still left without a precise definition of the term. Indeed, I have found it convenient to let the term "realism" itself alone, although what was meant by "reality" has at least been hinted at throughout the brief summation of "old" realism. As I have

19

tried to indicate by references to Pirandello, Verdi, and the verists, the term is a slippery one and probably cannot be defined in connection with art without first accepting the idea that we are talking about the relativity of artistic conventions.[12] The word "reality" is used through every discussion of neo-realism by critics, scriptwriters, directors and theorists, but is never actually defined. The use of the term shifts and slides a good deal, not only from writer to writer, but often within a single paragraph by a single writer. At times, the assumption is made that film as a medium is somehow "attracted" by its nature to, or has as its intrinsic goal, the expression of "reality". The fact that a camera will record whatever is in front of the lens, and that the processed film will then (depending upon the skill of the film maker) convince a spectator (always assuming the "willing suspension of disbelief" necessary for any aesthetic experience) of the "reality" of what he is seeing, should be enough to convince that film, like every other medium, has no natural "attractions" or "goals", independent of the creator. Film must of necessity be mani-.pulated by someone which implies that whatever "reality" is recorded on film is different from, and is only a fragment of, the endlessly wide and complex "reality" of common existence. Editing, camera placement, type of film stock, etc., involve choices, after all, even if such choices are seemingly left to chance. We are then left with an argument based on relative factors. Rossellini maintained that he "effaces" himself "as much as possible" — which is not quite the same thing as saying that as a director he was not there at all.

I indicated, when speaking of the use of actors and non-professionals in neo-realism, that one is actually discussing questions of convention, content, manner, and style. No one would argue that the "white telephone" films, or an MGM musical, are "more realistic" that neo-realism, simply because neo-realism *seems* less artificial, *seems* less stylized and manipulated. This is not only a matter of convention, but because neo-realist directors were paradoxically, more concerned to disguise their artifice, this would suggest rather more manipulation than less. Silvano Mangano was allowed to sweat, to be disheveled and dirty, in *Riso amaro*, while in *Gruppo di famiglia in un interno* she is elegantly coiffed and gowned. If she appears to be more "realistic" in the former, it is simply because we have grown to accept certain conventions of costuming and make-up: Miss Mangano is not less real in the later film. Indeed, it might be argued that she is more "realistic" in it because over the years she has become a less awkward and more convincing actress and is (in true neo-realistic theory) acting a role within the wealthy social milieu in which, both as a film star and the wife of powerful producer Dino De Laurentiis, she is more likely to move in "real" life.

There is, of course, something to be said for the "realistic" atmosphere to be gained by location shooting on real streets, in actual apartments, and so on, although here too we are dealing with conventions which audiences have learned to accept or reject according to their sophistication and experience in seeing films. Lubitsch was making a serious point when he joked that he preferred Paris, Paramount, to Paris, France. *Germania anno zero*, shot in the actual rubble of postwar Berlin, for example, is more *convincing* than, say, the same director's *Generale Della Rovere*, for which Rossellini was obliged to use sets of reconstructed rubble, but only because, in the latter, the artifice is self conscious, not because of the use of artifice itself. Some critics of neo-realism are willing to grant that they are, in actuality, speaking of conventions, or of "artistic realism", or of "cinematic realism" — that is, of the *way* the material is to be represented: many insist that the *only* way to treat material is in the neo-realist manner. This leads to some odd critical positions, and even odder films. As Luigi Chiarini points out, the subjects of some films cry out for another treatment, but because of the director's insistence on following the neo-realist method, such films become doubly false. In this way, inferior films are often valued over obviously superior works simply because the former are in the neo-realist manner. *Vivere in pace*, for example, is much praised, while *Senso* is denigrated. Most critics, however, including the "most pure" Zavattini, allow that neo-realism is but one way to make films, implicitly suggesting that, for all their insistence that film and "reality" are somehow naturally wedded, they are in fact speaking of artistic convention.

For some critics "reality" is, or implies, "social reality". The proper subject of neo-realism then becomes that which is actually happening in society, and in particular, the representation of the conditions of the poor, with the unemployed, prostitutes, and the destitute as typical characters suffering the problems of a class. The same critics also hold that such "reality" is to be analysed. We are once

21

more, however, evidently no longer speaking of an "objective" and "director-less" cinema, since *someone* must be analyst. Oddly enough, however, when directors attempted to "analyse reality" on other levels of society than that of the working class, the critics furiously denounced the directors for their decadence and involution. This is particularly true although, perhaps, for different reasons, when anything approaching psychologically-oriented analysis enters the films. It is as if the critics would accept only what Zola called Flaubert's *Education sentimentale*: "a verbal report dictated by the facts". Evidently, neither psychology nor classes other than the obviously exploited were "facts" of Italian reality. The point must be made, even though, as I have previously suggested, it is difficult to find neo-realist films (at least during the years of greatest activity in neo-realism) which deal directly with and "analyse" social problems.

This is not to say that social criticism is completely lacking in the films, but simply that it is rarely their main thrust. In *Ladri di biciclette*, the camera pans over rows of pawned wedding sheets while the protagonist attempts to pawn those of his wife, in order to buy a bicycle — an indication (no matter how obviously sentimental) of the protagonist's typicality of character and situation. Throughout the film we are indeed made aware of the thousands of others like the protagonist, all seeking work. Yet, although the problem is evoked through partial representation, nowhere in the film is the problem "analysed". The story, instead, turns most untypical as the protagonist turns thief himself, only to be humiliated and then "redeemed" by an act of forgiveness. At the end of the film we are moved by the man's plight — he still has no job and his prospects are even worse — but we are really no closer to an *understanding* of the "social reality" which neo-realists claimed was at the centre of the film. As is apparent in every film which De Sica made, his background was as an entertainer — any and every device to divert and move an audience was fair. How else can one explain the constant use of children as an entrée into the adult world he was supposedly attempting to analyse, save as emotional and theatrical devices to pull easy tears, tears indeed which are used as substitutes for analysis and understanding?[13]

Visconti's *La terra trema* comes closest to being the perfect neo-realist film in this regard. It is also of the highest quality on every other level as well. By its conclusion we are legitimately moved, but we also understand perfectly *how* the fishermen are exploited, how this "social reality" works to oppress people, who are at once both individuals and social types. We are moved by their plight due to Visconti's acute perception and honesty: clearly the characters are caught in a trap, but the way out of it is just as clear. 'Ntoni simply has not yet become aware of the need for unified action and has been momentarily defeated in his attempts to act outside his community. Visconti came to *La terra trema* after serving as assistant to Jean Renoir (De Sica's training was on the sets of the films of Camerini):

> The mythological vein which I had found in Verga no longer seemed adequate to me. I felt an impelling urge to find out for myself what were the historic, economic, and social foundations on which that Southern drama had been built. Reading Gramsci, I learned the truth that is still waiting to be resolved. Gramsci not only convinced me by the acuteness of his historical and political analysis, but his teaching also explained to me the character of Southern Italy as a great Social rupture and as a market for a colonialist type of exploitation by the ruling classes of the North. I saw in Gramsci, the founder of the Italian Communist Party, something that is not to be found in other studies of the South's problems: the indications of a realistic, political solution, in terms of the overall problem of the unity of our country: an alliance between the workers of the North and the peasants of the South, in order to break up the power of the agricultural and industrial capitalist block.[14]

La terra trema was admired widely and won a Venice Film Festival prize. It was also a financial disaster. It played abroad (when it was released abroad) in a mutilated version. Whether it was cut from distributor's fear that audiences would be unable to bear its starkness, because of its original length, or from exhibitor's greed for a shorter film which could be played more often each day, is unclear. On the other hand, *Ladri di biciclette* garnered international acclaim as a masterpiece and was hugely successful at the foreign box office. Small wonder, then, that neo-realism evolved into a popular entertainment dressed with realistic trappings, and that, after re-seeing many films of the period only a handful of titles still seem to represent an achievement of the first rank.

It is ironic that one of the greatest of the neo-realist films should have been based on a more-or-less faithful adaptation of a novel, just as Visconti's earlier masterpiece, *Ossessione*, had been based on an American novel which most critics even now consider to be almost beneath notice. It took a mind as sharp as Visconti's to see the stark quality of Cain's realism, while the critics, left-wing and bourgeois alike, with hardly an exception, courted the essentially naive and sentimental Hemingway. Neo-realistic theory holds that plot should disappear, for plot suggests a too-obvious manipulation of characters which blocks "reality" from being truly represented. Like most tenets of neo-realism, this too was more honoured in essays and speeches than in practice, although, again, one of the finest of the directors to emerge from neo-realism, Roberto Rossellini, carried this tenet to the core of his work by minimising narrative events in order to observe more clearly the "movements of the soul", and the "movements of ideas as they are born and acted upon".

Rossellini was much praised for this near-plotless fidelity to reality in the war trilogy (*Roma città aperta*, *Paisà* and *Germania anno zero*), yet, when he attempted to develop the theory further, he found himself attacked on all sides. Leaving aside *Paisà* — of which the fragmented, minimal narrative about the episodic movement of the Allied Army up the Italian peninsula could only have been structured in one way — this is particularly odd criticism, because in both *Roma città aperta* and *Germania anno zero* there are, in fact, more "plot manipulations" than in a good many of his later films. While it is true that *Roma città aperta* has no continuously developing plot, what can one make of the superhuman purity of the partisans, the priest, and the wife, Pina, as opposed to the equally superhuman villainy of the totally perverted and degenerate Nazis and their loathsome collaborators? Is this not exactly the same kind of "manipulation of reality" decried by those critics who warmly embraced *Roma città aperta* while rejecting, with contempt, *Stromboli* and *Viaggio in Italia*? In neither of these can there be said to be plots after the basic situation is given, nor as Manichean conception of character as in *Roma città aperta*.

24

V

Throughout the essays which follow, critics and directors alike often make what seem to me to be outrageous critical judgements, with which I have not argued in notes. Some of these, however, seem to be a result of the years in which they were made and thus deserve some comment. Many of the essays were written before 1953, the year De Sica and Zavattini collaborated on *Stazione termini*. Therefore, with few exceptions, De Sica received almost universal praise as *the* artist of neo-realistic cinema. Critical judgements might have been different had writers been able to foresee De Sica's later commercial films (which seem to me to be natural outgrowths of his earlier work). The degradation of neo-realist method is exemplified in his use of *La ciociara* (1960) as a star vehicle for Sophia Loren, and of Zavattini's glossy, empty comedy, *Ieri, oggi, domani* (1963) for the same star. The critics failed to see the ultimate cynicism of Zavattini's dialogue in De Sica's "international production" *Caccia alla volpe* (1966) in which an actor (Victor Mature) receives a proposition by telephone to act in a neo-realist film. Turning to the others in the room, he asks "A neo-realist film? What's that?" Answer: "Films you make when you have no money." It is a joke, perhaps, but one which Rossellini would have been incapable of making, even late in his career when he claimed he felt "little personal connection" with his early work.

Whether or not one responds to the films of Rossellini is not at issue. His films are not always easy to "like", and he certainly made a number of films which were far from masterpieces. The point is, that he did not compromise his aesthetic/moral view of what film should do. From his earliest films to his last, *The messiah* (1976), his interest in the movement of characters in their daily existence within a surrounding environment, and in the movement of new ideas as they burst upon the historical scene, remained the same. This led him from filming in real streets to reconstructions of history (indeed, it might be argued that he really began there) in which the way that Louis XIV arose in the morning and was dressed, or how he ate his meals, told us as much about the period and the historical importance of the idea of the Sun King (and his ideas) as what was said and done on a grander historical scale. An abiding interest in the "reality" of details that explode into an understanding of "social reality" was at the core of neo-realism, and remained at the core of Rossellini's work. In his last film, he said he kept his camera in constant motion over and about the plane of action in order to free the audience as much as possible so that they might pick up the details they considered important; in this way he asked the audience to collaborate with him in the creation of the film.

As to why Rossellini and his films were constantly under attack while those of De Sica were so highly praised, at least two reasons suggest themselves: the taste of most critics is not so very different (nor, perhaps, should it be) from that of the "average" filmgoer, and De Sica gave the public easy entertainment and emotional *divertissement* on a "high level" ("cultural" even), while Rossellini gave them films about which they had to think and which refused to "entertain" in the usual sense of the word. Secondly, until 1953, De Sica used the lower classes as subject matter, while Rossellini refused to continue shooting films about partisans, the resistance, and the more obvious "social problems" of the day. The one director thus attracted the admiration of critics who were the "guardians" of neo-realist social purity; the other alienated them. As Vittorini says in his apology for cultural diversity, a social and cultural danger is run when "truth" is regulated as an orthodox system, when any group decides it alone possesses *the* "truth" and *the* definition of "reality".

The neo-realist manner (style, if you like) somehow became detached from the movement itself, and from Italian cinema, so that Georges Sadoul, for example, could ask in *Cahiers du cinéma*: "Is there a Japanese neo-realism?" When Satyajit Ray's *Pather Panchali* was screened in 1956 at the Cannes Film Festival, those who had bothered to see it began at once to speak of "Indian neo-realism." Thus, neo-realism could no longer be treated as exclusively Italian, nor as the long hoped for "popular national" art form. Certainly Chiarini's suggestion that neo-realism had become one way of making films, even a mannerism, applicable to any subject in any nation, seems accurate.

In spite of the mildness of social criticism in most neo-realist films, even that was too harsh for a "restored" Italy under the Christian Democrats at the end of the Forties and in the early Fifties. The government was upset that such films displayed to the world the unemployed, the poverty, the deprivations, the poor housing, and the often general misery of the lower classes in Italy. The Church (which under Article Seven of the Constitution was *the* spiritual voice of Italy) decried everything from the "Communist content" of the films to the lack of respect shown Catholic priests and charities, and even accused them (as in the case of Rossellini's *Il miracolo*) of "blasphemy" and "insulting all Italian women".[15] Such attacks might have added to the prestige of neo-realism as being more strongly anti-establishment than it actually was. However, a number of things happened at once to cause the famous "crisis"; suddenly a wave of congresses, press conferences, and polemical essays swelled up in "defense" of the cinema in general and neo-realism in particular

The "crisis" had its roots in the situation of the entire Italian film industry. There was no definite pattern as to how well any single neo-realist film would do at the Italian box office. Many of them fared rather well, especially when the neo-realist manner served a sexual melodrama. As their production budgets were usually small, the films, in theory at least, did not have to become gigantic hits in order to recoup the money spent. Generally speaking, however, Italian audiences simply preferred not to see films which showed "their own reality as it was". For much the same reason that so many had voted for the Christian Democrat Party, they refused to attend films which had the goal of closely examining what had happened and what was happening in Italian society. They preferred the "restoration" of old cultural values because they seemed to bring peace and some level of prosperity. Audiences also wanted to escape that daily reality mirrored in neo-realist films, and crowded to see whatever purely escapist fare was offered, which was almost always American films.[16] The huge popularity and large influx of American films after the war, all but destroyed whatever financial basis the domestic market had for Italian films, neo-realist or otherwise. Thus, neo-realist producers and directors were obliged to rely heavily on foreign receipts. As Roberto Rossellini points out, in his series of reminiscences ("Ten years of cinema"), such funds were very often enough to cover the costs of an inexpensive film and even to show a small profit.

Producers, however, were greatly worried: commercial films were passing them by, fortunes were being lost. Furthermore, the film makers themselves were understandably upset that their intended audience preferred American films and escapist fare in general; the lack of a local audience made a mockery of a number of basic moral positions of neo-realism.

Several disastrous consequences for neo-realism resulted from this situation. First, there was the "crisis of involution": depending upon who used the term, it could mean either the supposed "betrayal" of directors like Antonioni, Rossellini, and Visconti who chose to widen their subject matter and method, or that many filmmakers tried to make "commercial" films under the guise of neo-realism. Chiarini's discussion of Genina's *Cielo sulla palude* is an important and central example of the latter.

The government acted immediately. Giulio Andreotti, then a Government Minister who was to become more famous later, was appointed to take charge of the film industry. The reaction of the film industry to what subsequently happened was mixed. Several new measures were aimed at the neo-realists and, naturally, most of the hostility to governmental actions and most of the "defenses of the Italian cinema" came from neo-realists. For a time, Italian film receipts went up because of better and more efficient distribution under Andreotti. A number of cinema unions listened with sympathy when he explained that more "popular" films would mean more films and more jobs. Actors, particularly, felt Andreotti could help them, since they had long feared that neo-realist doctrine about the use of non-professionals might be taken seriously in practice. The "Andreotti Law" was passed in December, 1949. Under the law, an official body with wide-ranging powers, the *Direzione Generale dell Spectacolo*, was established. It was impowered to subsidise "suitable" films. In order to be granted a loan for a production, producers were obliged to submit their script to a government-owned bank, which could then demand changes in script, cast, director, or simply refuse the loan outright. Andreotti could not only ban public screenings of films he determined were not in the "best interests of Italy", but, even more harmful to the neo-realists, he could, and did, ban any film for exportation on the basis that it maligned Italy and its people. This effectively cut off the foreign receipts on which many neo-realists depended.

The government's view of cinema can be summed up best by three quotations which were made publicly and officially. From the office of Mario Scelba, then Christian Democrat Prime Minister:

> Film is merchandise. If the government has the right to control the export of vegetables and fruits to make sure that they are not rotten, it also has the right, and the duty, to prevent the circulation of films infected with the spirit of neo-realism.

Minister Ponti: "Film is escape, relaxation, forgetfulness for the poor. The people have need of bread and circuses."

And, in the famous letter to De Sica concerning *Umberto D,* from Andreotti himself:

> We ask the man of culture to feel his social responsibility, which should not be limited to a description of the abuses and miseries of a system and a generation ... If it is true that evil can be fought by harshly spot-lighting its most miserable aspects, it is also true that De Sica has rendered bad service to his country if people throughout the world were to start thinking that Italy in the middle of the Twentieth century is the same as in *Umberto D.*

Italy joined NATO in 1949. However ultimately mild their social criticism, neo-realist films were anti-Fascist; it was a political stance which in some circles was, and still is, equated with Communism. Some directors and writers, of course, were and are politically and socially left. Nonetheless, Karel Reisz was absolutely accurate in stating that neo-realism and neo-realist films were political "only in the sense that they treat problems that are subject to the jurisdiction of political control; but they do not offer any solutions, nor have they got any particular programme". The sensitive government and the Church were determined, nonetheless, to quell all opposition, particularly if it seemed "tainted" with leftist ideas. George A. Huaco suggests, indeed, that: "The increasing distaste of the Italian government for the neo-realist cinema was at least in part a consequence of Italy's position in the 'cold war'."[17]

Still, in spite of Andreotti's repression, the depletion of bank credits and funds, and the problems of release, distribution, and exportation, neo-realist films continued to be made. They became, however, more and more commercially careful. Any strong "analysis" of social reality seemed more out of the question than before. Neo-realist directors continued to work, but the majority joined the commercial mainstream, or made films outside both commercial and neo-realist structures. Neo-realism, as a movement, dwindled away during the Fifties, but its influence continued to be felt, both internationally (as with the early films of Satyajit Ray, Elia Kazan, Jules Dassin, Robert Rossen, and Stanley Kramer) and in Italy itself.

Several new directors emerged during the Fifties and Sixties whose work can be traced directly to neo-realism. Ermanno Olmi, for example, came to feature films from industrial documentaries. His films *Il posto* (1961) and *I fidanzati* (1963) assumed the look of earlier neo-realist films, to discard all but the most minimal narrative, to treat ordinary people and situations, and to represent reality in social terms. Although they have modified their style considerably while maintaining a good deal of the original moral vision of neo-realism (as in *Padre Padrone*, 1977), the Taviani brothers clearly began as neo-realists with *San Miniato, Iuglio '44* (1954), made in collaboration with Zavattini, and *Un uomo da bruciare* (1962).

In fact, the most important figure to emerge in Italian cinema in the last two decades, Francesco Rosi, came out of neo-realism. He had been an assistant to Antonioni, Zampa, Gianini, Emmer, and most importantly to Visconti (*La terra trema, Senso*). Strictly speaking, he is not a neo-realist at all. His complicated editing, his use of flash-backs, his casting of stars and well-known actors, and his detailed dialogue, are all anathema to pure neo-realist theory. Yet, the neo-realist spirit is strong, and not simply because Rosi usually insists on filming on the actual locations where historical action took place. His films reflect precisely the profound analysis of which the neo-realists spoke so often. *Salvatore Giuliano* (1967) is, to my mind, the finest Italian film since the war. Its stark, unswerving search for the truth — modified consciously by the knowledge of the impossibility of finding it — is expressed through an unsettling analysis of the forces at work in society during the brief life of the Sicilian "bandit". In speaking about his relationship to neo-realism and *Salvatore Giuliano*, Rosi explains:

It's true that I have a rapport with the films of neo-realism. After all, everything started for me with Visconti and *La terra trema*. That was the 'first time I really did anything in the cinema and it was a very fundamental experience for me, that contact with reality: the reality of a small village in Sicily, with real fishermen who became our actors. Visconti followed a rigid structure; he had a very precise idea of what he wanted, and it was not in any way a documentary. I don't make documentaries either. I make documented films on a certain reality of life, and in this I do feel linked to the neo-realist experience. On the other hand, I make an effort — since *Salvatore Giuliano* — to interpret the facts and document. I don't try to represent life more or less exactly, but to interpret what I know of it . . . [*Salvatore Giuliano*] is about the pain of a Sicilian village, about people badly treated, used, exploited by different political powers. It is a film indeed, about a whole framework of politics which is central to all of Italy. Therefore I couldn't make a film just about a man. I profited by the character, Salvatore Giuliano, to make a sort of discourse about institutions, about the different forces of the police, but above all, about justice and the negation of justice. And, of course, about various versions, various interpretations of "the truth".

Since then, Rosi has made films about the corruption of city governments by land speculation (*Mani sulla città*, 1963), war as class oppression (*Uomini contri*, 1970), the hypocrisy and corruption involved in the "restoration" of the Naples government after the war by the American military (*Lucky Luciano*, 1973), and the disturbing manipulation of historical-social-political "truth" by both a reactionary government and the Italian Communist Party (*Cadaveri ecellenti*, 1975). His films are also sophisticated critiques of film itself as cultural fact. While neo-realism proper was by implication critical of previous Italian cinema (refusing, in Zavattini's words, the "lies and myths" of pre-war films), Rosi's films are often explicit statements concerning cinema and society, culture and politics. In *Lucky Luciano*, for example, he reduces the romantic and "exciting" gangster violence of fifty years of cinema into one jolting balletic sequence of bloodshed in order to suggest that such violence, while real enough, has been too long exploited by the "official" screens to mask the equally real and much more dangerously widespread violence and corruption by the "respectable" and "law-abiding" ruling classes.

In reading through the statements of directors, screenwriters, novelists, critics, and scholars, then, about a movement of a national cinema which has been pronounced "dead" for some twenty years, it is startling to discover that many of the basic arguments are still being carried on: the relationship of cinema to society and government, the function of cinema as either reflection of or as a motivating force in culture, the nature of realism, and the nature of cinema itself. These statements are also of interest in any attempt to understand current Italian cinema, for the very best of it began with and evolved from a neo-realism which after the war brought renewed vitality to the screen and new hope for cinema throughout the world.

Notes

1   It is not clear exactly where the term "neo-realism" came from, nor who was the first to use it. Morlion claims rather vaguely that it was invented by unnamed Catholic critics. Visconti claimed his editor Mario Serandrei first used it after seeing the rushes of *Ossessione*. Umberto Barbaro, evidently, was the first to use it in print in *Cinema* in 1942, but he applied it to French cinema.

2   Maurice Schérer and François Truffaut, *"Entretien avec Roberto Rossellini"*, *Cahiers du cinéma*, 37, July 1954.

3   I have leaned on a number of sources for this historical summary, including Denis Mack Smith, *The making of Italy 1796-1870*; Giuliano Procacci, *History of the Italian people*; Luigi Villari, *The liberation of Italy*; Norman Kogan, *A political history of postwar Italy*.

4   *History of the Italian people, op. cit.* p. 425.

5   Olindo Guerrini, *Le rime di Lorenzo Stecchetti*, quoted by G.M. Carsaniga, "Realism in Italy", *The age of realism, p. 329.*

6   Particularly useful is the discussion of the lack of social analysis in neo-realist cinema in the light of the ideas of Georg Lukacs and the films of

Francesco Rosi, *"Néo-réalisme et réalisme critique"* by Michel Ciment in his *Le dossier Rosi.*

7 See Parker Tyler's discussion of De Sica in *The shadow of an airplane climbs the Empire State Building: a world theory of film*, pp. 223-230.

8 David Overbey, "Rosi in context", *Sight and sound,* Summer, 1976.

9 Smith, *Making of Italy, op. cit.*

10 Carsaniga, "Realism in Italy", *op. cit.*, p. 331.

11 *Ibid*, p. 349.

12 For a succinct but solid discussion of the basic arguments about realism and cinema, see Andrew Tudor, *Theories of film.*

13 Eric Rhode, *A history of the cinema.*

14 Quoted by Roy Armes, *Patterns of realism.*

15 Governments in general seem particularly sensitive to the reputations of their female population. In 1964, for example, the French censor required Jean-Luc Godard to change the title of his *La femme mariée* to *Une femme mariée* before allowing its release. This gentlemanly concern evidently even crosses national borders: Joseph Losey's *The romantic Englishwoman* became *Une anglaise romantique* in France. Nor is Italy the only nation whose government officials could become upset over the display of apparently national problems in foreign cinemas. Claire Booth Luce, then U.S. Ambassadress to Italy, caused headlines with her outrage over the importation into Italy of Richard Brooks's *The blackboard jungle* from her native land in 1954.

16 This is neither a unique nor surprising phenomenon. One need only consider the American cinema during the Great Depression. The films of Satyajit Ray can never hope to attract more than a fraction of the audience which flocks to see popular musical films in India. Nor do the many foreign workers in France attend films about the plight of the North African workers in France, preferring instead to see Egyptian comedies, musicals, and melodramas.

17 *The sociology of film art.*

---

2. For Whom Do We Write?
by Alberto Moravia

Alberto Moravia (1907-   ) is probably the most famous of
20th Century Italian writers. His novels, short stories, and
essays have been translated internationally, and many of his
fictions have been adapted for films. In so far as his novels
and stories are concerned with moral, ethical, sexual, and
political problems of the Italian bourgeoisie, all of which
Moravia treats critically, his books were banned under Mussolini and put on the Index by the Roman Catholic Church in
1952. His essays on literature in general express his concern
over the gulf between the sensibilities of the artists and his
supposed audience.

It is difficult for an Italian writer to establish an intelligent relationship with his audience. If, alongside a general history of literature, a
history of Italian literature could be written, it would become
obvious that the reading public in all older societies was made up of
the courtly section of the community. In Italy, it was not replaced by
any other reading public, either bourgeois or popular. It is not that
people read less now; certainly people read even more. But the readers of the *ancien régime* existed within a humanistic culture in which
reading played a part. Today, on the other hand, the last traces of classical humanism have disappeared; very little if any, of the culture, in
a collective and social sense, still exists. Reading now, in its best
sense, is representative of an increase in individual culture — rather
disparate and anarchic — and, at worse, nothing more than an entertainment with little real informative value. The lack of a social climate, in which culture is a social fact, comes from the failure of our
bourgeoisie to establish a democracy in our country; a failure not
only moral, but political, economic, and, consequently, cultural as
well. It has not happened in Italy as it has happened elsewhere at different times and in different ways, in France, Germany, England,
America, and Russia: that diffusion of culture outside the circles of so-
called "good" society to the wider, popular masses. Some will maintain that this diffusion was made posible by an increase in the num-

ber of newspapers, periodicals, and cheap books that were published. That is a superficial, mechanical point of view. In reality, the diffusion of printed paper does not include, as an inevitable consequence, the diffusion of culture. What fostered the birth of democratic culture in those countries was the free experience of their people in political and moral domains; experience which was transformed into beliefs, modes, streams of sympathy and preferences, and which provides people with mental "vehicles" with which to approach works of culture and to benefit from them. It is the same for *persons* as it is for *people*. Reading becomes meaningful only if it is accompanied by a growth in human experience. If not, the acquisition of culture becomes a mere hobby, and there is no difference between the worker who reads *La domenica dell corriere* and the bourgeois who enjoys leafing listlessly through the pages of Gide or Huxley.

Whoever is a writer in Italy will have felt, while waiting for his book to be published, a sensation we all generally feel: that the book is marching towards the most unforeseeable and delusive adventures outside literary circles. In Italy, certainly, the myth of literary success, the great popular success, exists: but that success is almost always due to extrinsic causes; it is very seldom based upon even modest demands of a valid and genuine cultural character. That is to say, success too often, draws its origins from prurient curiosity, as happened with the erotic literature or the post-war period, or from various absurd and mysterious literary fads. The best evidence for this is the book which reaches the bourgeoisie but not the popular masses. The reading of such a book rarely leads to the reading of related books, nor to any great spiritual awakening. It is a question, in other words, of epidemic success on the same level of celebrity as that inhabited by actors, politicians, and other public personalities. This type of success does not prove the existence of some true curiosity in the public, strangely enough, but rather of a mental inertia too easily swayed by solicitations of an extra-cultural order. This was confirmed for me, once and for all, at the time of the fairly big success of my first book, a success due mainly to scandalised curiosity on the part of the public.[1] This was (and is) so true, that when I met not uncultured people they seemed to be unaware that I had written books since the first one! In fact, their enthusiasm did not lead them to seek out other books by the same author, nor even to interest themselves in the biography of the author — a cultural and moral history which at least would have clarified for the reader just why he had enjoyed the first book.

This "deafness", this lack of interest, leads logically to several results in the making of literature. Italian writers of quality do not trust such a childish and excitable public, and most prefer to think that they are writing for their colleagues — the only ones, in their opinion, who are able to appreciate the real value of their work. On the other hand, to write for men of letters logically leads to writing books in which the formal, technical, and "purely artistic" aspects prevail over content. I do not mean that this is the main reason for the particular direction taken by our most recent literature. I only mean that Italian writers never feel encouraged to speak to the public about problems concerning it, for the public, on the contrary, was the first to ignore, or worse, to scorn them. After all, literature is a kind of dialogue between author and reader, in the same language on both sides. When it is not, it is exactly like a meeting of two people who speak different languages. One says one thing, the other understands something else; the dialogue is too painful and immediately ceases.

When we speak of the "public", we are at least hinting at the so-called bourgeoisie, of course. Contrary to what happens in other countries, in Italy the masses are still a long way from making conscious, cultural demands. Our bourgeoisie is, in cultural matters, so diverse that it seems difficult at first sight to make a general statement about it. One passes through geographical, historical, and environmental differences which are enormous, from people who read absolutely nothing, and whose cultural baggage would make a retarded ten-year old blush, to people who, with far inferior economic means, possess libraries and acquire books assiduously. Nevertheless, the same confusion, the same uncertainty, the same cultural approximations are common to all. They begin where they are the most dangerous and inadmissable, in our classical literature: Machiavelli, Dante, Manzoni, Leopardi, Ariosto, and Boccaccio[2] are, for many, only illustrious names without meaning, or worse, names which evoke only boring scholastic studies. Too often, in the field of classical studies, one is confronted either with a conventional, exaggerated respect, or by a discouraging dilettantism. It is obvious that the first consideration for the understanding and appreciation of foreign literature is to understand and appreciate one's own national literature. I think that few people are as well-informed about foreign literature as are the Italians. Most of the time, however, it remains mere information, and as such neither illuminates nor enriches our own older literature; nor does it receive light from it in return. Hence a provincialism sets in which has no parallel in other countries, even in those where translations of foreign texts are scarcer, a provincialism which is noticeable not only in our public with its easy, rootless, infatuations, but often as well in the unhappy mimicry indulged in by several of our writers.

I would like to point out remedies for such consequential, serious, and painful evils. Undoubtedly, it is a problem for Italian culture that Italy is a country so predominantly based on an agricultural population. The rhetorical praise of the good earth, of the peasant with his simple rustic life — often turned out by the Fascist publicity mills — should be exchanged, for cultural purposes, for praise of the cities filled with inquisitive, restless men, and surrounded by factories and working-class suburbs. Italian towns, with a few exceptions, are inhabited by people who generally come from the countryside or have maintained strong links with the country. A man who works on the land is linked to a way of life based on continuity; he does not know what to do with culture. Do not think that, in the past, literary civilizations were based on a rustic economy. Athens, Rome and Florence were, in their own times, what Paris, London, and New York are now: cities with an industrial base, centres of intellectual urban life. We can deprecate the fact that modern cities have not kept that admirable balance between nature and artifice proper to cities, but we must reckon that the industrial civilizations are still, and always will be, those which forge the destiny of the world.

The first condition for the diffusion of culture in a democratic sense remains the one at which I hinted at the beginning: a deep and unifying experience of the entire nation in the political and moral field. That experience moulds the great mass of readers and at the same time provokes in writers the impulse to express it.

"La nuova Europa,"
December 10, 1944

Notes

1   Moravia's first novel, published in 1929, was *Gli indifferenti.* Concerned with middle-class corruption, the book caused a sensation as it was assumed, not entirely without reason, to be an attack on the Fascist state. It not only brought Moravia fame and money, but a fair number of difficulties with the government as well.

2   Alessandro Manzoni wrote, among other things, *I promessi sposi* (1840-42), which most authorities consider to be the finest Italian novel of the period, if not indeed in all of Italian literature.
   Giacomo Leopardi was a lyric poet whose formidable reputation rests on a relatively small output of verse.
   Ludovico Ariosto wrote *the* Italian epic, *Orlando furioso.*

---

3. Politics and Culture: A Letter to Togliatti
by Elio Vittorini

It is not yet entirely clear whether Elio Vittorini (1908-1966) will be remembered best for his novels or for his literary and cultural criticism and his insistence on debating central issues of cultural and political problems in public. In trouble with the Fascist government, which stopped the publication of his first, and prevented the distribution of his second novel, Vittorini kept himself alive during the period by translating American literature into Italian. From 1945 to 1947, he edited the first weekly and then quarterly *Politecnico*, devoted to the publication of new writers, translations, reviews, and articles about cultural and social matters.

The occasion for this essay was a series of exchanges between Vittorini, his readers, his critics, and several well-known leftist political figures. When the *Politecnico* evolved from a weekly to a quarterly, Vittorini wrote, in issues 31 and 32, a two-part essay concerning "Politics and culture" and a self-criticism of the review itself. This provoked many responses. Some non-Communists wrote letters and essays to take advantage of what they saw as a "break in the cultural ranks" of the Italian left-wing. Then, in the rival left-wing review *Rinascita*, Mario Alicata wrote a sharp attack criticizing *Politecnico* and Vittorini for, among other things, publishing a "reactionary scribbler like Ernest Hemingway". As Vittorini had spent a good part of his creative life translating such "scribblers" (including Saroyan, Faulkner, and Caldwell), it is one issue taken up very specifically by him, although it fits nicely into his main thesis that an open culture should remain independent of social programmes and that aesthetic judgements should be divorced from political ideology.

Before he could react in print to Alicata, Vittorini received a letter from Palmiro Togliatti, co-founder, with Antonio Gramsci, and head of the Italian Communist Party; he

41

deplored, with Alicata, the suggestion that there was a break in the solidarity of Communist position, reacted strongly to the charge that the Communist Party suppressed artistic freedom, commented on several "problems" in Vittorini's logic (referring him back with amused paternalism to "good old Hegel"), and hoped that the *Politecnico* would not go the way of other left-wing reviews through factionalism and the lack of a strong practical programme. Vittorini published the letter in *Politecnico* (No. 33/34), and in the following issue published this answer.

Dear Togliatti,

Instead of sticking directly to the argument of your letter with an answer either simply logical or polemical, I am taking this opportunity to discuss with you several problems born from, or directly concerning, our Party[1] — problems which seem to me to be open to a variety of solutions, and, for that reason, regarded by the Party with uncertainty and uneasiness, diffidence and hypocrisy, aversion and fear.

I would like to begin by telling you about the rather "special" way in which I am a Communist, a way which in Italy is a bit "special" for a good many militants. I did not register with the Italian Communist Party out of any ideological motivation. When I registered, I had yet to read anything by Marx, Lenin, or Stalin. I want to tell you that first, so that everything will be as clear as possible, for even the *Politecnico* has its cultural position. I am exactly the opposite of what might be described in Italy as a "man of culture". I have never been to university, nor to secondary school for that matter. I might almost say that I have no formal education at all. I know neither Greek nor Latin. Both my grandparents were workers; my father, a railroad man, hardly had the means to send me to the schools which were, for a time, called "technical". What I know, or think I know, I learned by myself, in the defective way one learns on one's own. I know foreign languages, for example, like a deaf and dumb man: I can read and write in them, translate from them, but I can neither speak them nor understand them when they are spoken to me.

42

I have to laugh when people reduce the problems of popular culture to mere problems of simplification. I remember the way in which I saw it solved by myself and the group of Syracusan workers with whom I exchanged books and ideas when we were thirteen, fifteen or sixteen years old. We were not put off by any difficulty in reading. For example, we too read *La scienza nuova* by Vico,[2] and if, after the first reading, we understood nothing, we read it again and understood a bit of something, and then a third time and understood a bit more .... My friends and I found the time to do that every day after eight hours of manual work. They were really geniuses. They are simply workers who can read anything and who can give a lot of trouble to anyone teaching Croce — they are particularly hard nuts to crack.

The method, however, of the self-taught person is vicious: it leaves behind bad habits, gaps, and irremediable imperfections. I know all of that from my own experience. While not refusing to be a part of culture, to actively support culture, to have cultural duties, it is not as a proper "cultural professional" that I write in the *Politecnico*, and it is not as a "cultural professional" that I am registered in the Party.

I must repeat that when I registered, I had not yet read a single work of Marx. During the time of my euphoric self-education, Marx's texts were not to be found in the world of books, at least not in Syracuse. The texts available to me came from the *Biblioteca Universale Sonzogno*. Marx, unfortunately, had not yet been distributed by the cultural wing of the Party in Italy. He had certainly never entered "culture" with a capital "C", and all those who were ten or twelve years old in 1922 simply had to discount him as they moved between the poles of Crocian idealism and whatever else there was.

Thus I did not accept a philosophy when I registered in our Party. Rather, I joined other men in a struggle. I knew what the Party was by seeing who the Communists were, beginning with Mario Alicata, who was the first Communist I knew. They were the best of all people I had known: better in daily life, the most honest, the most serious, the most sensitive, the most dedicated, and at the same time, the happiest and most vivid.

That is why I joined the Communist Party: to be with the only ones who were good and courageous, not dejected, not empty, to be with the only ones who had already (in 1941 and 1942) fought for and believed in their struggle; to be with the only ones who, when they reasoned, reasoned as revolutionaries.

It was not because I was a cultural Marxist. I started studying Marxist texts, but I won't call myself a Marxist because of that! Now I find in Marxism a spring of cultural richness which makes me richer. It gives life to my brain; properly, some *"acqua viva"* in the sense used by St. John the Evangelist; and sometimes, here and there, some *"acqua morta"*. But for me to call myself a Marxist it is not sufficient that I complete my studies only to support each and every point in Marxism, to accept it in all its consequences. That would be, for me, passive and useless, and certainly unproductive. I think that to call myself a Marxist, I should be able to bring something to Marxism and to myself, to enrich both and to be, myself, an *"acqua viva"* which merges with the Marxist stream of *"acqua viva"*.

I know more than one friend of late who at this moment would object: "Why, if you are not a Marxist, do you publish the *Politecnico*; why do you engage in debates, particularly with us, instead of restricting yourself to study?" That is to say, that since I am not a Marxist, I don't possess the truth, and so should not speak, so as not to break Communist solidarity. But I know that you, yourself, are the first to fight such thinking, particularly in our friends. The right to speak does not derive from "possessing the truth." It comes from the fact that one *looks* for the truth. And — watch out! — that may not be all. It may be that such people also want the security of "possessing the truth". And the presumption of "possessing the truth" means that only those who do not *seek* are qualified to speak: predicators, rhetoricians, Arcadians, academicians. Culture would once again become clerical, as it was before Protestantism, or it would present the same philistine spectacle which so disconcerted Karl Marx in the Germany of his time. If Marx thought that through his method one might definitively eliminate all forms of philistinism, it was because he thought his method should be one of "empirical research" not of "possession", and because he thought that speech and discussion should occur as a function of that research and not as a function of possession.

So I believe I can support our Party quietly, even without calling myself a Marxist, and be able to support it not by only listening and learning but also through talking, even writing, and by continuing to publish the *Politecnico*.

Marxism, by its very nature, reassures me. The fact that the Party has declared, in its Fifth National Congress, that it imposes no ideological obligations on its militants has had, for me, a much greater significance than a simple acknowledgement of reality, in which I have played a small part along with one hundred thousand others. The Party has understood that political action in Italy can correspond to the needs and desires of ten to twenty times the number of people involved, even those who remain ideologically unconvinced that they need it. The Party has also probably understood that it can satisfy, through its political actions, even those human demands manifested through non-Marxist ideologies, despite crises, "shipwrecks" and the gropings of ideologies different from Marxism.

But the pace of the Party cannot have been merely political and tactical. It would be unthinkable that a party of men would so open itself up and welcome us with all our problems of crisis, of inquiry for truth, and yet at the same time remain insensible to the problems, to the inquiry, and that it would want to remain in the state of coldness of those who "possess the truth." Whom would it serve? Political solidarity dies very quickly if it has a repugnant base. No one could have overlooked it even if the Party's eye been made of glass.

The step taken by the Communist Party at the Fifth Congress assumes a significance far beyond the limits of Italian political necessity. It does not mean that the Party should remove its ideology from the realm of political necessity. It does not mean that the Party, at that particular moment of Italian history, gives up being a philosophy and a culture. Hundreds of thousands like me can have wanted only to accept a policy in joining a party. But with its step at the Fifth Congress, the Party has offered us the possibility of joining a philosophy *and* a culture, to have a philosophy again without having to deny anything that, shall we say, *philosophically* was already a part of us. That is why the decision to open up the Party has such a profound meaning.

It has removed from its own heart the diffidence which threatened to keep it from understanding the contemporary expression of man. It has reckoned on having learned much (even ideologically) during its clandestine period. It has redirected Italian Marxism on its path; has recognised Marxism as a great open road of philosophy-as-inquiry, rather than as a cul-de-sac of systematic philsophy.

"Come to me", the Party said, "even if you are Kantians, Hegelians, Catholic Existentialists, or even Atheist Existentialists". With the invitations, it did not say merely that our political adhesion was the only important thing, and that it did not care what else we were. On the contrary! In my opinion, the Party told us that what we were was very important for it, both for what it is and what it can be. Through this openness, through open contact with other ideologies which show themselves to be extremely sensitive to the problems which today manifest themselves to man, and which are able to inform us of them, the Party can make the problems its own and set them in their proper perspectives. In other words, the Party has re-opened itself to every sort of contact, to every sort of ideological stimulus, in order to push itself again into the mainstream of life in which it can receive as well as give; can enrich itself and not just spend; can begin once again the process of inquiry, development and evolution. Admitting us all as Communists — even if Kantian, Hegelian and so on — the Party hoped that, through us, it would become something other than a closed system; not even a true and proper philosophy, but a force for the reformation of the world.

In this way, we shall be Communist in so far as our Kantian, Hegelian, or Existentialist outlook is turned towards this transformation. We shall be Communist in so far as our outlook will not paralyze us within a fixed system. We shall be Communist in so far as our outlook will be a function of philosophy in its original and basic meaning: inquiry after the truth, rather than "possession of the truth."

The Double Front of Culture

In my weekly *Politecnico*, we have not transposed to the general ground of Italian culture the requirements, demands, and hopes formulated by each non-Marxist Communist. Nonetheless, we have tried to remain sensitive to them, even when they originated with people who were ignorant of, neutral, or even hostile to our Party. We at the *Politecnico* want to attempt a new culture, but we know very well that the development of a new culture depends upon a "whole" culture. We have, therefore, first tried to sound a warning against the danger which threatens the existence of culture in Italy. I might analyse, self-critically, the reasons for which the weekly *Politecnico* remains an irritant even to leftist Italian culture, including Marxist groups, but our discussion transcends the limitations of self-criticism in mere defense of the weekly. In general, our argument concerns the relationship between politics and culture, and my experience at the *Politecnico* is useful only if it can be used profitably in dealing with our argument.

To begin with, I do not believe that politics and culture are totally distinct. On the contrary, I shall try to demonstrate that the two areas seem to me to be closely linked. Of course they are *two* activities, not one, but when the dynamism of one is decreased (for whatever reason) and becomes subsidiary to, or merely a component of, the other, a historical void comes into being. The culture that fails both to develop itself politically — in the proper sense of cultural inquiry — and to maintain itself forcefully through it, leaves the task of developing the entire culture unfulfilled. Even when politics itself would seem to demand a secondary relation for culture, the latter does not serve the development of politics. The influence that culture can exert, as a means through which politics can prosper, will always be of little consequence.

Culture best serves history objectively when it fulfills its own task by continuously raising new problems, discovering new goals, and asking new questions. From such questing, politics draws its incentive to new action. In the ordinary course of history, it is only autonomous culture that enriches politics and thus becomes a profitable basis for political action; whereas politicized culture, reduced to an instrument of political influence (or, at least, deprived of its own problem-raising strength) has no qualitative contribution to make and is of no use to political action, save perhaps as a foreman is of use in a factory.

It is as indispensable that culture should include a political understanding of the historical reality in which it is rooted, as it is indispensable for politics to perceive cultural problems and to incorporate them in its own actions. Culture cannot be the formal manifestation of what is commonly labelled "culture", which allows itself to be bypassed by the dynamics of history; it must itself be dynamic enough to guide events. This does not mean that culture should identify itself with politics. Neither, however, should culture lose touch with the masses. It should always be aware of their cultural needs as well as of the human needs which produce them. In the masses we have an exact historical measure of the proportion in which culture and life, civilization and life, stand in relation to one another and proceed, one translating itself into the other. Therefore, if the cultural level of the masses constitutes a properly political force within which it is a political task to use culture; if the elevation of such a level is a task in the current state of things which cannot again be part of political action; if we must refuse the pretence often advanced in politics that culture develops itself, at the cost of it no longer being inquiry or an immediate and direct educator; if we must claim that the great significance of a cultural idea or work can have that which is inaccessible to the masses (Dante or Cézanne, Macchiavelli or Marx) as a supplement to its importance as inquiry, as educator, even indirectly through inferior levels of culture or through politics itself: then we must be careful to see that culture does not lack (as a stimulus to search in the right historical directions) the contact with the cultural level of the masses, and that it does not lie beyond the experience of their human problems.

Culture must develop itself on a double front: on the one hand, it must progress in such a way that the masses remain attached to it, acquiring from it the incentive to accelerate their own pace and to drop those vestiges of old-fashioned culture which impede their historical dynamism; on the other hand, simultaneously, it must develop in such a way as not to stop the masses in their own development and to withdraw culturally as they have done recently.[3]

Politics can offer appropriate action according to the level of maturity reached by the masses — at one time marking time, at another, stopping — while culture constantly moves forward. It is in this difference of rhythm, I would say, that the distinction between culture and politics can be made. It is here, at any rate, that we can observe the two streams flowing separately throughout history.

A dynamic culture (in the sense of both historical idealism and historical materialism) which works continuously at the level of the cultural maturity of the masses, which keeps in step with them and explores with them, will be one which can truly call itself political. On the other hand, a non-dynamic culture for which we must still use the term "culture" will be that uncommitted to any form of direct action on the path of continual inquiry. If culture stops searching, probing, and asking questions, and becomes merely political, there will be no further human inquiry. If culture ceases, what will give politics its impetus? Will it receive it directly from "life"? In fact, of course, life will put culture into motion again, and culture will bring about political movement. That is to say it will translate itself into action. Meanwhile, we would have had a Middle Ages of automatism as we have had a Middle Ages of exploitation. And why? Why should we have it? Marxism is not only a method to use in fighting against exploitation. It is also the premise of the method to use in fighting against automatism. It seems to me that no political doctrine, no form of culture, can refuse any longer to share that premise with Marxism; a corollary of this regulates the relationship between culture and politics, guaranteeing culture the opportunity to develop properly on both the 'avant-garde' front and in the sense of problem-posing inquiry; on that level of contact with the masses in the sense of a revelation, but one with a quality of critical interrogation, never presuming to possess absolute truth. It must never take on the character of a catechism, which unfortunately is too often invested with the function of cultural revelation, covering the ground with the dead weight of the catechized.

I have been accused of having upheld a "false generalisation." Alas, I blush at the idea that I have so badly expressed myself that I could be so misunderstood. I wrote: "Politics acts generally in the area of daily existence and events, whereas culture cannot develop on the direct ground of history alone, but must stand outside every law of political tactic and strategy." This has been, unfortunately, understood to mean, "Politics is news; culture is history." Can my idea really become that when summarised? Perhaps, then, it might be better if I tried to clarify my position.

I intend to say nothing other than what I have frequently said before: politics, as it operates, takes into account reality even in its most contingent aspects, and conforms to those aspects; culture develops by acknowledging reality in its most historical aspects without needing to proportion itself to current contingencies. Politics (or culture translated into social action) must interpenetrate a whole range of basic necessities to be able to be action in the first place. Culture which remains research (either science or poetry) must limit itself to a degree by removing from itself any cognisance of the purely necessary in order to remain free to investigate and pose problems and goals.

Therefore, politics is as much history as is culture, save that culture is history which passes beyond politics as history in its contact with common events of daily existence, and therefore culture becomes a function of history. I do not think that the difference between culture and politics can be made with a one-to-one precision any more than a distinction can be made between a man of culture and a politician. What is a politician? He is the man of culture who moves from the area of inquiry into that of action. What is a man of culture? He is one who stands outside action in order to carry on the investigation and to pose problems.

Of course, in reality, it is difficult for one person to be either a wholly political man totally immersed in action, or wholly a man of culture totally immersed in research. The same man can be at times a mixture of the political and cultural, a man for whom a political act is both research and discovery, for whom the cultural act of research and discovery is at the same time a political act. We can never really tell where the politician leaves off to make room for the man of culture. Nor can we always tell whether the erring meaning of both politicians and men of culture is cultural or political in essence.

For the men of the American Revolution, for example, it was clear that the great political actions of Washington and the Federalists turned out to be so limited in capacity for development because of their indifference to culture. It is not equally clear, however, that the capacity for political development in Jefferson was due to his cultural, as opposed to political, grandeur. On the other hand, the example of Benedetto Croce, who declares Marxism out of date, is an example not only of cultural tradition which translates itself into political meaning, but also of culture which has declined into pseudo-culture. He paralyzed Italian culture with his regression, and prepared the ground for the political triumph of Fascism: he scattered the equivocations from which were born all the cultural lies which have justified the politics of Fascism in Italy. The fact that Croce has elected to retain culture's pomp, only proves that cultural pomp is not at all the same thing as culture.[4]

It is not only through politics, and through the total transforma-

50

tion of culture into politics, that culture can be stopped. When culture in itself turns into the "possession of the truth" and into a system, it is stopped. This is what happened with Saint Thomas; culture was finished until the birth of Protestantism. But I must reject any instant system of culture.

Instead, I will respect as culture, the opposition and resistance to Croce from the most enlightened heads of the working movement — those who have been called "mere politicians" — and will call this culture. That said, it is not the same as saying that political intransigence always produces fine results, but only that it may, when it unchains itself from a historic sensibility more acute than that implicit in the cultural position to which it is opposed. There are examples of political acts, based on their political necessity, which give birth to cultural inconveniences that in turn are harmful sooner or later to politics itself. There are also examples of cultural positions which give birth to political inconveniences which are sooner or later harmful to culture itself. Take Lenin's book about "empiric criticism". Lenin is the typical figure of a man both great in action and in thought. His book, whose stand against the political dangers of "empiric criticism" was of enormous political necessity and importance, gave birth to a cultural inconvenience which still marks popular Marxism today (as well as Trotskyism and Bukarinism) and which has not been entirely unharmful to the development of our Party up to now. All the reserved diffidence shown toward the Communist Party by many men of culture (some among the most lively of our time) stems primarily from their reaction to Lenin's book; a book which, considered in its cultural sense, seems to translate Marxism from a method into a system. It had become a necessity to link it positively to the science of the time, to assimilate the results of contemporary epistomology which had developed from empiric criticism, and which in science has taken the names quantum physics, atomic physics and biophysics.

That is why I find, at times, Stalin's doctrine more important than Lenin's. The former knows how to counterbalance the rigours of revolutionary duty and logic with a wisdom that counsels us against the impatience of scientific rationalism: every rational step is made after the preceding one has penetrated at least partially into the human psyche and has, in fact, assumed a non-rational nature.

51

Antonio Gramsci, in Italy, is great for that very reason. His works present every posible premise for a Marxist cultural position corresponding to the free and valid politics of the New Communist Party in Italy.[5]

Revolution and the "Culture of Power"

Let us move on to the distinction between the ordinary course of history, in which politics modify events only quantitatively, and the extraordinary moments in history in which politics modify them qualitatively. Previously, I have not expressed myself clearly on this point. I made a mistake, and it is only fair that I should be reminded of the "doctrine of good old Hegel" who taught us not to separate quantity from quality.[6] My mistake, however, lay in my conviction as to what comprised politics and culture, and what I am in history, as well as the relationship between politics and culture. Even with my aversion to the mechanical, and my sympathy for modern physics, I allowed myself to be trapped by a mechanical concept which sees qualitative mutation as a result of numerous quantitative mutations. Or, more simply, I imprisoned myself in a mental fiction. Similar slips often happen to someone who does not express himself through explicit reasoning. When he is compelled to do so, he can become more abstract than a formal logician. Have I then merely enclosed myself in a convenient abstraction?

The serious consequences of my distinction between the quantitative and the qualitative is to divide politics into two principles, one of which applies during its quantitative phase and identifies with daily events and existence, the other fulfills its mission during the qualitative phase by identifying with history. It has been deduced from this that I believe culture should be the "directing factor" during the stages of the so-called "quantitative phase". This is *not* what I believe, however, so I must have made a mistake in all that business of quantitative and qualitative.

I have never believed that it was the function of culture to direct. Had I so believed, I would have been maintaining that culture should transform itself into politics, for there is hardly a difference

52

between "directing" and "acting". To say "culture which directs" is to say "politics." A "direction" in society always exists: as much in revolution as in the phases of simple evolution, or even involution; for a class already in power as for a class which seeks to gain power. What does "to direct" in politics mean, concerning the rest of culture?

It means that politics can — with political means and political intentions — limit research, can force it to take one direction rather than another, can stop it at any point, urge it forward at another, and in fact make it a slave to its own action. From what I have said before, it should be clear that I refuse such an interpretation, for it would then lead to a total politicization of culture, and the consequent progressive impoverishment of politics itself. It should be clear that I ask for an autonomy of culture in order that it may play freely its proper non-political role, even accounting for those errors which any research is bound to make. I am also aware, of course, that at the most acute moments of revolution, politics coincides so much with cultural research that it becomes impossible to make a clear distinction between the two, which makes an autonomous culture impossible. This is the reason for my artificial distinction between quantitative and qualitative: so that culture can be claimed to be autonomous in relation to political action, except in the decisive moments of revolution. This is not the same as saying that in period X the direction should be left to culture, and in period Y it should be left to politics. If I did not make myself clear before, I trust I do now, and that my distinction is useful, at least in that it is an indication of the necessity to deepen the question and to clarify it at the same time. Certainly, it must be conceded, that the relationship of culture to politics does not always remain the same. It varies in a number of ways at different times, never more especially than in those periods of fluctuation between a phase of rapid historical movement and a phase of comparative calm.

Giuseppe Ferrara called revolution "each step in history, even a backward step". The institution of the Podestà in the medieval communes he called "the revolution of the Podestà." The same for the "Gonfalonieri" which he called "the revolution of the gonfalonieri".[7] In thinking of revolution, however, we usually think of such great social upheavals as the Revolution of England in the 17th century, in France in the 18th century, and in the Russia of our own. Culture craves these upheavals. It leans towards revolution. Why? Because objective inquiry into the nature of truth (which exists in spite of the Roman "philosopher", Pontius Pilate) is the function of culture, which thereby introduces choice into the determinism of world history. Culture is truth which develops itself through change, not only as a co-function of the concrete changes in the world, but as a function of its own impulse to change. It is a human force which uncovers in the world those demands for change, and makes the world conscious of it. It thereby seeks the transformation of the world.

But in seeking to transform the world, it aspires to reorder it, so that it can never again slide under the domination of economic interests, political necessities, or automatism. On the other hand, it identifies itself with truth, philosophy, art, as well as science. Culture aspires to revolution as a possibility of taking power through politics, culture transformed into politics, which is quite different from economic interests transformed into politics, or class privilege transformed into politics, or necessity transformed into politics. Such aspiration is evident, for example, in the culture which preceded the French Revolution. Robespierre lost his head because he wanted to be a man of politics (culture transformed into politics) without any compromise with the necessity or the interests of the social forces which were agitated in the revolution. Both he and the Jacobites were deluded in thinking that the French Revolution was *the* Revolution, and that all they had to do was to exert power for culture on the basis of society's development. That is, they attempted to force society's development to correspond directly to that of culture, rather than allowing it to develop as a social force to correspond to the progressive capacity of political action. Yet Burckhardt tells us, more than seventy years later, that the old aspiration of culture to take power (in the sense of continuous realisation rather than the immobilization of a moment) has become a reality with the rise to power of the parliamentary democracy in France.

Marx, on the other hand, knew better how to see beyond delusion. He shows us what is beneath such parliamentary democracy. He does not suggest we relinquish our aspirations. Rather, he suggests that we can be part of and can perpetrate an extraordinary revolution, a revolution for truly revolutionary goals: to assure the predominance of choice over automatism, of research over a set system, of culture over political necessity, culture translated into politics rather than privilege transformed into politics. Marx maintains that in a classless society, culture will have been liberated once and for all. Nonetheless, Marx does not exclude the danger, even in a classless society, of culture becoming estranged from independent inquiry, and taking possession of Truth, fortifying itself into a system, forcing the world to march with a new automatism. Marx knows very well that a world, freed of political necessity by culture, can always descend into slavery through culture itself.

The Catholic Church is a typical example of how culture can crystallize itself into a doctrine and then can move into politics to imprison the world, working within the limitations of economic automatism today, and moving outside those limitations for tomorrow. The elimination of economic automatism, therefore, is no insurance, by itself, against every automatism.

It comes back then to the Marxist vision that the struggle against exploitation is also a struggle against this or that form of automatism, of strict systems, inside culture as inside politics. It will continue to be so until society liberates itself from both political and cultural necessity. Marxism demands that we engage ourselves in a spirited struggle against exploitative factors which grew out of Protestantism. Marx did not profess the Jewish religion; he was educated as a Protestant Christian. If he identified the Protestant Revolution with the rise of the bourgeoisie, he did not identify the spirit of Protestantism with its spirit but rather with that of the *ascendance* of the bourgeoisie — a spirit at once critical-constructive, non-conformist, anti-philistine, and problematic. It has, ultimately, little to do with the regrettable fact that the bourgeoisie abandoned its position for the equivalent of a rigid Catholicism.

Marx aspires to an "extraordinary" revolution in which man acquires the definite spirit of ascent. We can say, therefore, that the spirit of Protestantism is a function and a source for a human conquest which, once made, is permanent. Marxism also contains it. Its historical presupposition is the inheritor of that spirit, and is in turn developed by it. One might, indeed, wonder if Marxism does not find itself exposed to certain limiting consequences each time it confronts a reality never before encountered by the Protestant experience. Those who consider Marxism as a conception of a millenium, who consider that a classless society is its sole and ultimate goal, are enemies. They seem to explain Marxism as a development of Judaism. To consider Maxism mystically, without understanding that essential anti-automatism which is the contrary of a millenary concession, is to be an enemy of Marxism. It is not a development of Judaism but of Protestantism. Very often, Marx's personal contentious assertions are confounded with the aim of Marxism, and his distaste for "history as it is" with his presumed taste for "history as it must be". Marx affirms that the activity of man develops under the dominion of economics, but is it understood that he aims at liberating man from such dominion? Marx affirms that collective manifestations have a certain weight in history, but is it understood that his aims forward a history in which *individual* manifestations would exert the deciding influence? There is a confusion in some minds between the majestic "moral idealism" of Marx and the powerful weapon of his realism. It is not generally understood that, while teaching us that we cannot achieve true liberation of the individual without a collective effort, Marx supports a revolution whose aim is not collective in essence, but rather individualistic; indeed, for the first time in recorded history, he advocates a revolution with a properly individualistic aim. Involved in the struggle for the achievement of a classless society, Marxism has not yet developed itself in the direction of intrinsic significance. A way of avoiding the slide towards one or another automatism in culture and politics, and of keeping alive in man the will to ascend, which has been established, has not yet been discovered. A society, even a classless one, in which man lacks that spirit, would be a society in which no new Marx, no new philosopher, no new poet, no new politician would have a reason to be born and to live. This would be contrary to the society envisioned by Marx, in which the individual is qualitatively motivated to live. That is why it is so necessary for culture always to have the opportunity to search, to raise problems, and to renew itself. That is why it is necessary for culture always to have a consciousness of the danger of becoming a system translated into politics, the risk of moving further and further in the direction of being research translated into politics. Hence it is necessary that the relationship between politics and culture should not be regulated by either politics or culture, but should be free to develop a reciprocal interdependence, according to the constant changes in phases that history goes through in its approach to a classless society and the liberty of man.

To Play the Fife for Revolution?

I could end the argument here, but I have not yet really said what seems to me to be particularly important.

The words of your letter express, above all, a feeling of good will. May I now take advantage of it? I wish to express in full the perplexity in which so many intellectuals find themselves (I include even those intellectuals not registered with the Italian Communist Party) who are confronted today with something which keeps the relationship between politics and culture, both within and outside the Party, from being more vivid. I have never heard it said that politicians should not interfere in matters of culture, but that they must keep from interfering, especially with political criteria, including arguments and political intimidation. As a man of culture, as a man of research, however, he cannot but participate in cultural battles, but only on grounds of culture and only with cultural criteria. Observe the Marxist reaction to Croce. It was developed culturally and culminated in the work of Gramsci, who re-established the full activity of Marxism, but not without having welcomed some of Croce's objections to it, not without having profited from them, not without drawing an opportunity of development or, at least, of clarification of the Marxist position through them. Now imagine that the reaction had been developed politically; not with the assasination of Croce or with an imposition of silence on him, nor with the pressures of a general strike or the force of an action or decree, but with a formal and scornful 'No', with political reasons hidden behind cultural ones, with lies. The Italian Marxist would have remained in the situation he was in in 1908,[8] chained hand and foot to positivism; the politics of our Party today would be that much poorer, and they would certainly not be that of the New Communist Party. As for the *Politecnico*, if I accept your criticism (and that of men like Alicata), I do not yet accept the purely political criteria with which many arguments falsify the grounds for discussion. Such a purely political position leads to a writer like Hemingway being categorized as a "small impressionist", one whose acquaintance we can do without. I am opposed to this tendency to transpose considerations of a proper political nature into cultural matters and to disguise them as cultural judgements; the result is only a distortion of the relationship between culture and politics to the detriment of both. To use a cultural lie is the equivalent of an act of force, and can be translated into an obscurantism which produces a lack of sincerity, an aridity and lack of life, and the final and absolute stagnation of culture. It is not to engage in the cultural battle by progressing through the use of one's own reason, to move forward in culture, to transform and to be transformed. To use a cultural lie is, rather, to attempt to affect culture while remaining removed from its problems. It is to act on, and not within, culture. At the present time, there exists no such danger between living Italian culture and our Party. Indeed, the dangers seem to disappear more and more daily. However, we have centuries of Catholicism behind us to overcome. Moreover, it is latent in several countries in the world, sometimes in France or America. That is a danger which we Communists, in particular, run, and we must struggle against it with a watchful conscience. Take America: on more than one occasion the best novelists, poets, and scientists have worked in a quasi-Communist direction. The current quarterly review *Science and Society* still offers us an example of the richness of the problems which American culture can raise for itself in its contacts with Marxism. America's men of culture have become politically agnostic — even if they might once have been Communist or quasi-Communist — while others, remaining Communist, have temporarily lost their cultural importance.

Hemingway, Steinbeck, Caldwell, Dos Passos, Richard Wright, and James T. Farrell have abdicated their positions as writers supporting our political movement, to other men of less than first rank: Howard Fast, Albert Maltz, and the like. Yet we cannot say that they have changed direction as writers, or that they have sided with the reactionaries. Some, undoubtedly, have committed political errors — Hemingway, for example, has falsified, in some of his worst passages, the figure of a great revolutionary — but the entire complex of their work is still of revolutionary importance. It is by his cultural pertinence, after all, and not by his more or less accidental political statements, that a writer must be judged. If a writer speaks slightingly of Garibaldi, is that sufficient reason to judge him as a counter-revolutionary? Many political men speak boldly in criticism of revolutionary writers, but the writers themselves do not then call them counter-revolutionary politicians. Giuseppe Mazzini, to give an example, wrote that Leopardi was a decadent poet when compared to the great Civil War poet (imagine!) G.B. Niccolini.[9] Yet no man of culture has ever dreamed of treating Mazzini as a reactionary. We merely suppose that Mazzini was unable to understand the renovative value of Leopardi's poetry. The politicians almost never exercise the same indulgence.

We should question those vices and defects in our attitude towards the relationship between culture and politics which might contribute to its dessication. Perhaps such defects stem from the fact that the spiritual nourishment in Marxism attracts to itself too many small-minded intellectuals who, unable to lead a proper life of their own, become the watchdogs of the Party, ever ready to use Marxism as a code of politics and culture and to affirm their conformist and squalid adhesion devoid of problems and inquiry. Each different demand, each problem not yet solved, which a writer puts into his work with his own vitality, can thus provoke a wave of abstract accusations which sooner or later frighten him into avoiding them. "Petit-bourgeois", "decadent", "individualistic" are the terms with which the poets and thinkers were worried by the adherents of a supposed Marxism, for many years, in more than one occidental country. Now I find in Marxism examples by which to guide oneself. In the last few months, while America has run the risk of returning to the thought of Calhoun and the doctrine of slavery, *New masses*, a responsible serious weekly, published a superficial and sectarian diatribe against the greatest progressive thinker beyond the Atlantic, John Dewey. Yet how valuable his work was in opposition to the conservative philosophies of Jaspers and Croce.

The line which divides progress from reaction on a cultural basis is not easily identified as the same line which makes the same division in politics. Either one is ready to understand, or one is not, or does not want to. As it happens, we do not want to judge a poet by his political declarations deciding whether his poetry is progressive or reactionary in tendency. If we condemn Dostoevsky as a reactionary on the basis of his more superficial statements, we fail to enrich ourselves with the profoundly progressive forces in his work, and we allow instead the reactionaries to enrich themselves first and then use it to their advantage. In the Nineteenth Century, Marxism knew how to grasp what was of implicit progressive value in the work of the time — Hoelderlin, Heine, Dickens, Balzac — without examining them to see if they were politically to the right or to the left. Today there is a tendency to reject or ignore the great writers of our time. We completely ignore Kafka, who described the pompous force of the conditions under which man is reduced to living in contemporary society. We totally reject the work of Hemingway, yet in concrete terms it throws light on so many problems for which man needs a revolutionary transformation of the world. If Hemingway compromises himself politically, we can consider him our enemy, but his books are not our enemies. They are still our friends. I do not deny that in Hemingway, and other writers of the kind, there is present, even in a cultural or political sense, something that more recent authors tend to transcend. Man, in Hemingway's books, is still a sort of "superman", not a real man. But we cannot describe as all black something which is merely spotted, and we cannot describe something as all gold because it contains a few flecks of it. That is an obscurantist criterion which we cannot adopt in support of culture. It is now the turn of actual works of a newer poetry and a newer culture to cancel out, or to reduce in importance, the works of Hemingway and others like him. Hearing some first-class writers being treated as "scribblers", we gain the impression that everything is diminished, that our own work is diminished, and that our culture is diminished; that indeed, our revolutionary efforts can never be counted as such by our political fellows. What does it mean for a writer to be a revolutionary? During my acquaintance with political friends, I have noticed that they tend to acknowledge us as "revolutionaries" in so far as we "play the fife" for revolutionary problems raised by politics; in so far — and just so far — as we take problems from politics and translate them into *bel canto*, dress them up in images, words, and figures. That is, in my opinion, something other than revolutionary; it seems rather to be Arcadian or academic.

An Effort which avoids "Arcadia"

"Arcadia" does not mean "art for art's sake". There can also be an "Arcady" as well as an "Academy of Art for Art's Sake," but the formula is not in itself an Arcadian formula. We find it historically old-fashioned as a protection from conformism or a development of a new conception in life, whether in Victorian England or France during the Second Empire. Victorian England, like France of the Second Empire, pretended that art served to inculcate, directly or indirectly, the principle of the dominant societal morality. "Art for art's sake", on the other hand, defended the liberty to express new visions of life. Swinburne and Baudelaire, Flaubert and Thomas Hardy, even Oscar Wilde, had a progressive function. They opened a passage through conformity; they opened the mind to receive new teachings. Their lesson was not that art *must not* teach, but that it must teach beyond the limits imposed by society. It is Arcady, on the contrary, which does not teach. Arcady is the art that Victorian England or Second Empire France wanted: the Art of Conformity. And I maintain that, in so far as it teaches nothing that it has not already discovered itself; in so far as it has nothing new to say on its own account, but is content to limit itself to repetition of common morality, it does not teach.

Speaking of Arcady, in general, we think of only one form of Arcadian art: pastoral variations on the theme of love. But this form of Arcadian art is not Arcadian before it deals with love. Even the *"stilnovisti"*[10] who dealt with love were not Arcadian. The Arcadian form is Arcadian because instead of taking inspiration from the direct reality of human passion, it deals with the conventional conception that society formed through habit. It is Arcadian because it does not adhere completely to life, and instead of developing itself from life reflects one or another abstract pattern of already asserted and deduced truth, so that the work of art is a mere illustration and magnification of such a pattern. The aestheticism of Arcady implies a distinction between art and poetry by which truth is conceived as existing outside poetry, and poetry itself as something other than a search for truth. The cultural position which most encourages the slippage from art to Arcadian aestheticism is abstract rationalism which measures everything in small, visibly rational, obvious steps and which

61

does not want to recognize as rational the larger or less visible steps. It appeals to writers as a simple philosophy and as simple politics. It induces poets to say: "Let us become the servants of truth." It is not realized that this means inducing them not to work for truth, not to fulfill their task of the proper discovery of truth, not to seek their own truth. It prevails upon them to "play the fife" for a predetermined form of truth. The fact that the fife is played on themes of politics, science, or civil ideology, or even themes of amorous ideology, does not change the Arcadian character of the music.

Many of the poetic compositions written by Italian Arcadians of the Eighteenth Century concern themselves with civil themes: Vencenzo Monti writes about balloonists or the activities of court as an Arcadian.[11] The *Risorgimento* created Arcadians. The patriotic poets whom Mazzini preferred to Leopardi, wrote as Arcadians and as "pastors" of politics. He who plays the fife for revolutionary politics is not less an Arcadian than he who plays the fife for reactionary or conservative politics. The poets of the American revolution, John Trumbell, Phillip Freneau, and Timothy Dwight, were not less Arcadian than those in London who played the fife for the suppression of the colonies. The subject of a work can be a great revolutionary problem, but if it does not come to the writer directly from life, if it comes through politics and ideology, if it comes to him as "argument", he will "play the fife" for it, and will be an Arcadian. A fife player is not a revolutionary writer. In the best of cases, if he has a lyrical temperament he will provide us with lyricism instead of the pastoral and he will be, say, a Maiakovski. But it is certainly not lyricism that makes a revolutionary writer. A writer is revolutionary when he succeeds in communicating revolutionary demands different from those which politics makes; internal, secret demands, the hidden demands of man which only *he*, the writer, can discover; demands which it is proper to him, as a revolutionary writer, to place *before* those of politics. When I speak of efforts from us writers in a revolutionary sense, I am speaking of efforts to express such demands. If I accuse our political fellows of not acknowledging our efforts as truly revolutionary ones, out of fear, it is because I see them recognising, instead, the Arcadian literature by those playing the fife for revolution. To ignore the best writers of what is often called "crisis" literature means to reject all the literature concerned with true problems, born from the crisis of our contemporary occidental society. Is this refusal to acknowledge those problems the opposite of revolutionary?

Undoubtedly, much of the literature of crisis comes from the bourgeoisie, and from a Romanticism drenched in individualism and decadence. But it is also charged with the necessity of escaping from it. It can be called bourgeois literature only in the sense that it is auto-critical of the bourgeoisie. Its motivating force is a sense of shame in its own bourgeois origins. Therefore, it can be called revolutionary, in spite of itself, just as English and French literature of the Eighteenth Century can be called revolutionary, in spite of its aristocratic vices. This desperate shame is reflected in the work of writers both inside and outside our Party. Their motives are not very different from those of Sartre and Camus.

There are also those who comprise only an Arcady of Party and who write a Lyricism of Party. Soviet literature itself, as far as we can judge it in translation, is also Lyrical Arcadianism. It is part of an Arcady of the weakest kind, although it partakes of the best sort of lyricism; a fact which demonstrates that the crisis of culture is world-wide, in capitalism's "insufficient politicisation" as well as in socialism's "political saturation". In one society, one runs the risk of becoming involved in reactionary politics, and in the other, of being drawn into a no less serious automatism. The revolutionary writer in a capitalist country must be awake to both dangers. The revolutionary writers who support our Party will have to refuse the aesthetic tendencies of the USSR because, as Italians, they come from a western country in a different phase of socialistic construction, and because the Russian way is not the way of the Italian or French socialist construction. Certainly, we writers of the Party are prepared for the eventuality of having to limit our work on the day that such an action should be indispensible for the construction of a classless society. Indeed, I would say that we are prepared to give up our work entirely. In this sacrifice lies the only difference between us and those who belong to no party at all. We know what happened to politics and culture during every great revolution: poetry became Arcadian, and culture the handmaiden of politics. We accept that the same will happen without revolution. From the teachings of Marx, however, we can take hope that our revolution will be different and extraordinary. It can happen that culture will not stagnate, that poetry will not enter Arcady. We must at least make the effort to act in such a way as to make this happen.

"Politica e cultura: lettera a Togliatti",
Politecnico, 35, January-March 1947.

Notes

1   The problems in 1947 "directly concerning" the Italian Communist Party were many, the most important of which was the direction in which the Party would move, particularly as it became clear that it was going to be kept out of the government. Togliatti clung to the idea of "class solidarity" with the Soviet Union, although he had been influenced by the ideas of Gramsci and believed as well in a uniquely Italian socialist experience. He, therefore, made a series of compromises, regarding representative democracy as one road to that particularly Italian socialism-to-be, and was clever enough to realize, with Vittorini, that a good many of the political problems were directly related to cultural ones.

2   Giambattista Vico (1668-1744) was an Italian philosopher who rejected the perfect understanding of a rigid system for an imperfect understanding of reality. He suggested that, since man can understand only that which he has made, philosophy should concern itself with investigating the principles underlying the foundations of nation-states. His *Principi di una scienza nuova d'intorno alla natura delle nazioni* was first published in 1725 and was followed by revisions in 1729-30 and 1744.

3   This is hardly a new problem, but it seems particularly relevant to neo-realism in terms of audience taste and the pressures against "pure" neo-realist theory. One of the defenses used by directors later accused of "involution" was the necessity of "staying in contact with the cultural level of the masses". A related problem arises with Vittorini's discussion of Arcady; Chiarini's arguments concerning "mannerism" parallel those of Vittorini here.

4   Benedetto Croce published an article in 1908 in the *Giornale d'Italia* in which he claimed that Marxism was no longer relevant to the modern world. Aside from the fact that Vittorini held opposing views concerning the relationship between literature and society, and would no doubt have considered Croce's cultural power and position dangerous, he would later also hold Croce responsible, in part, for Fascism at a philosophical level; he labelled him, in comparison with the Communists as something of a pseudo-anti-Fascist. He also regarded Croce as the author of a series of gutless political compromises (which were accepted by Togliatti) concerning the abdication of the King.

5   Many of the ideas expressed about culture and politics by an open Marxism not yet hardened into a system are, very likely, outgrowths of Vittorini's reading of Antonio Gramsci. Social and literary critic, political philosopher, as well as co-founder of the CPI, Gramsci insisted that the experience of any Communist or socialist in Italy must be "popular-national" in character as opposed to "imitation Soviet". The degeneration of the Russian revolution into bureaucratic "automatism" greatly worried him.

6   It is ironic that Togliatti should refer Vittorini back to Hegel, considering the points of view expressed by each in the debate. The influence of Hegel's "dialectical idealism" on Marx is well-known. At the end of the nineteenth century in Italy, however, positivism spread throughout the intellectual and artistic climate. Much of the contemporary polemicising over literature, which was later reflected in the arguments over realism and naturalism in neo-realism, grew out of positivism and an interest in "scientific objectivity". The Hegelians, with Bernardo Spaventa in Naples at their centre, were the last to argue this viewpoint. Arturo Labricola was Spaventa's student; when he "discovered" Marx, he interpreted the latter's ideology as one which would evolve by opening itself and release further premises for other ideologies. He was a major influence on Gramsci and thus on both Vittorini and (to a lesser degree) on Togliatti.

7   A *podestà* was a town magistrate appointed in the place of a monarch to regulate administrative matters in the medieval communes. The *gonfalonieri* were standard-bearers who carried the *gonfalone* of their town or *contrade* (district) as an emblem of local identity and at least some degree of governmental independence.

8   1908 was the year of Croce's statement to the effect that Marxism was
     dead. If not moribund, the socialist movement had split in two as a
     result of triumph and collapse. Italy was experiencing an economic cri-
     sis marked by the growing monopolistic ownership of major industry.
     Arturo Labriola and Alceste de Ambris led an agricultural strike in the
     Parma region which lasted for months. The temporary success of the
     strike led to the real beginnings of organized contact between indus-
     trial workers and the peasants in the South. When the strike in Parma
     finally failed, the less activist-oriented wing of the movement gained
     control.

9   Giuseppe Mazzini (1805-1872) was a revolutionary who spent most of
     his life in exile, and who actively supported the demand for an inde-
     pendent and united Italian Republic. For a time he was called back to
     serve in the Roman Republic of 1848, and then, bitterly opposed to
     Cavour, he went back into exile.
        As has been noted, the reputation of Giacomo Leopardi (1798-1872),
     who is often cited as the best lyric poet in nineteenth century Italian
     literature, is based on a very small number of poems and a few prose
     works. His poetry, while not ignoring society completely, concerns
     itself primarily with personal considerations of man's insignificance
     in the face of an indifferent universe.
        Giambattista Niccolini (1782-1861) was a minor but prolific writer
     of plays and verse. His most famous theatre pieces, *Giovanni da Pro-
     cida* (1830) and *Arnaldo da Brescia* (1843), are romantically patrio-
     tic. Mazzini is undoubtedly alone in preferring the latter to the former.

10   Those poets who belonged to the *"Dolce stil nuova"* (sweet new style)
     movement, including Francesco Petrarch. It is unclear why Vittorini
     excepts Petrarch from the charge of "Arcadianism", save that Petrarch
     set, perfected, and moved with profound freedom within the poetic
     conventions of the school. Substitute "manner" for "Arcady" and the
     same line of reasoning is used by Chiarini in his discussion of neo-real-
     ism.

11   Vencenzo Monti (1745-1828) was, for fifteen years, the official poet of
     the Papal court at Rome. He wrote a great many occasional poems to
     commemorate, among other happenings, Pius VI's travels, land recla-
     mation, and the first Italian ascent in a balloon. His verse is always for-
     mally elegant, verse and plays both being modelled along classical
     lines. Evidently, he espoused no political convictions, for he wrote on
     politics from every possible point of view.

---

4. A Thesis on Neo-Realism
by Cesare Zavattini

This essay is actually made up of three articles by Zavattini: "*Alcune idee sul cinema*", *Revista del cinema italiano*, December, 1952; "*Tesi sul neorealismo*", *Emilia*, 21 November, 1953; "*Il neorealismo secondo me*", first delivered at the Congress of Parma on Neo-Realism, December 3, 4, 5, 1953, and later printed in *Rivista del cinema italiano*, 3, March 1954.

Zavattini has several basic ideas about neo-realism and the cinema ("which I will repeat until everyone listens"). These turn up again and again in his articles and in the various interviews with him, often with very little modification in either phrasing or illustrative examples. Thus the three articles named have been edited together here to avoid the repetition which would have resulted in printing all three. No violence has been done to any of his ideas. This essay as it now stands encompasses his central ideas; his examples impart the flavour of the man himself.

There is no doubt that our first, and most superficial, reaction to daily existence is boredom. Reality seems deprived of all interest as long as we cannot succeed in surmounting and overcoming our moral and intellectual sloth. It is, therefore, not surprising that the cinema has always felt the "natural" and practically inevitable necessity of inserting a story into reality in order to make it thrilling and spectacular. It is evident that in this manner one could spontaneously escape from reality; it is as if nothing could be done to prevent the interference of the imagination.

The most important characteristic of neo-realism, i.e. its essential innovation, is, for me, the discovery that this need to use a story was just an unconscious means of masking human defeat in the face of reality; imagination, in its own manner of functioning, merely superimposes death schemes onto living events and situations.

Yet, in fact, we are now aware that reality is extremely rich. We simply had to learn how to look at it. The task of the artist — the neo-realist artist at least — does not consist in bringing the audience to tears and indignation by means of transference, but, on the contrary, it consists in bringing them to reflect (and *then*, if you will, to stir up emotions and indignation) upon what they are doing and upon what others are doing; that is, to think about reality precisely as it is.

From a profound and unconscious lack of confidence in confronting reality, from an illusory and ambiguous evasion, we have gone on to an unlimited confidence in things, events, and in men.

Naturally, this taking of sides requires us to dig deeply, to give reality the power and faculty of communication, the radiance, which, up until the time of neo-realism, we didn't believe it could possess.

It has often been written that the war was the keystone for neo-realism. This overwhelming event upset men's souls; film directors, each in his own way, tried to transpose this overwhelming emotion onto the screen. As we saw absolutely no reason for participating in it, the war seemed particularly monstrous for us Italians. We had far more reasons for not becoming involved. This rebellion, however, was not limited to that particular war; it went much further. It was the absolute — I would even say the eternal — revelation that war always violates those fundamental human needs and values which are so dear to us. This revelation was, in my opinion, the starting point of a vast human uprising.

You might reply that this revelation was not the distinction of Italy alone. I would tend to agree. Nonetheless, those very qualities which many take to be the faults of our people, but which are actually our essential virtues — extreme individualism, a lack of overweening social pride, and so on — urge us towards a full and passionate reaction against the supreme evil of war. It was not "historical man" who acted — that abstract character in novels which follows a course of action that is unrelated to a specific time and deals with dates of past, present and future wars indiscriminately — on the contrary, it was the real, deep thinking, hidden man who acted. You might object by pointing out that "historical man" and the man without a label exist side by side. That is true enough, except that they co-exist *usefully* only when, by the principle of clear channels of communication, they find a common level and merge; that is to say that the former, with his awareness, and the latter, with his profoundly original drive to live, must be in real contact. The need to live, when it is rich and happy, can transcend its limits more easily when, as in this case, it inspires and enlightens an entire fallen people who seemingly could no longer make the smallest contribution to humanity.

I dare to think that *other* peoples, even after the war, have shown that they continued to consider man as a historical *subject*, as historical material, with determined, almost inevitable, actions. This is why they, unlike the Italians, did not give the cinema its freedom. For them, everything continued; for us, everything began. For them the war had been just another war; for us, it had been the last war. What were the discoveries and the consequences of this rush of post-war pioneers, which were new, not because they had never before been known, but because they had never been felt in such a collective and tenacious manner? The results were the endless possibility of studying man that we see opening before us, a non-abstract and concrete study of man, as concrete as the men who provoked and underwent the war. We needed to know and to see how these terrible events could have occurred. The cinema was the most direct and immediate way of making this sort of study. It was preferable to other art forms which did not possess a language which would readily express our reactions against the lies of those old, generalized ideas in which we found ourselves clothed at the outbreak of the war, and which had prevented us from attempting the smallest rebellion.

This powerful desire of the cinema to see and to analyse, this hunger for reality, for truth, is a kind of concrete homage to other people, that is, to all who exist. This, among other things, is what distinguishes neo-realism from the American cinema. In effect, the American position is diametrically opposed to our own: whereas we are attracted by the truth, by the reality which touches us and which we want to know and understand directly and thoroughly, the Americans continue to satisfy themselves with a sweetened version of truth produced through transpositions.

That is why the Americans are undergoing a crisis; they have no idea what subjects to use. This is not possible in Italy, for here, there can never be a lack of truth. Every hour of the day, every place, every person, can be portrayed if they are shown in a manner which reveals and emphasizes the collective elements which continually shape them.

This is why one cannot speak of a crisis of subjects (facts), but only of the possibility, as the case may be, of a crisis of content (the interpretation of facts).

This essential difference was very clearly expressed by an American producer who told me:

> In America, the scene of a plane passing over is shown in this sequence: a plane passes, machine-gun fire opens, the plane falls. In Italy: a plane passes, it passes again, and then again.

It is the absolute truth. But it is still not enough. It is not enough to have the plane pass by three times; it must pass by twenty times. We work, therefore, to extricate ourselves from abstractions.

In a novel, the protagonists were heroes; the shoes of the hero were special shoes. We, on the other hand, are trying to find out what our characters have in common; in my shoes, in his, in those of the rich, in those of the poor, we find the same elements: the same labour of man.

Let us move on to style. How can we express this reality (truth) in the cinema? First, I would like to repeat what I have often said: The contents always engender their own expression, their own technique. Imagination, therefore, is allowed, but only on the condition that it exercise itself within reality and not on the periphery. Let me be clear: I do not intend to give the impression that only "news items" matter to me. I have tried to concentrate on these with the intention of putting them together again in the most faithful way, using a bit of imagination, which comes from a perfect understanding of the event, situation, or fact itself. Obviously, it would be more coherent for the camera to catch them at the moment they develop. This is what I intend to do when I make my film on Italy.[1] It should never be forgotten, of course, that any relationship with an idea one wishes to express implies a choice which is part of the creative act, but that choice must be made in relationship with the subject on the spot rather than the subject being a reconstruction following an imaginatice choice. This is what I call the "cinema of encounter". This method of working should lead logically to two results: first, from an ethical point of view, directors would leave the studio in search of direct contact with reality. Therefore, we will create a system of production which will bring with it the freshness of collective awareness. The number of films we make also plays an important part. If we make one hundred films a year which are inspired by these criteria, we would change the very conditions of production; if we only make three, we will have to submit to the conditions of production as they exist today.

This awareness of reality, which constitutes neo-realism, has two consequences in terms of narrative construction:

(1) Whereas in the past, cinema portrayed a situation from which a second was derived, and then a third from that, and so on, each scene being created only to be forgotten the next moment, today, when we imagine a scene, we feel the need to "stay" there inside it; we now know that it has within itself all the potential of being reborn and of having important effects. We can calmly say: give us an ordinary situation and from it we will make a spectacle. Centrifugal force which constituted (both from a technical and a moral point of view) the fundamental aspects of traditional cinema has now transformed itself into centripetal force.

(2) Whereas the cinema always told of life's external aspects, today neo-realism affirms that we should not be content with illusion, but should move toward analysis, or better, should move towards a synthesis within analysis.

For example: let us take two people who are looking for an apartment. In the past, the film-maker would have made that the starting point, using it as a simple and external pretext to base something else on. Today, one can use that simple situation of hunting for an apartment as the entire subject of the film. It must be understood, of course, that this is true only if the situation is always emphasized with all the echoes, reflections, and reverberations which are present in it.

We are, we recognize, still far from that necessary and true analysis. Now we can only speak of analysis simply in opposition to the vulgar artificiality of current production. For the time being we have only an analytic "attitude", but this attitude brings with it a powerful movement towards facts, a desire for comprehension, for adhesion, for participation, and for co-existence.

This principle of analysis arises in the consideration of style, in the most narrow sense, and is opposed to bourgeois synthesis. In the bourgeois cinema, directors choose the most representative aspects of a situation of well-being and privilege of a part of Italian culture. To understand critically the range of neo-realism, one must stress the role played by Italian culture. Given the increasingly important collaboration of writers in the creation of the cinema, it could not be otherwise. But this collaboration cannot limit itself to the furnishing of novels as a basis for film; writers should rather contribute to the enrichment of cinematic expression, an expression rich with as much potential as literary language. If writers can involve themselves in a less tentative way than they usually do, they can bring great progress to the cinema and involve the whole of Italian culture.

It should, therefore, be clear that contrary to what was done before the war, the neo-realist movement recognized that the cinema should take as its subject the daily existence and condition of the Italian people, without introducing the coloration of the imagination, and thereby, force itself to analyze it for whatever human, historical, determining and definite factors it encompasses.

I believe that the world continues to evolve towards evil because we do not know the truth: we remain unaware of reality. The most necessary task for a man today consists in attempting to resolve, as best he can, the problem of this knowledge and lack of awareness. That is why the most urgent need of our times is social contact, social awareness. But no matter how artistically successful it may be, moral allegory is no longer enough. This awareness and contact must be direct. A hungry man, a downtrodden man, must be shown as he is, with his own first and last names. A story should never be constructed in which the hungry and the oppressed merely appear, for then everything changes, becomes less effective, and far less moral.

The true function of the arts has always been that of expressing the needs of the times; it is towards this function that we should redirect them. No other means of expression has the potential which the cinema possesses for making things known directly, for making contact immediately, to the largest number of people. It was, of course, natural that even those who understood such things were still obliged, for all sorts of reasons — some valid, others not, to compose stories invented according to tradition, and even more natural that they sought to add to the stories some elements of what they themselves had discovered.

In effect, this is what neo-realism is currently in Italy.

Roma città aperta, Paisà, Sciusià, Ladri di biciclette, and *La terra trema* are films which contain passages of great significance. They were inspired by the possibility of telling everything, but, in a certain sense, they still involve translation because they tell stories and do not apply the documentary spirit simply and fully. In films like *Umberto D,* the analytical fact is much more evident, but the analysis is set within the framework of traditional narrative. We have not yet come to real neo-realism.

The neo-realism of today is like an army prepared to march. the soldiers are prepared: Rossellini, De Sica, Visconti. They must lead the assault; it is the only way the war can be won. The important fact is that the movement has begun; now either we go forward to the very end, or we will have missed a great opportunity. Ahead of neo-realism vast perspectives are opening, perspectives beyond our imagination. We must grasp our chance. It will not be easy. Transforming every day situations into spectacle is not an easy thing to do; intensity of vision is required from both the director and the audience. It is a dialogue in which one must give life, reality, its historical importance, which exists in each instant.

As for recent productions, I can speak about those in which I was involved. I assure you that I do not hold *Stazione termini* as an important example of a human document in my neo-realistic career. The existence of a co-production[2] reduced to practically nothing the basic and original inspiration, which made the first conception of the film an examination of a precise and limited time and place.

My next film *Italia mia* has neo-realist origins in the most precise sense of the term. It began with my need to know and to understand my own country thoroughly, and my absolute confidence in the adventures and encounters I would meet. Aspects of neo-realism are contained in the central ideas of *Amore in città* and *Siamo donne.*[3] In the latter, at least, there is a certain moral idea in the need for communication which inspires actors and their confessions to the audience. In the presence of these confessions, the audience should be able to liberate itself from the inferiority complex caused by the mythic idea of the "star".

Attacks on these films, like the attacks on other films based on a neo-realistic idea, indeed on neo-realism itself, have come in various guises. Here are the principle ones:

Neo-realism describes only misery. Neo-realism can, and must, study misery as well as luxury. We have begun with misery because it is one of the most vivid realities of our time. I defy anyone to prove the contrary. To believe, or to feign belief, that after a half dozen films about poverty the theme has been exhausted is either an error or sophistry. The theme of poverty (of both the rich and the poor) is one to which a person could devote a lifetime. We have only just begun. If the rich raised their eyebrows at *Miracolo a Milano*, which is only a fable, they will soon see better than that. I place myself among the rich. What riches we have are not simply money (which is only the most apparent aspect of richness); we are also rich in the injustice and violence which money engenders. There is also a moral position which might be counted as a man's riches.

Neo-realism offers no solutions, shows no new roads, gives no conclusions; the films are totally evasive. I deny this with all of my being. Every moment of each of our films is a continual response to such accusations. As for solutions, it is not up to the artist to examine them. It is enough for him to make the need urgently felt.

Every day occurrences are not interesting; they do not constitute a dramatic spectacle. When a director evades the analysis of "every day occurrences" he obeys the more or less expressed desires of the capitalistic system of cinema production; he gives in to the public's wish to escape reality; he is lazy. The putting together of one situation after another in a narrative line is not so very difficult. The analysis of a situation or an action in depth is extremely difficult. If it is done, however, it is dramatic and a spectacle.

We have the illusion — call it that if you like — that with us something completely different and new is beginning. Today a man who suffers before my eyes is absolutely different from a man who suffered a hundred years ago. I must concentrate all my attention on the man of today. The historical baggage that I carry within myself, and from which, by the way, I neither can nor want to free myself, must not prevent me from being what I wish to be, nor from using the means I have at hand to deliver this man from his pain. This man — and this is one of my basic and fixed ideas — has a first name and a last name. He is part of society in a way that concerns us, make no mistake about that. I feel his fascination. I must feel it in such a way that I

74

am urgently obliged to speak to him or of him, but not as a character of my imagination's invention; it is exactly at that moment one must beware, for it is then that the imagination attempts to come between reality and the self.

I have often had to explain that I do not wish to prohibit actors from playing in films. Of course actors have a place in films, it is simply that they have very little to do with neo-realistic cinema. The neo-realistic cinema does not ask those men in whom it is interested to have the talents of actors; their professional aptitudes have to do with the profession of being men. They need to be made aware of this, of course, which is the responsibility of the cinema. It is evident that this awareness can only be created or reinforced through the knowledge we give them of themselves, knowledge which we will attain through neo-realistic cinema.

How, then, does the imagination, the creative act, enter neo-realism? It is, of course, a very particular sort of imagination, and the creative act is a very new method of using that imagination.

For example: a woman goes to a shoe store to buy shoes for her son. The shoes cost 7,000 lire. The woman bargains to get them cheaper. The scene lasts ten minutes, whereas I have to make a film two hours long (we will discuss the commercial "rules" of distribution and exhibition which dictated that a film be of a certain length at another time). What then do I do? I analyze all the elements which go to make up the situation, what happened beforehand, what will come afterwards, and what is really happening while the situation exists. The woman buys the shoes, but what is happening to her son at the moment? What is happening in India which might be related to this particular pair of shoes? The shoes cost 7,000 lire. How did the woman get that money? What pain have they cost her? What do they represent for her? And the shoe shop owner who sells them: who is he? What relationship is created between these two people? There might be two other sons also there eating and chattering. Would you like to hear their conversation? Here they are. And it goes on.

It is the act of getting to the bottom of things, of showing the relationships between the situations and the process through which the situations come into being. If we analyze the purchase of a pair of shoes, we see before us a complex and vast world, rich in scope and possibilities, rich in practical, social, economic and psychological motifs. The banal disappears, for it never really existed.

I am against exceptional persons, heroes. I have always felt an instinctive hate towards them. I feel offended by their presence, excluded from their world as are millions of others like me. We are all characters. Heroes create inferiority complexes throughout an audience. The time has come to tell each member of the audience that he is the true protagonist of life. The result would be a constant emphasis on the responsability and dignity of every human being. This is exactly the ambition of neo-realism: to strengthen everyone, and to give everyone the proper awareness of a human being.

The term neo-realism, in its larger sense, implies the elimination of technical-professional collaboration, including that of the screen writer. Manuals, grammars, syntax no longer have any meaning, no more than the terms "first take", "reaction shot" and all the rest. Each of us will "direct" in his own way, "compose a scenario" in his own way. Neo-realism shatters all schemes, shuns all dogmas. There can be no "first takes" nor "reaction shots" *a priori*. The subject, the adaptation, the direction cannot, in neo-realism, be three distinct phases of the same work. It is true that they are so today, but this is an anomaly. In neo-realism, the screen writer and the writer of dialogue disappear; there will be no scenario written beforehand, and no dialogue to adapt.

We must come to terms with the unique *auteur*, the director, but he will, in the long run, have little in common with either the theatre or cinema directors of today.

Everything is in flux. Everything is moving. Someone makes his film: everything is continually possible and everything is full of infinite potentiality, not only during the shooting, but during the editing, the mixing, throughout the entire process as well.

I have been working in the Italian cinema since 1934. I know that I have contributed to the destruction of a few of the usual and traditional schemes. If I place myself among those who believe that neo-realism is one of the most powerful forces to which we can address ourselves, it is not by any lack of imagination. On the contrary, I must constantly pull myself to a halt with both hands so as to refuse my imagination entrance into my work. I have enough imagination in the traditional sense of the word to sell and resell, but neo-realism requires us to allow our imagination to exercise itself only *in loco* and through reality, for the situations increase their natural imaginative force when they are studies in depth. It is only then that they can become dramatic spectacles, because it is then that they become revelations.

I know very well that one can make marvelous films like those of Charlie Chaplin, and that they are not neo-realist works. I know very well that there are Americans, Russians, Frenchmen, and so forth, who have made masterpieces which bring honour to humanity. They have certainly not wasted film. And God knows how many distinguished works they will continue to produce, depending upon their genius, using stars, studios, and the adaptations of novels. But the men of the Italian cinema, in order to continue to search for and to conserve their own style and inspiration, having once courageously set ajar the doors of reality and truth, must now open them wide.

Notes

1   *Italia mia*, a film which was never made. It came from Zavattini's idea to make a film about a trip around the world, and then developed into a project for a film about a journey throughout Italy. He was particularly enthusiastic about the project in 1951 and 1952. His idea was to move through various social environments filming brief episodes and fragments of Italian life, allowing all sorts of people to tell their stories. In 1953, he described the project: "A time will come when in the cinema we will share a man's everyday preoccupations, observe him doing the most ordinary tasks, and we will follow all of this with the same attention the Greeks gave to their great playwrights."

2   For reasons best known to himself — his films represented the opposite end of the cinematic spectrum from neo-realism — David O. Selznick, throughout the Fifties, attempted to interest various neo-realists in making films for him. In 1949, he tried to sign Roberto Rossellini to a contract, perhaps to "protect" Ingrid Bergman whom he had "discovered" for American films in 1939; Rossellini refused, going back to Italy to make *Stromboli* and several other films with Bergman, but without Selznick. The producer then approached De Sica in the early Fifties. the result was *Stazione termini* (U.S. title: *Indiscretion of an*

American wife), with a script by Zavattini, directed by De Sica, and starring Jennifer Jones, who was then both Mrs. Selznick and Selznick's most valuable star.

The 1954 film had a huge budget (for Italy and De Sica), two major Hollywood stars (Montgomery Clift played Miss Jones's lover), and "additional dialogue" by Truman Capote. Whatever Zavattini-De Sica's original intent (or that of Selznick, for that matter), the film became an over-produced, semi-glossy melodrama of hysterical adultery in Rome's central train station. There were three versions of the film when it was released: in Europe outside of Italy, the film was shortened by about half an hour; in America it was shortened by one third; the Italian version maintained the original length, but was entirely dubbed into Italian. The film was a critical and financial failure in all three versions.

This film, however, marked the beginning of De Sica and Zavattini's move away from neo-realism towards comedies and melodramas with big budgets and stars.

3 Zavattini produced (with Riccardo Ghione and Marco Ferreri) *Amore in città*, and collaborated on one of the episodes (with Franco Maselli): "*Storia di Caterina*". *Siamo donne* was also an episode film partially written by Zavattini and Luigi Chiarini. The idea was to have several stars "play" themselves (Ingrid Bergman, Anna Magnani, Alida Valli, and others) in short "revelatory" and "realistic" episodes directed by several directors (Rossellini, Visconti, and others). The episodes ranged from interesting personality studies to fully scripted and artificial "star turns".

5. Concerning a Film about the River Po
by Michelangelo Antonioni

Michelangelo Antonioni (1912-   ) was first a film critic
(for *Corriere padano* and *Cinema*), then an assistant director
(for Marcel Carné), and finally a director who has gained a
well-merited international reputation as one of the most
important artists in the Italian cinema. This essay was written for *Cinema* as a description of intention some time before
he became active in making films.

It is not ridiculous to say that the people of the Po Valley are in love
with the Po. In fact the river is surrounded by a halo of instinctive
attraction, even of love, and, to a certain extent, the Po can be
regarded as the despot of its valley. The people of the valley "feel" the
Po. How this feeling comes to reification, we do not know. We only
know that it is "in the air" and is felt as a subtle bewitchment.

Actually, this is a commonplace phenomenon in many places
which are intersected by large rivers; it is as if it were the destiny of
such lands to terminate in a river. There, life is endowed with particular customs and tendencies. A new, limited economy arises from the
river. Children choose it for their favourite, often forbidden, games.
In other words, a special intimacy, fed by different factors, is established, among which is the common struggle of the population
against the waters. Almost every year, at the beginning of summer or
of autumn, the waters set themselves against the population,
through floods that are always tragically superb and forceful.

This flood is, therefore, a basic divining force in our hypothetical
film. It is basic for two reasons: for the spectacle itself, and because it
reveals the essence, the substance, of that love hinted at before. This
attachment is strange; so is the steadfastness which resists the ordeals
imposed by the floods. If today the floods leave the people in relative
peace because of the new jetties and easily built shelters, we must not
assume that the floods of the past have always receded without sco-
ring deep marks. Very often the floods took human victims; they left

a horrible prospect of muddy fields and villages, of heaps of furniture, crockery, and other domestic objects on the roads, and reeds and uprooted trees in abundance rising from the foaming eddies. Yet, in spite of everything, the sons of the Po have not found a way to escape it. They have struggled and suffered, and struggle and suffer still, but obviously they can reintegrate the pain into the natural order of things, and, on top of this, can derive from this sense of order an incentive for the struggle.

There is another significant point of interest which comes from reflecting particularly on the civilization of the people of the river. A long time ago, the river used to look more serenely romantic: a thick vegetation, numerous fishermen's cabins, floating mills (of which we still have examples today), rudimentary ferries and bridges made of barges; the whole of it immersed in an amnesia-inducing and ecstatic aura, in a powerful force that seemed to ooze from the vast waters to mark everything.

The population — solid folk with slow and heavy gestures — were well-acquainted with long rests along the banks and with wandering through the woods which cover them; they knew ponds full of fish and young girls hidden under weeping willows, the branches of which licked the water. But they left that slow life, busying themselves with carrying goods and people, with taking care of the mills, and above all fishing. Neither for men nor for things did the years pass in vain, and for the river too came the time to awaken.

Then it was iron bridges, on which trains clattered along by day and night; it was five-storied buildings spotted with large windows which vomited noise and dust; it was steam boats, factories, smokey chimneys and added channels with concrete piers. In fact, it was a whole modern world, mechanical and industralized, which had come to upset the old one.

Yet, in the midst of the destruction of their old world, the population had no regrets. Perhaps they might have liked to feel regret because their own nature, harsh and contemplative, had not yet become accustomed to the new situation, but they never succeeded. At a certain point, the evolution not only did not disturb them, but in a certain way pleased them. They started considering the river from a functional point of view. They felt it had become valorous and they were proud of it. They understood that it had become precious and their ambition was satisfied.

All of this can seem to be literature; it is not. It is, or wants to be, cinema. Now, it remains for us to see how it can be translated into action. First of all there is the basic question: should it be a documentary or a story film?

Without any doubt, the former appeals to me a good deal. The material is suggestive and rich; it moves *from* large sections of river, huge as lakes, and sometimes interrupted by small islands, *to* small passages where the Po, surrounded by wild plants, looks like some African landscape. From the squalid huts along the piers with the usual pool in the middle of the yard in front of the door, to the modern villas with their chalets near the water which on certain nights become animated by light rhythmical music; from the floating mills to the imposing factories; from the steep jetties to the pleasant beaches pretending to be worldly; from the barges to the motor boats, to the hydroplanes of the Pavia-Venezia . . .

This is rich material, but dangerous, because it lends itself to rhetoric. Consequently, if we are seduced by the memory of a wonderful documentary about the Mississippi, *The river,*[1] we are left perplexed by the trite formulas of "what was, is what is" and "the eternal river".

The introduction of a light narrative thread would not entirely suffice either. We must be very cautious about hybrids in general, and in particular those of the screen, where the form which dictates precise directions and does not allow for uncertainties can never be overpraised. Either one way or the other, the essential is to know exactly what we want. Flaherty, although a very distinguished *auteur*, provides us with a rather recent example, in fact, with his *Elephant boy*[2] because of the clash between documentary and narrative. The lyrical impulses of the work, this sort of religion of the jungle, finds its most genuine expression in the documentary sequences in which there is only the torment of poetic discovery, which is elsewhere disturbed by the narrative.

Thus, we must be careful not to welcome a fiction film too quickly. Between you and me, I feel a good deal of sympathy for a filmed fiction/document without any label, but we must not hurry. Even here there is no lack of obstacles. The first is to idealize a thread of plot which corresponds completely to the motives already mentioned. The Americans, from whom no theme can escape, have already tackled it. Two of their films, the first being a very old one, *The river*, and — released some years ago — *La canzone del fiume*, were successful, especially the first; from a thematic point of view, it is the best. Yet both were far from my own conception and my own sensibility.

But here I do not want to advise anyone, nor to suggest any thread for a story. I need only say that I would like a film with the Po as the central character, in which the spirit of the river would provide the interest of the film; that is to say, a film which is the sum total of its moral and psychological elements, rather than a heap of its folkloric, exterior, decorative elements.

I would like a film in which commercial demands are not essential, but in which intelligence prevails.[3]

"Per un film sul fiume Po", Cinema, 68,
April 25, 1939.

Notes

1   *The river* (1937), directed by Pare Lorentz, with a narration spoken by Thomas Chalmers and a musical score by Virgil Thomson, was produced by the Farm Security Administration of the (U.S.) Department of Agriculture. It was intended to explain government projects for flood prevention and soil preservation. Its main thrust, however, is an epic portrait of the Mississippi River from its headwaters in Canada to the Gulf of Mexico.

2   *Elephant boy* (1937) was only partially directed by Robert Flaherty; the "dramatic" sections were directed by Zoltan Korda. The British film was based on Kipling's *Toomai of the elephants* and starred Sabu.

3   Antonioni began his documentary *Gente del Po* in 1943 and finished it in 1947. In 1948, Alberto Lattuada directed a fictional film which used the Po as its setting, *Il mulino del Po*. Other films have, of course, also used the Po as background for at least part of their action; the most celebrated is the Po episode in Rossellini's *Paisà*.

6. Anthropomorphic Cinema
by Luchino Visconti

Luchino Visconti (1906-1977) was both an aristocrat and a Marxist, a double commitment which was reflected in his work in which social analysis and elegance of style merged.

What led me towards creative activity in the cinema? (Creative Activity: the work of a man living among other men. It is clear by this term that I do not mean something limited only to the artist's domain. Every worker who lives, creates, provided that the conditions of his time are free and open. This is as true for the worker and artisan as it is for the artist.)

It was not the strong call of a vocation — a romantic concept far removed from reality, an abstract term coined by artists to contrast the privilege of their activity with the next man's. While a "vocation" does not exist, the consciousness of one's own experience, the dialectical development of a man's life in contact with that of other men, does.

I think that it is only through painful experience which is continuously stimulated by an objective study of humanity that one can achieve specialization. To reach it, however, does not mean enclosing oneself in it and breaking off every concrete social link, as has happened to so many artists. Very often, that very specialization leads them to escape from reality, in other words to a lack of commitment.

I do not mean that every work is not a particular work and to a certain extent a "trade"; rather, that it is valuable only in so far as it is the product of a life's testimony or is a manifestation of that life.

I was attracted by the cinema because it coordinates so many demands and enthusiasms that lead to a better, more complex, work. Because of this, it is all the more obvious that the human responsibility of the director is truly important; only as long as that responsibility is not corrupted by a decadent vision of existence will it lead us in the right way.

I was drawn to the cinema because I wanted, above all, to tell stories of living men, of living men *among* things, not of things *per se*. What I am interested in is an "anthropomorphic" cinema.

Among all my activities in the cinema, my favourite is working with actors; with the human material from which we build those living men who give birth to a new reality, the reality of art. The actor is above all a man possessing key human qualities. I try to base my work upon those qualities and to graduate them in the creation of my characters so as to make a unity of the man-actor and the man-character.

Until now, the Italian cinema has had to endure actors; it has left them free to magnify their vanity and errors, while the real problem is to use the originality and actuality of their true nature. To a certain extent is is important that actors, so-called professionals, should present themselves to the director with all the deformities born from their personal experiences. Even if it is often hard work, it is worth capturing the nucleus of a distorted personality; a human being is always at bottom, "free-able" and "re-educatable". We want the actor to speak his own instinctive language, abstracting himself from previous systems, from any memory of school or method. If such language exists at all, it will not be sterile (even if hidden under a hundred veils) if the actor has "character". I do not mean to imply, of course, that great actors should not have such qualities, but that less famous actors (who must all the same attract our attention) possess these qualities as much as the others.

And what of non-professionals? Not only do they possess a fascinating simplicity, but they often have more genuinely sane qualities because, being less corrupt, they are often better men. The important thing is to discover them and to focus their qualities. In this case the director has to become a "water diviner" in both circumstances.

My experience has taught me that the heft of a human being, his presence, is the only thing which really fills the frame; that *he* creates the atmosphere with his living presence. He acquires truth and character thanks to the emotion he undergoes, while his temporary absence from the screen will cause things to return to the state of non-animated nature.

The most humble gesture of a man, his face, his hesitations and his impulses, impart poetry and life to the things which surround him and to the setting in which they take place. Every other solution to the problem will always seem to me an offense against reality as it unfolds itself before our eyes: made by man and continuously unmade by him.

The discussion has hardly begun, but I would like to make my position clear before having to conclude: I could make a film in front of a wall if I knew how to find the data of man's true humanity and how to express it.

"Cinema antropomorfico", Cinema, 173/174, September 25/October 25, 1943.

7. Why *Ladri di Biciclette?*
by Vittorio De Sica

Vittorio De Sica was born in Naples and became first a music hall entertainer, then a film actor, and finally a director himself, usually working in collaboration with Cesare Zavattini.

Why did I make that film? Well, after *Sciuscià*, I read some thirty or forty scripts, each more "beautiful" than the one before, full of facts and interesting situations. But I was looking for action which would be less apparently "extraordinary", which could happen to anyone (above all to the poor), action which no newspaper wants to talk about.

Anyway, everything happened as follows: one evening Zavattini called me to tell me he had read a beautiful book, *Ladri di biciclette*, by Luigi Bartolini, and that the book had inspired him to write a story for me. The next day I read the first draft of the story.

The story differs from the book fairly radically; the latter is really rather cheerful, colourful, and picaresque. It suffices to note that the protagonist of the film is not Bartonini's, but a bill poster who wanders through Rome in a desperate search for his means of transport. From that point, there is another atmosphere, other interests, more adapted to my own means and scope. Why did we then acquire the title and the rights to a book from which we planned a free adaptation? To acknowledge a remarkable writer who, with his vivid style, has given me inspirational motivation for my new film. My scope is to trace the "dramatic" in every-day situations, the wonderful in small events, what many consider to be artificially embellished trivia.

What is the importance, after all, of stealing a bicycle, one which is far from bright and new? In Rome many are stolen every day and nobody cares, since it is of no importance to the rest of the city. Yet, to lose a bicycle is a grave event, a tragic circumstance, for those who have nothing else, who use it to go to work, who cherish it in the turmoil of city life. Why seek extraordinary adventures when we are presented daily with artless people who are filled with real distress?

It has been a long time since literature first discovered that modern dimension given to small things, that state of mind considered too "common". Thanks to the camera, the cinema has the means to capture that dimension. That is how I understand realism, which cannot be, in my opinion, mere documentation. If there is absurdity in this theory, it is the absurdity of those social contradictions which society wants to ignore. It is the absurdity of incomprehension through which it is difficult for truth and good to penetrate. Thus, my film is dedicated to the suffering of the humble.

"Perché Ladri di biciclette?", La fiera letteraria,
February 6, 1948.

8. A Few Words about Neo-realism.
by Roberto Rossellini

Roberto Rossellini (1906-1977) is one of the toweringly important figures in Italian and international cinema. He began working in documentaries at the *Instituto Nazionale Luce* during the Fascist period, came into his own as a director immediately after the war, and continued making films outside the usual commercial structure until his death following his heart attack soon after serving on the Jury at the Cannes Film Festival.

I am a director, not an aesthete, and I doubt whether I am capable of indicating with absolute precision what realism and neo-realism are. Nevertheless, even if there are probably those who can talk about it better than I, I can describe what I perceive neo-realism to be and what I have done. Neo-realism is the greatest possible curiosity about individuals: a need, appropriate to modern man, to speak of things as they are, to be aware of reality, in an absolutely concrete manner, conforming to that typically contemporary interest in statistical and scentific results; a sincere need, as well, to see men with humility, as they are, without resorting to stratagems in order to invent the extraordinary; to be aware of being able to arrive at the extraordinary through inquiry itself; a reality, whatever it is, in order to attain an understanding of things. To give anything its true value means to have understood its authentic and universal meaning.

There are those who still think of neo-realism as something external, as going out into the open air, as a contemplation of misery and suffering. For me, it is nothing other than the artistic form of truth. When truth is regained, we can arrive at expressing it. If the truth is a sham you can feel the falseness, and truth of expression is not achieved. Holding these ideas, I cannot believe in an entertainment film as it is understood in some industrial circles, of course, even outside Europe, if it is not a film which is at last partially capable of attaining the truth.

The subject of neo-realist film is the world; not story or narrative. It contains no preconceived thesis, because ideas are born *in* the film *from* the subject. It has no affinity with the superfluous and the merely spectacular, which it refuses, but is attracted to the concrete. It does not remain on the surface, but seeks out the most subtle aspects of the soul. It refuses recipes and formulas in its search for the motivating forces in each of us. Briefly, neo-realism poses problems for us and for itself in an attempt to make people think. We found ourselves, after the war, face-to-face with this commitment. What counted for us was the enquiry into truth, the correspondence to the real. For the first so-called Italian neo-realist directors, it was a real act of courage, and no one will deny that. After the innovators came the popularizers. They had nothing to transform, and perhaps they were able to explain themselves better; they provided a larger conception of neo-realism. In so far as they spread it, perhaps they are more important. Then, as was inevitable, came the deviations and transformations, but by then neo-realism had already travelled a long way on its road.

The birth of neo-realism is to be found first in certain romanticized film documents about the war, then in "true" war films, and eventually in minor films in which the formula (if I may call it that) of neo-realism is achieved through the spontaneous creations of the actors. Neo-realism was born unconsciously as dialectical film, after which it acquired a heart-felt consciousness of the social, human problems during the war and the post-war period. As an example of dialectical cinema, neo-realism hearkens back to less immediate predecessors. With *Roma città aperta,* so-called neo-realism revealed itself to the world in an impressive way. From then on, from my first documentaries really, there has been only one direction.

I have no formulas or preconceptions, but if I were to look back at my films, undoubtedly I would come across elements which are in themselves constant, and which are repeated not systematically but naturally, especially the aspects of the chorus. Realistic film is in itself a chorale. The sailors of *La nave bianca* are as important as the refugees at the end of *L'Uomo della croce,* as the population of *Roma città aperta,* the partisans of *Paisà* and the monks of *Francesco, giullare di Dio. La nave bianca* is an example of a choral film: from the first scene of the sailors' letters from home, to that of the battle, to that of the wounded who attend mass or play music and sing. There is also the pitiless cruelty of the machine in relation to man in the film: that supposedly unheroic aspect of the man who lives inside the ship in almost total darkness, in the midst of death, seeing only dials and gauges, wheels and levers; an aspect without apparent heroism or lyricism, and yet heroic to a tremendous degree.

Then there is the documentary attitude of observation and analysis, which I had learned in shooting my first short films, and which stood me in good stead when I later shot *Germania anno zero* and *Stromboli*.

Then, the perpetual return, even in the most rigorous documentary, to fantasy, for in man there is one part which leans toward the concrete and another which is attracted by pure imagination. The first tendency must not suffocate the second. From it comes the fantastic, even fabulous, aspects of *Il miracolo*, or *La macchina ammazzacattivi*, even of *Paisà* if you like, as well as of *Francesco, giullare di Dio*: the rain at the beginning, the young monk jostled by the soldiers, Saint Clare near the hut. Even the ending in the snow must have a properly fantastic appearance.

Finally, spirituality: I am not alluding to the religious aspects of *Stromboli* so much, nor to the heroine's cry to a divine power at the end, as to themes which I had already developed. How can it be denied that there was effective spirituality in *La nave bianca*, in *L'Uomo della croce*, in *Paisà*, in *Francesco, giullare di Dio* and *Il miracolo*?

Anyway, it cannot be doubted that I *began* by putting the accent on the collective above all. It was the war itself which motivated me; war and resistance are collective actions by definition. If from the collective I then passed to an examination of personality, as in the case of the child in *Germania anno zero* and the refugee of *Stromboli*, that was part of my natural evolution as a director.

In the narrative cinema, "waiting" is essential. Every solution is born from waiting. It is waiting which makes people live, which unchains reality; it is waiting which, after the preparation, gives liberation.

"Due parole sul neorealismo",
Retrospettive, 4, April 1953.

9. Ten Years of Cinema
by Roberto Rossellini

I

After the War

In 1944, immediately after the war, everything was destroyed in Italy. The cinema was no exception. Almost all the producers had disappeared. Here and there of course, there were some who were making attempts, but their ambitions were extremely limited. Therefore one enjoyed an immense liberty; the absence of an organized industry favoured the least routine enterprizes and all initiative was good. It was this situation which permitted us to embark on work of an experimental nature. Anyway, it soon became clear that these films, in spite of their experimental aspects, were on the way to becoming important at a cultural level as well as from a commercial point of view.

Under these circumstances, I started to shoot *Roma città aperta,* for which I had written the scenario with some friends[1] at the time the Germans were still occupying the country. I made the film with very little money, which we raised in small sums as we went along. There was just enough to pay for film stock: no question of paying a laboratory to develop it. There was, therefore, no chance to see the "rushes" before the end of the shooting. Sometime later, having found a bit of money, I put the film together and showed it to some movie people, critics and friends. Most of them were very disappointed.

Roma città aperta was first shown in September 1945 with the help of a small festival, and those spectators who were in the auditorium whistled.[2] You might say that the critical reception was frankly and unanimously unfavourable. It was just at that time that I proposed to many of my colleagues that we found an association modelled on United Artists[3] in order to avoid the "deforestation" which would certainly come with the reorganization of the Italian film industry by producers and businessmen. But no one wanted to be associated with the director of *Roma città aperta,* who by all appearances was, no artist.

That was the atmosphere in which I made *Paisà*. When it was shown at the Venice Festival the reception was disastrous. At the Cannes Festival in 1946, for want of anything better, *Roma città aperta* was presented as an official entry by the Italian delegation, which nonetheless had a profound contempt for the film. It was shown in the afternoon and, if I recall the press of the time correctly, it was hardly a big news item.

Then, two months later in Paris, both of my films provoked a surge of enthusiasm, something which by that time I no longer even hoped for. Their success there was so great that the cinema people in Italy had to reconsider their opinion of me, only to abuse me anew when . . . but let's not anticipate. A little after that, Burstyn, the producer of *The little fugitive*,[4] brought out *Roma città aperta* with well-known happy results.[5]

The Word "Commercial"

Italian films thrust themselves on the entire world at a moment when the American cinema was undergoing a fairly serious crisis. That crisis was perfectly understandable, for it was the result of what happens to national production when the ideas which gave it its vitality are worn out. American producers did not want to face facts, but the crisis was nontheless quite real. The disaffection of the public accentuated it, but the producers lazily blamed television. It was difficult for them to confess that they themselves had caused the crisis.

The Italian cinema became stronger and reorganized itself, but not in the way I had wanted. Italian films were made very cheaply, and so recouped their costs easily, particularly because of the foreign markets. The American market was especially important; when *Roma città aperta* and *Paisà* were distributed there, they were received in triumph by critics and a rather specialized audience. The receipts for Italian films in the United States were modest compared to those of Hollywood's own super-productions, but they were enormous if you remember the low cost of neo-realist films. Nevertheless, Italian producers were weak and didn't like the films; they wanted only to make once more those films they called "commercial". My friend Jean Renoir recently told me that the word "commercial" in the minds of producers does not correspond as one might think to potential profits, but to a certain aesthetic. Producers of "big" films believe they have made a commercial film even if they never get back their expenses; those same producers will maintain at the same time that *La strada* is not a "commercial" film.[6] It was inevitable that the Italian cinema would again fall into the same old aesthetic as the Hollywood industry; it was, after all, reorganized and directed by the old money-men who had returned after running away during the war, or by new ones who were motivated by the same ideas.

The Crisis of Italian Cinema

One should never forget the presence of American films in the market. These films are generally productions with a medium budget, very well made and well received by the public. The American cinema has one of the best national markets for getting back the cost of its films; it also has a powerful and direct commercial organisation throughout the entire world, which is to say that it makes as much money as it is possible to make from a film, like squeezing a lemon to the last drop. Obviously, then, the battle between the American and European cinemas is hardly equal; competition is hardly possible. As I see it, the only chance for us is to make films intended for a much smaller audience, to reduce costs as much as possible, and to think carefully about how best to launch an *avant-garde* film (by which I mean a film made outside the usual formulas) in every market, including America. It is too easy to forget that on the other side of the Atlantic there is a public composed of connoisseurs, of specialists, which is extremely important. That public comes to see films which have something new to say. If an Italian neo-realist film brings in from its American distribution no more than $100,000, $50,000, or even $30,000 — thanks to "art cinemas" for example — that is already a considerable return considering the low budgets of such films.

It seems to me there is only one real reason for the crisis in the Italian cinema: the producers believe that if a neo-realist film which costs pennies can bring in so much money, then a super-production with a budget ten times as big will bring in ten times as much. This is, of course, a stupid line of reasoning; you can't make films on such

95

an idiotic basis. Another absolutely mad idea: dubbing Italian films into English and attempting to distribute them as in America. Failure is assured.[7] The policy of the Italian film industry — far more than in the rest of Europe — is to copy Hollywood formulas. The result is simply that costs are driven up so high that even foreign sales are insufficient to recoup expenses. The reasons for this are rather complex, but I will try to analyse them a bit later.

The cinema which plays such an important role in everyday life is *also* an art: commerce which *becomes*, at least sometimes, an art. Everything remains to be discovered. That is the great good luck of a filmmaker; that is what should inspire him to work on the level of every other form of artistic expression and not to lag behind. The public is curious, and it is that curiosity which should be satisfied. Take, for instance, *The little fugitive*. It happens to be an American film which was released in the United States with no great success. Then it was a huge success at the Venice Festival. The critics and public were so enthusiastic that the film, which had been consigned to the margins of the usual distribution process, that it became a financial success in Europe, as well as in America where it was re-released.

The Art of Waiting

Personally, I don't believe that in the course of my career I have ever been reduced to compromise. I have, of course, always kept outside the normal production system. From what happened with *Roma città aperta* I learned that in order to defend myself and my work I would have to suffer criticism and attacks without flinching. When the Italian film industry was reorganized, the industralists at the top immediately wanted to lop off the heads of all those who were out in front. That is a normal fact of life and happens all the time; they found it necessary to make everyone equal by reducing them to the lowest possible level, and to make everyone start over again in the ranks. I think it is because I would not give in to this that the attacks against me have been more violent than against the others.

The fact that I am my own producer allowed me to make my films very fast and with a very modest budget. I think that is the only solution, and I find it works very well for me. Time is what costs most in the cinema, but what is that time used for? Usually to satisfy the finicky instincts of the director, of the cameraman, of the actors, of God-knows-who. I have been in this profession now for 25 years and I have always been shocked by what happens when the rushes are projected. Everyone appears to be filled with wonder and admiration at seeing something on the screen, and that something must be indubitably good in order to astound the financial "sleeping partners" who are there to see their money transformed into images. Everyone is happy at the projection; everyone is pleased at seeing each shot, at the superb sequences. Then you edit together fifty magnificent bits and — surprise! — the film is a disaster. It is no longer anything, and everyone looks stupified. People seem to have a complex about technique: they turn on the radio, tune in to a music station, and then take themselves for Toscanini!

Beautiful shots! That is the one thing that makes me sick! A film must be well-directed; that is the least one can expect of a filmmaker, but a single shot need not be beautiful.

The only thing that is important is rhythm, and that cannot be learnt; you carry it inside yourself. I believe in the importance of the scene; it resolves itself, it completes itself, at a certain point. In general, directors love to develop that point. As far as I am concerned, I think that is an error dramatically. Neo-realism consists of following someone with love and watching all his discoveries and impressions; an ordinary man dominated by something which suddenly strikes him a terrible blow at the precise moment when he finds himself free in the world. He never expects whatever it is. What is important for me is the waiting. That is what it is necessary to develop; the blow, the fall, must stay intact. Take, for example, the tuna fishing sequence in *Stromboli*. For the fishermen, it is all just waiting under the sun. Then they suddenly shout "They're coming! They're coming!" They have thrown out their nets, and suddenly the water is alive and death is striking the tuna. That is the final point of the scene. In the same way, there is the death of the child in *Europa '51*. There had been a failed suicide; the child is recovering and all is calm; then suddenly, like a blow, at the moment you would no longer possibly expect it, he dies.

Naturally, this waiting manifests itself in the movement and rhythm of my films, since my work consists of following the characters. Usually in the traditional cinema a scene is constructed like this: an establishing shot in which the environment is defined; the discovery of an individual in that environment; you move closer to him (medium shot); then a two-shot; a close-up, and the story begins. I proceed in a manner which is exactly opposite to that: I always begin with a close-up; then the movement of the character determines the movement of the camera. The camera does not leave the actor, and in this way the camera effects the most complex journeys.

The Direction of Actors

It is too often believed that neo-realism consists in finding an unemployed person to play an unemployed person. I choose actors solely by the way they look. You can choose anyone in the street. I prefer non-professional actors because they have no preconceived ideas. I watch a man in life and fix him in my memory. When he finds himself before the camera, he is usually completely lost and tries to "act", which is exactly what must be avoided at all costs. There are gestures which belong to this man, the ones he makes with the same muscles which become paralyzed before the lens. It is as if he forgets himself, as if he never knew himself. He believes he has become a very exceptional person because someone is going to film him. My task is to return him to his original nature, to reconstruct him, to *reteach* him his usual movements.

II
Germania anno zero

I have already explained that the world-wide success of *Roma città aperta* and *Paisà* started in France. In 1947 I found myself in Paris with the idea of asking the French Government for permission to shoot a film in Berlin about Germany after the Armistice. Thus *Germania anno zero* came into being as the third panel of the triptych on the war.

I arranged the finances with *Union Génerale Cinematographique* and, without any preconceived ideas, I left for Germany, not to shoot, but to get an idea for a scenario.

I arrived in Berlin in March, by car, at about five in the afternoon, just as the sun was going down. It was necessary to cross the entire city to get to the French sector. The city was deserted. The grey of the sky flowed back into the streets, and from about the height of a man one could look over fallen roofs. To find the streets again under the ruins, people had cleared away the rubble and piled it up. Grass had begun to grow through the cracks in the asphalt. Silence reigned; each noise intensified the silence. A sickish sweet odour of rotting organic matter exuded from the piled-up rubble. It was as if we were floating over Berlin. I started off down a wide avenue. On the horizon, a huge yellow advertisement was the only sign of "life". I slowly came up to this immense sign which was attached to a stone block in front of a store with a tiny façade. It said "Israel Bazaar". The first Jews had come back to Berlin; it was the symbol of the end of Nazism.

The four occupying nations were very hospitable and permitted me to wander everywhere, so that I returned to Paris with a very clear idea of the film in my head. In every country, more-or-less "funny stories" are related which can tell one a good deal about life in that country. At that time this story was being told in Germany. A man arrived in Berlin and someone put him up. The first morning he was asked if he had slept well. "Yes, in spite of those trains which kept passing under my window." "But you must have been dreaming; there are no trains." "But there are. I heard the steam and the water pumps." The host took the guest to the window and showed him there were no trains. The following morning, the guest was awakened by the same noise. He got up, looked out of the window, and saw old women in men's clothing clearing away the rubble. As they passed bricks to one another along a line: "Danke schönen" — "Bitte schonen" — "Danke schönen". That is the sort of story which gives you a proper point of view.

The Germans were human beings like all the rest. What was it that could have carried them to this disaster? A false philosophy, the essence of Nazism; the abandoning of humility for a cult of heroics; the exaltation of strength over weakness, vaingloriousness over simplicity? That is why I chose to tell the story of a child, an innocent, who through the distortion of a utopian education was brought to the point of commiting a crime while believing he was accomplishing something heroic. But a small ethical flame still burned within him; he killed himself to escape his sense of moral disquiet.

Finally, I was able to make *Germania anno zero* exactly as I had intended. Whenever I see the film again now, I come out of the screening upset; I think my judgement of Germany was right, not complete, but right. For all that, and contrary to all experience, *Germania anno zero* was badly received. It was then that I began to ask myself some questions.

The world of the cinema had reorganized itself, and had returned to its pre-war habits and styles. *Germania anno zero* was judged according to the pre-war aesthetic, even though *Roma città aperta* and *Paisà* had been admired for what they had done in terms of a new style. The political world had also reorganized itself, and the film was judged politically. The critics of *Germania anno zero* taught me that what the respective journalists (or more likely the editors of their newspapers) thought about the problem of Germany, but they gave me nothing useful on the level of film criticism. At that moment I found myself in a dilemma: either prostitution or sincerity.

I Chose Sincerity

I have already said that I believe cinema is a new art and has the potential for making many discoveries. It is that potential which makes being a film director intoxicating. It was in that spirit that I made *"Una voce umana"*[8] from the play by Jean Cocteau.

The cinema is also a microscope in that it can take us by the hand and lead us to the discovery of things the eye alone could never perceive (be it close-up, small details, and so on). More than other subjects *Una voce umana* offered me the change to use the microscopic camera. The phenomenon to be examined was Anna Magnani. Only the novel, poetry, and the cinema permit us to rummage through a personality to discover reactions and motives for actions.

This experience, pushed to an extreme in *Una voce umana*, was useful to me later in all my films, since at one moment or another in shooting I feel the need to cast the scenario to one side in order to follow a character in his most secret thoughts, those which are perhaps not even conscious. It is also this "microscopic aspect" of cinema which made neo-realism; it is a moral approach which becomes an aesthetic fact.

When I had finished "*Una voce umana*" I found myself with a film forty minutes long. As we are the slaves of commercial programming, it was practically unsaleable. I therefore had to look for another story of about the same length. Federico Fellini, who often worked with me, wrote a story which I filmed under the title "*Il miracolo*". According to Fellini, it was taken from a Russian short story but he claimed he had forgotten both the author and the original title. When he saw that I was much taken with the story but that I was searching desperately for the original text so that I could make legal arrangements for the rights, he confessed that he had invented the story down to the smallest details. He had lied at first because he was afraid that I would find the story ridiculous.

After a time, both stories were released under the title *Amore*. The Italian critics said that "*Una voce umana*" was not cinema. It was certainly the only time I have ever seen critics affirm anything so unanimously.

"*Il miracolo*" was the object of very serious accusations.[9] An American priest, whom I met in Italy, told me that it was manifestly clear that I had wanted to make money by exploiting blasphemy for blasphemers. He was unfamiliar with a sermon of Saint Bernadin of Siena. It concerned a saint named Bonino. A peasant went to the countryside with his two-year-old son and a dog. He left the boy and the dog in the shade of an oak and went to work. When he returned he found the child with his throat cut and with the marks of teeth around his wound. In his grief, the father killed the dog. It was only at that moment he saw a huge snake and understood his error. Conscience stricken at his injustice, he buried the dog in the rocks close by and engraved an inscription on the tomb: "Here Lies Bonino: Killed by the Ferocity of Man". Several centuries went by, and the road passed by the tomb. Travellers who stopped in the shade of the oak read the inscription. Little by little they began to pray there, to ask for relief from their unhappiness. Then miracles began to happen, so many that the people of the area built a beautiful church and a new tomb to enshrine the body of Bonino. As they were transferring the remains, they discovered he was a dog.

You can see that the story of "*Il miracolo*" is rather similar. It is about a poor mad woman who has a sort of religious mania, but she has faith as well, a real and profound faith. She could have believed anything she liked. I admit that what she believed was rather blasphemous, but her faith was immense, and that faith was her recompense. Her action is absolutely human and normal: to suckle her child. I believe "*Il miracolo*" is an absolutely Catholic work.

A theme which obsesses me, and which can be found again in *Stromboli*, is that of the absolute lack of faith, the absence of a desire to fight for anything, which was typical of the post-war period. What bothers me is the sort of cowardice which brings people to gather together like sheep under the staff of some pastor or other. However, the character played by Anna Magnani in "*Il miracolo*" is the exact opposite. She is mad, but in the midst of her mental confusion, she has a faith, deluded if you like, *but a faith*. Once, a politician said to me with a great deal of bitterness: "Men want to have less social justice provided they also have less freedom." It is that mentality which even today obsesses me and frightens me, in spite of certain signs lately which might indicate a return of conscience.

A Letter from Ingrid Bergman

It was at this time that I received some concrete offers to work in the United States. These offers came from David O. Selznick and were extremely attractive. Selznick, who has a very forceful personality, would have been a valuable patron for my career as a director had my goal been a "career". After long negotiations, I decided to stay in Italy. Four years later, Selznick and I became very good friends, and he is a man I appreciate for his great human qualities. One thing which held me back and influenced my refusal was simply that in Italy there is hardly enough work already and I was afraid of betraying my friends and the people who usually worked with me, in this way.

On May 8, 1946, I received a letter from Ingrid Bergman. She had seen *Roma città aperta* and *Paisà* and wanted to make a film with me. The 8th of May is my birthday. On the evening of the 7th, I got a phone call from Mr. Potsius of Minerva Films who told me that he wanted to see me in order to give me a beautiful present. I thought he was referring to my birthday, especially as I had sold him the rights to *Roma città aperta* for a mouthful of bread when it was a "bomb" and he had then profitably exploited it as a "masterpiece". The next day he brought me the letter from Ingrid. He had already read it, for it seems that Minerva had just burned all its accumulated correspondence and that he had opened all the letters without first checking to see if they were addressed to him. I answered the letter at once, and on 17 January, 1949, exactly five years to the day of the first turning of the camera for *Roma città aperta*, I arrived in Hollywood to discuss the idea of *Stromboli* with Ingrid.

A big producer showed a very great interest in our project and we had long conversations over a number of breakfasts, lunches, and dinners. That is how I learned English, since the same words came up interminably over and over in our conversations. I must make one point clear: all these conversations I had with him were of an aesthetic order. He explained to me all that his great experience in the cinema had taught him, and he tried to convince me of the necessity of working with a detailed shooting script. Some of his arguments were extremely judicious, but I was absolutely opposed to the idea that it was necessary to work from a detailed script for reasons I have explained a hundred times already.

As I shoot in real interiors and unretouched exteriors to begin with, I can only improvise my direction to correspond to the settings I find myself in. Therefore the left hand column of a shooting script would be left blank even if I had to make one. Then, I choose my secondary actors at the time and place of the shooting. Therefore I cannot, before seeing them, write their dialogue. Otherwise it would of necessity be theatrical and false. The column on the right side would therefore also be left blank. Finally, I believe strongly in the inspiration of the moment.

Anyway, one evening Ingrid and I were summoned by telephone to another meeting in his office. He had called a press conference and announced the production of the film to the newspaper. Very surprised, we took our places anyway and were photographed signing a phoney contract. From that day the discussions between the producer and myself took a decided turn for the worse, to such a degree, that a short time later I refused his proposition.

I felt out of my element in Hollywood, the city with the highest density of intellectuals. I hardly understood that atmosphere of contempt, wounded pride, and frenzied chauvinism. I must say anyway that I made some good friends there, but the atmosphere was directly hostile without the reasons for it — at least at that time — being at all clear to me. One day, Ingrid was invited to a reception at which she was the guest of honour. When she returned she told me with complete amazement, that on her right was sitting a Hollywood big shot.[10] This man, after trying to dissuade her from making a film with me, told her that I had come to see him a year before in Europe to beg him to take me to Hollywood, and that I was so insistent that he had to treat me very rudely to get rid of me, and that finally he had me thrown out, telling me he had no use for a guy like me. Now obviously I knew this man only by reputation. When he was pointed out to me in a restaurant in Paris last year I could only remark with astonishment that a man as sly as twenty foxes managed somehow to look smaller than even one.

At the beginning of March, having put the production of *Stromboli* on the road, I returned to Italy, where Ingrid joined me on the 19th.

III
Stromboli, Little Island

At the beginning of April, we began to shoot the film on the island of Stromboli, and, at the same time, the scandal over our private life exploded.[11] What was the reason for all of that? Why was there a resounding scandal over a simple divorce and remarriage, especially in the world of the cinema, and, in particular, the American cinema, where divorce had for a long time been an institution which everyone treated like a routine, everyday matter? I have already said that in a general way the atmosphere of Hollywood was not friendly to me. Ingrid was an actress, I was a director; it was normal that we should arrange to do a film together. The world of Hollywood received this news as if it were an insult and a blow to its prestige.

Stromboli was a small island, very isolated from the rest of the world. There was no telephone, no electricity, and a connection to the mainland by boat only once a week. News of the outside therefore came to us very late, and we didn't realize that a scandal had burst until we saw the arrivals of journalists, photographers, and even friends — not forgetting the "experts" from the distribution company, "experts" in publicity and public relations — all come to give us their advice as to what was best for the "common interest". It was then in my life that I had the surprise of learning that in the world there were many hitherto unsuspected professions, "specialists" of the most precise sort. Every wave of sensational news doubtless had but one purpose: to frighten us. In the face of constantly repeated "sensations", the "experts" suggested only one solution: deny everything.

When Ingrid and I offered to suspend production, or even purely and simply to give up the film, in order to deal with the situation after a period of reflection, when we would be at our ease, and free from all other responsibilites, the "experts" absolutely disagreed. Above all: work! Friends and "experts" busied themselves in pointing out the grave dangers that the scandal threatened to our respective careers. If they had calculated on our cowardice and hypocrisy by underscoring the danger we were running, they had evidently miscalculated. For us, Europeans, and for me who had no experience in these matters, it was difficult to describe what American journalism was.

Many American journalist are merely guardians of the established order, a militia ready to bludgeon anyone who dares to break that order. I had been struck, during my stay in Hollywood, by how the appearance of a certain newspaper, a certain radio broadcast, could make everyone hold their breath. Every day, hearts would beat rapidly when the newspaper came out, and life would stop for the broadcast. At that time in Hollywood, there was a story going around which, for all its being invented, is still revealing.

A famous lady broadcaster, as she was finishing her weekly programme saw one of her "hunting dogs" bring in a final bit of gossip hastily scratched on a bit of paper. Already a bit senile, she clamped on her glasses, assumed a pathetic voice which barely hid the sadistic joy she was feeling at being the first to deliver this dismaying news and read from the paper: "Janet Smith is getting a divorce." On this sorry note the programme ended, and the assistant, who was finally able to speak, explained that in his haste he had made a mistake: the item should have read "Joe" instead of "Janet" Smith. A few minutes later, Janet Smith and her husband telephoned, upset but deferential and submissive, and begged the broadcaster to retract the false report. But the scandal-monger, whose imagination was never at a loss, rather than retract — which would have been a blow to her prestige — proposed a bargain with Janet Smith from which everyone would get something. Janet's husband was to move to a hotel at the expense of the broadcaster, who several days later would then announce the couple's reconciliation with a lot of publicity. She would exalt love with all its torments and paradoxes, the boundlessness of an artist's emotions, the lyricism of their feelings, and so on. Janet Smith and her husband evidently didn't dare refuse. There was nothing to do except give in and hope. The same evening, installed in the hotel, the husband began to receive phone calls from all his friends congratulating him on finally understanding what a slut he had married. The whole affair naturally ended in a divorce, which the broadcaster took pleasure in announcing just as everyone began to think it would never happen.

Sentiments after the War

To return to *Stromboli*: what interested me in the film was treating the theme of cynicism, a sentiment which represented the greatest danger after the war. Karin gambled on the ingenuousness of the love of a poor, primitive soldier and married him with the sole purpose of getting out of the internment camp. She trades the barbed wire for the island, but once there she finds herself even more enclosed. She had dreamed of something entirely different. A strong but determined woman who had gone through all the difficulties and trouble of the war and had always pulled herself through more or less all right, she was now the victim of small, stupid things: a crude husband, a small island without vegetation. She is doubly a prisoner in that she is pregnant. For her, being pregnant is stupid, humiliating, ignoble, and bestial. She therefore decides to leave, but at the top of the volcano she must climb over to get to the small port on the other side of the island, in the midst of hostile nature, broken by fatigue, bowed down by a primitive terror, in animal despair, she unconsciously calls upon God. "My God" is the simplest appeal, the most primitive and the most common that can escape from the mouth of someone overcome with suffering. It can be a mechanical invocation, or an expression of a very high truth. In one case as in the other, it is always the expression of a profound mortification which might also be the first glimmering of a conversion. This is the construction of the film. It wasn't difficult to figure out my intentions, I would even have explained my intentions, if people just took the trouble to read the Biblical verse which is printed on the screen after the credits of *Stromboli*: "I will answer those who ask for nothing; I will be found by those who seek me not." (*Isaiah* 65).

Many people were dead set against the film, particularly the ending, for diverse reasons. All of them joined together, however, to demonstrate that I was a cretin. The film was mutilated in America. I have not seen what "they" did, but I understand that thirty-five minutes are missing, that there is now a "lyrical" commentary on the action, and that at the end it seems Karin has the intention of returning to her nice little husband who is waiting for her at home.

When the shooting was finished, I made a cut of the film very quickly so that the American studio people would have an idea of how to edit their negative (I kept a second negative myself). The copy which I had not had time to perfect was then released in Europe. It seemed absurd to me to show the film in a version that had been so hastily edited. Still, I had to go to court just to obtain what is normally asked of us as directors — a bit of thought about the editing and a bit of advice in order to make the necessary modifications. All of that was refused me. I would perhaps have obtained satisfaction if it had been possible for me to pursue the long legal process. I only won the case as far as the Italian version was concerned; in the end, this version differed only slightly from the one released in the rest of Europe, but it was drastically different from the American version.

Stromboli won the *Prix de Rome* and although a number of critics defended it, the majority attacked it violently. What I had felt and suspected when *Germania anno zero* was released, was now very clear to me. The critics were reacting politically and were no longer even bothering to hide it. A limited group, politically involved, infatuated by the cinema, but amateurs nonetheless (there are too many amateurs in film criticism) had with the aid of a particular terminology created a critical movement which looked attractive from the outside and had a strong following in Italy, especially amongst journalists without taste, intuition, or sensibility. In this way, they were able to seize upon a popular critical vocabulary in place of making intelligent critical judgements.

That is why I also attribute political reasons to the reversal of critical opinion today which has benefited *Roma città aperta* and *Paisà*. I think that this group by its activities and by creating an enormous critical confusion, has contributed in large measure to the current crisis in the Italian cinema, feeding the divisions between filmmakers, by encouraging producers even indirectly, to persist in commercial or would-be commercial productions.

A Small "True Incident"

To illustrate what I am talking about, I will tell you a small "true incident" that seems significant to me. A very important film man who shared the ideas of this critical group wanted to collaborate with me. He invited me to revisit the swamps at the mouth of the Po river where I had shot the last episode of *Paisà*. It was November, cold and raining. Cigolani whom I had hanged in *Paisà* seven years before,[12] was very happy to see me again. One day as we walked on the banks of the Po, which was rapidly rising, he said to me: "What do you bet that this year the Po is going to overflow the banks on the other side again, and that those sons-of-bitches are going to have the benefits they had from the last flood?"

What had happened was that the year before the Po had overrun the other bank, and the people who lived on that side, after getting through the tragedy, had benefitted from all sorts of assistance which had practically changed their lives, while those on the unflooded side of the river got nothing and were forced to continue living in the same conditions they always had. When I told this story to my film-making friend and would-be collaborator, his eyes clouded over and he accused me of wanting to make a pro-government film.

Men usually adopt a political or moral position by choosing it from the range of "truths" with which they are presented. This choice is rarely made from personal conviction, but is the fruit of chance, of worry about getting ahead, or from a desire to live peacefully. Once committed to a cause, they are obliged to defend it and prove it has been worth devoting their lives to. That is generally how movements of public opinion are formed, and how philosophic, aesthetic, and moral movements win followers. Everything is sacrificed to consistency to the point of maniac pigheadedness, which kills all liberty and all imagination.

To return to the release of *Stromboli*: ranged against a small nucleus of defenders and myself, was a hostile front composed of the critical group without precise ideas, the defenders of justice and morality, sensational writers and journalists, and other general social nuisances. All were duly represented. From this confrontation came all the epithets that were used against me: Communist and pro-clerical, anarchist and devout, imbecile and clever. My films were judged to be sublime and ignoble. They talked as much about my evolution as about my involution. Then a certain newspaper joined in this chorus of judgements and I was able to read all sorts of remarkable things, each more unbelievable than the one before. *"Il miracolo"*, for example, was said to be the product of perfect Communist technique which was intended to "divide and rule", and the film was an insult to all Italian women. After they had finished with the work, they started on the man. They said that I was the "head of a gang directed by Mao Tse-Tung which had the sole goal of destroying the brains of American film-goers", and that I was either head over heels in debt or was living "like a Renaissance prince". The judgements that I have collected whether hostile or adulatory, were varied, funny, and often very eloquent. I have only given examples of the most ridiculous ones as I prefer to forget the most serious injustices.

Freedom of the Press

I remember that when the Allies either "liberated" or "invaded" Italy they distributed "occupation lire" on which were printed the four basic freedoms to which everyone was entitled, among them the freedom of the press. I will always defend the freedom of the press, even if I have been inconvenienced by it. Nonetheless, if my experiences serve for anything, as I sincerely believe they do, I must tell an anecdote which illustrates the morality of a certain type of newspaper.

At one time in our lives, my wife and I were literally besieged by press photographers. For four months Ingrid and my son could not leave the apartment. The photographers did everything to violate our privacy. What they wanted was one particular photograph. One night, at about one in the morning, the door bell rang. The maid, who was frightened, asked through the door who was there. They answered that it was the police. She opened the door and two men, one carrying a camera, pushed their way in. She managed to push them back out to the landing and called down the porter for help. He came out on the stairs and demanded how they had got in without his knowledge. The two "journalists" evaded his blows and escaped the same way they had come in, by scaling the fence at the entrance to the courtyard.

There was only one way to put an end to the siege: to publish the photograph they were seeking so desperately. I finally decided I wanted some peace and took the photograph myself. I gave it as a gift to the press agency which had bothered us the least and which had even gone so far as to deplore the behaviour of the others. The siege was lifted, but not without an accumulation of bitterness. A rumour circulated and finally came back to me that I had *sold* the photograph at a very high price. I thought at the time that the story had been invented by the rival agencies that had been frustrated.

Three years later, I told this entire misadventure to some friends in Paris. They were a very sympathetic couple; he was the director of a large daily newspaper. He told me that his newspaper had published the photograph, having acquired it at an exorbitant price. The agency had justified the incredible price by saying that it had been necessary to pay *me* a fortune for it!

"Dix ans de cinéma"
I: *Cahiers du cinéma*, 50, April/September 1955
II: *Cahiers du cinéma*, 52, November 1955
III: *Cahiers du cinéma*, 55, January 1956

Notes

1 According to the writing credits of the film, these "friends" would have been Sergio Amidei, Alberto Consiglio, Federico Fellini, and Rossellini himself.

2 In Europe, unlike America, whistling signifies displeasure.

3 The original United Artists Corporation was founded in 1919 by Mary Pickford, Douglas Fairbanks, Charles Chaplin, and D.W. Griffith, with the object of producing and distributing their own and the productions of other directors in order to control both the making and the selling of their work.

4 *The little fugitive* (1953) was directed by Ray Ashley; it was an independent production with a very small budget. As Rossellini points out later, the film was widely distributed after its success at the Venice Film Festival.

5 *Roma città aperta* was a huge success throughout the world. In America, for example, it was widely distributed and played in cinemas and towns not usually given to screening foreign films. Its commercial and critical success led to a small flurry of semi-documentary films in pseudo-neo-realistic manner in America.

6 *La strada* (1954) was a gigantic critical and commercial success everywhere, and was the film which made its director, Federico Fellini, internationally famous.

7 In this case, Roberto Rossellini was less than a great prophet. Dubbed versions of commercial Italian films have done well in the United States, and even less-commercial films often play outside the large cities in dubbed versions. In the last two decades, the practice has been to avoid making an "original version" at all. Films are often shot silently in Italy, with soundtracks in various languages laid in afterwards. A second method still, but less widely used, is to shoot each scene in each language. A third is to shoot an "international" version, with each actor speaking his own language, and to dub the film into other languages. Rossellini changed his mind about dubbing later in

his career, and even accused critics who objected to the practice of being "cinematic fetishists". His own last film *The Messiah* (1975) was dubbed into the language of which ever country it was to be released in, with Rossellini himself supervising each version.

8   *Amore* is made up of two stories: *"Una voce umana"* with only Anna Magnani and a telephone in the cast, and *"Il miracolo"* with Magnani and Federico Fellini.

9   *The miracle*, as the film was known in English-speaking countries, was the object of a good deal of controversy. It was condemned by the Catholic Legion of Decency and denounced by Cardinal Spellman (who later admitted not ever having seen it). As local censorship boards (and local cinema owners who were afraid of "offending" their audience) followed the lead of the Legion in banning the film to non-Catholics as well as to the Catholics who, in theory, were not going to attend the "condemned" film anyway, a series of court cases came about. These resulted in a landmark legal decision that films could not be banned on the grounds of "blasphemy". By then, however, it was too late to save the film commercially, at least in the United States. It played in a few large cities, where it was often picketed by the Legion, but was never widely distributed because of the "controversy".

10   Rossellini's note: "This is the second time I have talked about a famous person without giving his name. I am not writing these reminiscences either to scandalize or to provoke controversy; for this reason, neither have I asked the reader to excuse my discretion."
     Nonetheless, Rossellini's reference a bit later to the man in question as being "as sly as *20 foxes*" is enough of a hint for one to guess easily the man's identity.

11   The "scandal" was simply that Ingrid Bergman and Roberto Rossellini were in love and openly living together, although Miss Bergman was still married to Peter Lindstrom. When she was divorced, Miss Bergman was pregnant with Mr. Rossellini's son; a little later they married. The furore which this provoked internationally is now unbelievable. The films which Miss Bergman had made were boycotted by women's groups, by "morality" organizations, and finally by exhibitors. When *Stromboli* was released in a mutilated version in the United States (the centre of the commotion), however, the distributors and exhibitors tried to use the "scandal" to sell the film to a large audience

(for whom the film was never intended); although the advertisements and posters blazed "Flaming Volcano! Flaming Emotions!" few went to see it. Ironically, the exploitative handling of the film kept away the discriminating audience which would have found the film more than interesting.

The reasons the affair received publicity, particularly the bad publicity directed personally at Miss Bergman, were various. It was well timed so that the conservative guardians of public morality could once again blame the cinema for societal "problems". The audience, in rather childlike fashion, had also confounded the actress with the virtuous roles she had played in her most popular films (nuns, saints, suffering wives) while they tended to forget that she had also played semi-"wicked" characters (although those were her least popular films). The Hollywood publicity mills which had ground out hundreds of articles about Miss Bergman as symbolising the ideal of married bliss and motherhood also added to the "shock". The fires were fanned by Hollywood's own watchdogs of the female variety (Louella Parsons and Hedda Hopper leading the pack). In reading again their hysterical attacks, however, one gets the feeling that it was not the marital "scandal" which bothered them so much as the fact that an established star had "deserted" the system which had made her, and that Miss Bergman had the temerity to complain at the low artistic level of the films the system had had her act in. All of this combined with Rossellini's popular reputation as the "sinful blasphemer" who had made *The miracle* was enough.

One of the most unfortunate results of the "scandal" and the subsequent financial failure of *Stromboli*, was that the series of films which Bergman and Rossellini made later were rarely released and distributed outside Europe — films which are among the finest Rossellini made and certainly the best with which Miss Bergman was ever associated.

12   Cigolani was a non-professional who played the partisan in the last episode of *Paisà*; in the film the character he played was hanged.

10. The Philosophical Basis of Neo-Realism
by Felix A. Morlion, O.P.

In relation to the various national cinemas, the post-war period is marked by the fact that the American, English, and French cinemas, while still active, show no substantial renewal; the German and Russian cinemas have been a thing of the past for the last fifteen years. Only in Italy has a new school been born whose message has impressed people on both sides of the Atlantic. With its tough frankness, this Italian school is different from the somewhat "sophisticated" American school, the main goal of which is to please all audiences and every censor. In its artistic and intellectual severity, the Italian cinema is distinguished from the French school, which is always dressed up with plastic and literary embellishments. Again the Italian school differs in its freshness and spontaneity from the new English "documentary school", which, in the hands of Carol Reed, David Lean, and Harry Watt, remains rather cold.[1]

Among international film critics, the Catholics (whose reservations are so often of an ideological nature) are the ones who most vehemently defend what they call "the neo-realist Italian school".[2] I know of no Catholic critic, in Europe or the United States, who did not react with an instinctive sympathy to Rossellini's *Roma città aperta* and *Paisà*, Blasetti's *Un giorno nella vita* and *Quattro passi fra le nuvole*, De Sica'a *Sciuscià* and *La porta del cielo*, to Zampa's *Vivere in pace* and *L'Onorevole Angelina*, and to the last sequences of Aldo Vergano's *Il sole sorge ancora*.

There was not the least hesitation on the part of the members of the Jury of UCIC[3] at the Brussels Festival (June, 1947) in deciding which work promoted the spiritual and moral progress of mankind with greatest vigour. The prize was given to *Vivere in pace*, a film from which all mysticism is excluded, but which, on the other hand contains a number of scenes realistically depicting the superstitions of a peasant's wife.

When the American critics, who are often far removed from Catholic ideology, awarded their first "best foreign film" prize to that very same *Vivere in pace,* they confirmed the value of the Catholic jury's judgements for a second time (the first was *Roma città aperta* which received the same two prizes).

The public, of course, does not forgive a critic who is unable to explain why a film is beautiful or why it is not. The public is right. A critic must be able to defend and define, or at least to distinguish from among other values "the cinematically beautiful", in the name of which we hold discussions and pass judgements. And since we Catholic critics have invented the term "neo-realist school of cinema", we shall have to demonstrate and defend just what it is we find of substance in this artistic trend.

The Philosophy of the "Cinematically Beautiful"

We can discover the essential nature of the beautiful if we begin with a psychological fact: the aesthetic vision. This aesthetic vision is then differentiated from other forms of knowledge because: (a) it is a knowledge of the senses (of sight or hearing or both) which is simultaneously (b) an intellectual knowledge which (in the perception of universal or spiritual value) goes beyond the simple perception of the individual given by the external and internal senses (imagination and memory), and which is simultaneously (c) a pleasure which sets in motion man's emotional faculties, either of the senses or of the spirit.

The function of the knowledge of the senses in the intellect is to differentiate the aesthetic vision as intuitive knowledge (which presents us with the Idea in its own substance), from the aesthetic vision as abstract knowledge (which purifies us, but which denudes the Idea of its substance).

The conjunction of pleasure and knowledge results in a disinterested pleasure derived from aesthetic vision; that is to say, in enjoyment inherent to the cognitive faculties, as distinct from enjoyment which manifests itself in the will, when the conscious subject has become conscious of an object which he regards as belonging to him, which suits him, or responds in any way to his natural leanings.

The whole philosophy of the "beautiful" comes from the answer to that simple question: "What must be the nature of a known thing (the beautiful) in order to produce enjoyment in the faculties of the senses and the intellect as it unites with man's intuition?" The only possible answer is that the nature of the thing which is seen (that is to say, the beautiful) must be essentially similar to the nature of the man who sees.

Now the nature of man is to be an essential unity in spirit and substance; that is to say, to exist as a compound substance which derives its substantial form, its deep unity, from a spiritual principle, superior to that substance, which we call the soul. Thus it is a compound material which receives its essential form, its deep unity, from a spiritual principle superior to the substance.

This definition of the beautiful is a corollary of the metaphysics of Aristotle and St. Thomas Aquinas. We must conclude that neither Aristotle nor Aquinas elaborated a treatise on aesthetics because they did not have access to all the aesthetic experiences, since they did not know the greatest forms of painting, the novel, music, and cinema, all of which developed only after the Renaissance. At any rate, their metaphysical principles form a "*philosophia perennis*" in which common sense and empiric experience supply the substance which sets in motion the cognizant spirit which moves towards the knowledge of what is.

Considering the current state of civilization, many of the conclusions reached by the Stagirite and the scholastics are out of date.[4] However, through an analysis of their metaphysical principles concerning the fundamental constitution of the aesthetic phenomenon, "*Bellum est id quod visum placet*" (the beautiful is that which we have pleasure in knowing), we can reach a definition which will impart the secret of the nature of the beautiful, and especially of the beautiful in cinema.

It is often said that the art of cinema is a synthesis of all the arts; moreover, that it is *the* art in which all other arts sacrifice their own nature to constitute a specific new beauty. There are three types of beauty which correspond to three artistic techniques:

(1) *Material beauty:* beauty typical of lines and colour, both two-dimensional (photographs, drawing, pictorial beauty) and three-dimensional (sculpture and architecture), as well as of the sonorous modulations of music which are developed in the so-called fourth dimension, time. Material beauty is independant of the represen-

tation of the exterior object — which explains the beauty of Cubism, Impressionism, plastic art, and that music falsely termed "abstract" — and does not require the expression of a universal idea, thus freeing us to enjoy a painting or a sonata without having to wonder about the artist's "intended meaning".

(2) *Spiritual beauty:* the beauty of an entire idea in movement: that is to say, of quantity which transcends the apprehension of the senses but which acquires materiality in its relationship to the material world. A literary work differs from a scientific one because science tends to *dis*incarnate an idea while literature tends to incarnate it. A beautiful poem: an idea in motion charged with the emotional connotations of verbal music. A beautiful novel, drama, or comedy contains characters, or groups of characters, who either move closer or further apart along a given line of exterior events. A beautiful speech or treatise (and here I am thinking of St. Thomas Aquinas's work concerning the nature of human knowledge, the nature of angels, and the nature of God) is an expression of general ideas which become more precise and significant, and which open new horizons in the unity of their synthesis (like man himself, the unity of a great principle working within a variety-compound).

(3) *Expressive beauty:* the beauty of that living substance born when natural forms become instruments of the expression of spiritual forms. Beato Angelico's *San Domenico* is a beautiful figure, and is also the creation of lines and colours which possess their own material beauty, but which at the same time transcend this material field. It expresses, through the ingenious impulse of the figure's gesture towards the cross, the entire gift of being, to give to others everything he had received. The foreshortenings of El Greco, Rouault, Servens, and E. Nolde are deprived of any material beauty, but are nonetheless intensely expressive, particularly of the drama of the Man-God who has become, as the prophet says, "a squashed worm", "rubbish", "an expiatory victim".

Cinematic art needs plastic art, musical art, and literary art, but it uses them for its own ends as instruments to express a human reality. In fact, there are two principles which make a new thing of the art of the cinema: (a) the shot, which, in space, chooses the whole or part of the body, a group, a room, a town, a street, a landscape, which corresponds to the ends of the artist, the director; (b) the rhythm of editing which chooses, in time, the succession of faces, gestures, words or silences, visual or sonorous accessories, according to the dialectic of the movement of the mind required for representation on the screen.

Film differs from a succession of images, words, or musical modulations precisely because each element is chosen only for its expressiveness in regard to the theme to be communicated to the audience. With its alternations of shots, from the close-up to the panoramic, with its monologues or dialogues, its musical commentary or its silence, film stresses only what the artist has found essential in the narrative-become-scenario.

It should be necessary to develop these elements, to analyse one after the other, the photographic, pictorial/plastic, or musical/literary elements which cease to be isolated splendours as soon as they are integrated into the film. Nonetheless, two examples must suffice:

(1) *Rain* (1929), the masterpiece of the Dutch master Joris Ivens. In their depiction of all the harmonic variations of light and shadow on the water, on the roofs, in streets, cafés, shops, and the gutters of Amsterdam, a simple display of stills from the film would result in a great art exhibition. Ivens has combined all these photographs in a filmic order. He started with a monotonous light rain swelling to become an invading misty sadness. Then the sun's rays appear, weaving in and out, eventually to triumph over the city, which then recovers its orginal optimistic, busy rhythm. The photographs have become movement; not only physical movement, but movement of the mind, which ranges from surprise to a monotonous sadness to a rejoicing in victorious vitality. Each frame, as photograph, partakes of an individual beauty which expresses no precise idea, nor any need to be beautiful. Enwrapped in cinematic movement, however, the beautiful photographs themselves vanish to express a deeper reality, a human spiritual reality superior to their own limited nature: that hymn of quiet joy which shines in the human soul, through and above the impact of a turbulent atmosphere.

(2) *Henry V* (1945), Laurence Olivier's masterful film of Shakespeare's drama, is great cinema. Thanks to the beautiful language of the brilliant dialogue, its vigorously dramatic or comic climaxes and episodes, the speeches of the King, the actions of his enemies, of his soldiers, of the queens and princesses, and of Falstaff and company, the drama is a masterwork of the literature of all ages. The film is

only a part of the play, but it is something more as well. Literature has become one element among many used to express in filmic terms the central theme of Shakespeare's play. Above all, Olivier wanted to capture the historical atmosphere within which Shakespeare's people lived and breathed. The famous soliloquy of the royal conscience concerning his decisions and the life and death of multitudes acquires in the film an intensity which is never achieved in a reading of the play or in its theatrical performances.

That is the secret of the cinema: the material, plastic beauty of its bodies, costumes, and sets; the intellectual beauty of its words and music; its dramatic and intellectual invention: all exist transformed by the most expressive scenes, filmed from the best angles, or edited into a rhythm chosen to make the greatest impact on the audience, allowing them to see into the heart of that "man for all seasons".

From this, one can see that the beauty of the cinema is a new beauty, composed of the most complex substance, in which a multiplicity of objects is used in a precise context because of their vital nature. These objects — from the inanimate, to actors who move within a predetermined narrative — express human reality through the principle of artistic unity.

The Philosophy of Neo-Realism

What the creators of the new school have understood, more or less consciously, can be expressed in a single sentence: The means of expression must sacrifice itself to what is to be expressed.

The film director has discovered a deep, dynamic, and truly human reality in the fact of the war (*Un giorno nella vita, Roma città aperta, Paisà, Vivere in pace, Il sole sorge ancora*), in the post-war environment (*Scuscià, Germania anno zero*), in small groups (representing thousands) on the train to Loreto (*La porta del cielo*), and in the commonplace anecdote of a salesman, neither heroic nor wicked, who, by chance, encounters a girl on a train (*Quattro passi fra le nuvole*). The director has understood and wants to show us how the most common events can contain spiritual riches. He eschews lighting effects which tend to become an end in themselves — as in the Mexican school represented by Emilio Fernandez and Gabriel

Figueroa, for example[5] — for he cares nothing for sophisticated artifice. Unlike the directors of many French and Argentinian films, the Italian neo-realist director prefers simplicity. He is not eager to obtain effects through sensational editing in the manner of Eisenstein and Orson Welles. His goals are different: humble cinematography, seemingly unoriginal editing, simplicity in his choice of shots and his use of plastic material: all go to give his interior vision substance.

Moreover, not only does he have contempt for material beauty, but he seems often enough to neglect intellectual and spiritual beauty in the sense defined above. A French critic has suggested that "when we read Italian scenarios, most of them seem ridiculous. When reduced to plot, the films are very often nothing more than moralizing melodramas." In this regard, we must admit that Rossellini (and others) may have gone too far in trusting to the inspiration of the moment — a typical Italian attitude — in their attempts to establish fresh and vigorous contact with the "real", the true subject of the films. Yet we can also see that a precisely prepared screenplay is only a means to an end. Often, a screenplay that is too-well-prepared prevents the director from creating with his own means those gestures, or showing those faces which comprise the very soul of simple men in groups, which is the authentic "screenplay" of their dramas.

The Italian neo-realist school is based on a single thesis diametrically opposed to that thesis which regards the cinema only in terms of lighting effects, words, and purely imaginary situations. Neo-realism's thesis is that the screen is a magic window which opens out on to the "real"; that cinematic art is the art of recreating, through the exercise of free choice upon the material world, the most intense vision possible of the invisible reality inherent in the movements of the mind. The basis of every good work of art is not what people *think* about reality, but what reality actually is. Through a shared vision of existence, both artists and audiences forget with pleasure those artistic inventions which merely served as a means for the creation of that new-born thing (and here I am thinking of a mother's forgetting the process by which she arrived at her happiness in giving birth to a son, a new being).

The neo-realist school has taken a great step forward. It has forsworn vanity to reach the true aim of cinema: to express reality. René

Clair, who has made no secret of his admiration for the new Italian masters, recently shrewdly observed: "The Italian cinema produces masterpieces because it has few resources, but that will soon end because the Italian cinema will soon be rich." Clair will be proved right if the Italian school as a collective effort does not develop a philosophy which will perpetuate neo-realism as a source of inspiration. This philosophy is nearing its fulfillment, and the ideas which I have described comprise only the ideological substructure of what is being created in the nation of ancient culture, in this country which is, miraculously, the only country to rejuvenate itself after a dictatorship and a war.

As a foreigner who discovered Italy after working in thirty countries of Europe, America, and Africa, it is only here that I have regained my optimism about Western culture. In Italy, intelligence, imagination, and sensitivity are immensely creative because they are linked to a simple and rich human tradition, the fruit of twenty centuries of heroism and sacrifice: the Christian tradition.

There is only one danger for the neo-realist school: a loss of contact with the deep source of human reality, which in Italy is either Christian or non-existent.

As Luigi Chiarini has indicated — ideas which I do not hesitate to repeat — in Italian art, as in the Italian mind, there is not yet a division between the left and right, or to put it better, between materialism and the spiritual. Human reality is a spiritual reality, even for the man who is not a disciplined church-goer. That is why the Italian cinema will not have its *La bête humaine, Quai des brumes,* or its *Le jour se lève.*[6]

"The sun rises again"[7] in Italy because, beyond the sad realities of human perversity, tyranny, and social injustice, the soul of the Italian people — the soul of the same family of that Father Who is in Heaven, and Who is always there to help man free himself from evil — knows and believes that reality is Eternal.

*"Le basi filosofiche
del neorealismo cinematografico italiano",*
Bianco e nero, IX, 4, June 1948.

Notes

1   This particular conjoining of names makes it a bit difficult to see *exactly* what Morlion has in mind by "English documentary school". While Harry Watt is a key name in the documentary movement in England from the late Thirties, and into the war, he made feature films into the Fifties. He worked with the GPO (General Post Office) Film Unit, and directed one of the best-known war-time documentaries, *Target for tonight* (1941); neither Carol Reed nor David Lean, are particularly connected with the "documentary school". Morlion may, of course, be allowing the term to spread a bit to include English "realistic" fiction films of the same general period. Certainly, at the time Morlion was writing this essay, Lean was best known for *Brief encounter* (1946) and Reed for *Odd man out* (1946).

2   With few exceptions, "neo-realism" is what everyone called the movement. What Morlion is claiming, as he does explicitly three paragraphs later, is that the term was invented by Catholic critics, a claim which is difficult to document and which is probably irrelevant anyway.

3   *Ufficio Cattolico Internazionale Cinematografico*: International Catholic Office of the Cinema.

4   The "Stagirite" is Aristotle, so called after Stagira, the city in ancient Macedonia where he was born. While "scholastics" can include most of the philosophers of medieval Christian Europe, Morlion obviously has more specifically in mind the Thirteenth century, during which age Aristotle became known in Western Europe and Thomas Aquinas formulated his synthesis of Aristotelian rationalism and Christianity.

5   Fernandez is the director of many films, the most famous of which are probably *Isle of passion* (1941) and *The pearl* (1945). Figueroa is a well-known cinematographer who worked in Hollywood with Gregg Toland, and in Mexico on most of the films Luis Bunuel made there. Fernandez and Figueroa worked together on *MacLovia* (1950).

6   Morlion evidently objects to Renoir's *La bête humaine* and Marcel Carné-Jacques Prévert's *Quai des brumes* and *Le jour se lève* because

of their intense pessimism and lack of "spiritual" hope; the latter film would probably be anathema to a Catholic priest considering the protagonist's suicide.

7   *"Il sole sorge ancora"* means "the sun rises again"; it is also the title of Aldo Vergano's film, which allows for Morlion's mild play on words. While it is not clear why, earlier in the essay Morlion goes out of his way to slight the early and middle sections of the film, it is easy to see why the final sequences appealed to him. A partisan leader and a sympathetic priest are about to be executed by German soldiers. As an act of defiance and continuing hope, the villagers who are being forced to witness the execution respond aloud in unison to the priest's prayer: on the surface at least, a scene made-to-order to illustrate Morlion's final points.

11. **Towards an Italian Landscape**
by Giuseppe De Santis

Giuseppe De Santis (1917-   ) began working during the war as a critic for *Cinema,* and then collaborated on the scenarios for such films as *Ossessione* (Visconti, 1943), *Desiderio* (Rossellini, Pagliero, 1943), and *Il sole sorge ancora* (Vergano, 1948). In 1949 his second film *Riso amaro* was an international box office hit.

Both the choice and the importance of a landscape as the fundamental elements with which characters should live are two aspects of a problem which is never resolved in Italy, although solutions seem always to be found abroad. These two aspects should, in fact, reflect one another as they did in the work of our greatest painters when they wanted mainly to underscore either the feeling in a portrait or the dramatic qualities of a composition.

If we consider that a great number of films among those most valued belong to a genre in which landscape has a primordial importance — *White shadows in the South Seas, Tabu, Que viva Mexico, Storm over Asia*[1] — then it is clear that the cinema has an even greater need to use the same element of landscape which communicates most immediately with the spectator who, above all, wants to "see". If we ignore the particular character of each of the films mentioned, it becomes clear that their strongest appeal comes from an atmosphere impossible to create artificially and to which our inner personality responds, thanks to wonderful and extraordinary Nature which, associated with the actions of the characters, unfolds itself before our eyes.

How would it be possible to understand and interpret man if he were to be separated from those elements in which he lives every day, and with which he is in constant communication? These elements are: (1) Either the walls of his house, which must show the marks of his hands, his taste, his nature, and so on, or, (2) the streets of his town, in which he meets other men (such meetings must not be occasional, but must be underscored by the special character that such an act carries with it). We cannot forget here, by the way, Grüne's *Die Strasse* or Vidor's *The crowd*.[2] Or (3) his timid profession and his identification with the nature which surrounds him, on which he depends so much that he becomes moulded in its image.

Obviously, it is not very original to note that the place where we were born and where we have lived has contributed to making us different from one another. God is responsible for that, but unfortunately He is often betrayed to such an extent that a peasant from Sicily can often become identical to one living in the Alps — less in life, of course, than in the cinema.

Since cinema is the art which stimulates all our senses simultaneously, its central preoccupation should be to create an authenticity (even a fantastic one) of both gesture and atmosphere; in other words, an authenticity of the factors which must be used to express the world in which men live. Later on, this trend which was first used by the Americans in the Western (although born unconsciously and too often within the confines of "show business") was used more aesthetically by the Russians.

I think that a nearly perfect balance was found recently by the French. Jean Renoir, son of Auguste Renoir the painter, created sequences in several films which will remain classic examples in the history of the cinema. It would be very difficult to find an atmosphere to equal that in Renoir's films, where everything helps to determine the drama of the characters, and in which both the figurative elements and the interior movements expressed by the actors participate in the creation of that atmosphere. It would seem that Renoir wants to point out the existence of feelings which men cannot express; therefore, it is necessary to use everything around him to express those feelings. Thus the trip made by the French prisoners across Germany in *La grande illusion* is conveyed through a gradual transformation of the landscape as it is perceived through the eyes of the prisoners themselves. The dispute between the two hungry and exhausted fugitives, when they have nearly reached the Swiss border, becomes more dreadful in a barren and desolate winter landscape. In *La bête humaine,* the crisis of conscience which dawns upon Jacques Lantier (Jean Gabin) as he is about to strangle the girl beside the railroad tracks, comes to an end thanks to the unexpected rumbling of a train against a tormented sky. Later on in the film, there are the bare and empty stations in the north-west of France, the rows of willows like olive trees standing along the railway where the train passes by. It was not by mere chance that Renoir expressed himself in such a poetic way.

I intended just now to allude to Renoir's father without asserting that being the son of a famous painter necessarily implies an inheritance of the father's genius. Yet such an artistic upbringing has doubtless served the director well. It has opened his eyes to an essential world, one unknown to many people. Perhaps our own directors have never realized the importance of studying painting — or must we think that Italy lacks painters as famous as Renoir? Is there perhaps a lack of landscape in Italy? Isn't Italy the country which everyone envies for its beauty? It is no use possessing a beautiful thing if we neither deserve nor like it.

The only time that we could speak of a true Italian cinema was with Ruttmann's *Acciaio*,[3] Blasetti's *1860* and *Vecchia guardia* which, if not perfect films, should have formed the first nucleus of an authentic Italian spirit. But whose fault is it that this did not happen?

Piccolo mondo antico by Mario Soldati gives us new hope.[4] For the first time in the history of our cinema, we saw a landscape which was neither rarified nor picturesque, but which corresponded to the humanity of the characters either as an emotive element or as a clue to their feelings. I am thinking of Franco leaving for Milan at dawn. Luisa, who has come with him, remains behind on the edge of the lake, and he watches her disappear with the landscape, waving like the movement of the boat which takes him away from her across the lake. To my mind, then, the most important sequences of the film are those in which all the elements I have mentioned before are present. First, the ball in the country, then Ombretta's death, then Luisa's meeting with the Marquise, and finally the three women running along the steps of the village when they come to tell Luisa about the accident. Conversely, do you recall how, in Duvivier's *Carnet du bal*, the exact same landscape was neglected and remained cold?

Eventually, we should stop considering the documentary as a genre apart. It is only by blending the two elements that, in such a landscape as our own, we will find the formula for a true and genuine Italian cinema. The best evidence for this was given by De Robertis's

Uomini sul fondo. The landscape will never have any importance when deprived of the presence of man; but the reverse is just as true.

"Per un paesaggio italiano",
Cinema, 116, April 25, 1941.

Notes

1   *White shadows in the South Seas* (USA, 1927) was co-written and co-directed by Robert Flaherty and W.S. Van Dyke. It is a fiction film with documentary overtones.
    Tabu (USA, 1931) was directed by Robert Flaherty and F.W. Murnau, and was also a mixture of fiction and "staged" documentary.
    Que viva México (1931) is the unfinished semi-documentary directed by Sergei Eisenstein. The footage — or part of it at least, since more has recently been "discovered" in the USSR — has been edited and shown in various versions by various hands: *Thunder over Mexico* (Sol Lesser), *Death day* (Upton Sinclair), and *Time in the sun* (Marie Seton).
    Storm over Asia (USSR, 1929), directed by V.I. Pudovkin, is an epic melodrama with a strong ideological base in which the landscape plays an important role, finally becoming an ideological force itself.

2   Karl Grüne's *Die Strasse* (1923) is a semi-expressionist film in which the street is really the central character. See Lotte H. Eisner, *The haunted screen* for the most authoritative discussion of the film and its use of "landscape".
    King Vidor's *The crowd* (1928) is a picture of the dehumanization caused by city life in which New York is all-important as the setting.

3   The German documentarist Walter Ruttmann was brought to Italy by Emilio Cecchi (then artistic director of the Cines company) to make *Acciaio* in 1933.

4   In Alicata — De Santis's essay "Truth and poetry", Soldati is taken to task for having based films on the work of Fogazzaro, whose novel *Pic-*

cola mondo antico was adapted for Soldati's *here* much-praised film. Either De Santis changed his mind about the film in the seven months between essays, or it was primarily Alicata who had objections to the film, or (most likely) it was a matter of shifting focus to make polemical points. In this essay it is primarily painting which De Santis is stressing as a source of inspiration, while in "Truth and poetry" it is Verga who is being put forward.

12. Truth and Poetry:
Verga and the Italian Cinema
by Mario Alicata and Giuseppe De Santis

When most of its technical problems were solved, the cinema — which has moved from documentary to narrative — realised that its destiny was linked with literature. In spite of the silly pretensions of "pure" filmmakers, marginal relationships at least have always been maintained between cinema and literature, to the extent that it is possible to state that the history of cinema is only one chapter in the history of Twentieth Century art and literature. Examples of this co-existent relationship are so well-known that it seems unnecessary to mention them. However:

In America, the tracking shots behind the famous rides of W.S. Hart, Hoot Gibson, and Tom Mix depend upon the typical and popular tradition of the western stories of O'Henry and Bret Harte. In Europe, Wiene, the obsessed poet of *Das Kabinett des Dr Caligari*, was a contemporary of the Expressionist writers in Germany and of Kokoschka and Grosz.[1] René Clair created *Entr'acte* in the very same year that André Breton published the *Surrealist manifesto*.[2] Eventually the numerous symbolists, from Man Ray (*L'Etoile de mer*) to Machaty,[3] traced the course of a persistent symbolist experience in which so much contemporary poetry struggled. At this point it seems relevant to remind the "pure" filmmakers that Wiene, Clair, Man Ray, and other men of letters solved many technical problems which currently seem to have acquired an aspect of hermetic "ivory-towerism".

At any rate, it is necessary to make clear that the cinema finds its best direction in the realistic tradition because of its strict narrative nature; as a matter of fact, realism is the true and eternal measure of every narrative significance — realism intended not as the passive homage to an objective, static truth, but as the imaginative and creative power to fashion a story composed of real characters and events. It remains evident that when the cinema began to create characters, and to examine the change in men's souls in relationship to their con-

131

crete environment, it was necessarily influenced by Nineteenth Century European realism.

In fact, from Flaubert to Chekhov, from Maupassant to Verga, from Dickens to Ibsen, realism seems to have achieved a perfect syntax of psychology and of sentiment and, at the same time, a poetic image of the society in which these men lived. The great realistic dramas of the cinema were born like that, simultaneous with the birth of Buster Keaton's metaphysical farces and the realistic romances of René Clair.

In Germany, Dupont's *Varieté* was created in collaboration with a number of violent and crude-faced actors, thereby fixing the terms of a genuine narrative language in the compact block of its poetic framework.[4] The European novel and drama gave everything to *Varieté*: the acute need to investigate the intimate life of the characters thoroughly, the capacity to make us feel the tensions of certain situations or certain unexpected flashes of truth, the moral commitment to display the causes of spiritual and social crisis of the first post-war period. From that point of view, Dupont represents, with Clair, the highest level of performance in the first period of the history of European cinemas.

Subsequently, Pabst's realism tones down the primitive, desolate sincerity of Dupont, perhaps the better to exploit, thanks to the invention of sound, a more refined technique. *Abwege*, for example, is a drama of limited, almost decadent, perspective; the same is true of *Kameradschaft*, in spite of the grandeur and originality of its commitment.[5]

It was America which carried on the realistic experience of the European cinema; the America of Sherwood Anderson and William Faulkner, authors who renewed once more the great tradition of realistic narrative, and who succeeded in creating a story-stereotype which, within a few years, was to fascinate a classical and more worldly Europe. The realism of the American cinema was endowed with the undiluted, crude hues of uneasy, restless, and still maturing society. Moreover, these were the solemn and tragic years of the Great Depression. With the violent action of the drunken Negroes in *Sanctuary* came the rat-a-tat of the gangster's machine-gun in the streets and the lines of unemployed, so silent and gloomy. In rapid succession, King Vidor made *The crowd, Hallelujah!*, and *Our daily bread,*[6] all stories written with a confident hand. Fantasy and imagination redeemed the bits of vivid, social polemic in a wonderfully simple style which could, in the accents of an oratorio, exalt the waters flowing to the rescue of destitute homesteaders from drought and death.

Vidor found his faith in life through poetry. Yet in spite of the hope which always rises like a hymn from his work, American realism also wrote sadder and more sordid pages. Among its best films are those inspired by the hapless, violent life of the gangsters. It was Mamoulian with *City streets* who gave us *the* masterpiece in the genre.[7]

If, in this brief history of cinematic realism, every nation is represented at a particular moment with a particular trend in its production, in the last few years it is France that has demonstrated the existence of a typical "school", of a common method of understanding and solving the problems of cinematic narrative. We should not wonder that the French cinema, at a certain point in its development, found its salvation in realism. After years of insignificant and anonymous production, Duvivier, Carné, and Renoir brought back to the cinema an atmosphere, a rhetoric, and a style through a thorough rereading of Maupassant and Zola.

Of course, it is obvious that genuine poetry has not always corresponded to a realist brand of the poetic. Apart from Pépé's "invasion" of Algiers at the end of *Pépé le Moko* and the Maupassantian trip into the country of *La belle équipe,*[8] we can dismiss Duvivier and his satellites without regret. But it is also clear that it is an easy commonplace to claim an indicative relationship between the morbid violence of both Carné and Renoir and the corruption and disintegration of French society in the early years of its greatest military defeat. We need only add that because of texts such as those by Zola and Renard,[9] and because of the strong passions which created such a turmoil in French society, cinematic realism decisively adopted the tone of naturalism — we will not insist on great differences between realistic and naturalistic attitudes and taste — gaining thereby its interest in the pathological aspects of reality, even to the extent of merging all its scientific, experimental facets in a decadent hyper-sensitivity.

Even if criticism, in bad faith, denied that some of Renoir's sequences are fervently poetic, it remains true that the cruelty and the self-satisfied horror of a number of passages sometimes gives to Renoir's images the appearance of troubled case-histories rather than representations executed by the imagination. Those sequences of Renoir which we have in mind are, for example, the course of the train through the deserted countryside in *La bête humaine* or the suspended passion of the fugitive and the lonely German woman in *La grande illusion*.[10]

It is obvious that our blind faith in a realistic credo includes precise estimation of that lucid balance between intelligence and moral strength which supports and elevates the realism of directors like Dupont and Vidor. Thus what we ask of the Italian cinema is that it possess a faith in truth and in the poetry of truth, a faith in man and in the poetry of man.

This is a simple request and a modest programme. We become ever more attached to that simple modesty when, glancing over the history of our cinema, we see its development being trapped amongst the rhetoric of D'Annunzio, the archaeology of *Cabiria*, and the flight to the middle-class paradise of night clubs along the *via Nazionale*,[11] where the homely boldness of our sentimental comedies finds relief. We see the only genuine and noble traditions of our cinema, that tradition linked to actor Emilio Ghione's tormented and ardent face and to the genuine passion of Martoglio's *Sperduti nel buio*, being lost or forgotten; we see the clever Camerini abandoning the sad, simple and vigorous style of *Rotaie* for the correctly orthodox but ever so much easier and more commonplace style of *Una romantica avventura*; we see Mario Soldati[12] who has written some of the most imaginative, powerful, and free Italian stories in contemporary literature, abandoning his taverns and harbours, his dark and oppressed scenes, his colourful and pure landscapes for the *risotti con i tartufi*[13] of Antonio Fogazzaro.[14] In fact, even in its choice of a literary tradition, the Italian cinema reveals strange predilections: Fogazzaro, Girolamo Rovetta, and even more minor realists.[15] This very choice would seem tacitly to confirm that stupid legend which has it that there is no narrative tradition in Italian literature.

It is, perhaps, helpful to indicate in the cinema that instead of the more habitual use of back doors to realism, there is a main entrance. The most intelligent readers, of course, will have already understood that our argument leads us necessarily to one name: Giovanni Verga. Not only did he create a great body of poetry, but he created a country as well, an epoch, a society. Since we believe in an art which above all creates truth, the Homeric, legendary Sicily of *I malavoglia, Maestro Don Gesualdo, L'Amante di Gramigna,* and *Jeli il pastore*[16] offers us both the human experience and a concrete atmosphere. Miraculously stark and real, it could give inspiration to the imagination of our cinema which looks for things in the space-time of reality to redeem itself from the easy suggestions of a moribund bourgeois state.

For those who ask for artificiality, rhetoric, and badly-coined medals and awards, for those who seek to follow the example of other cinematic productions whose technical perfection provides no salvation from their miserable humanity and poverty for reason, Giovanni Verga's works will perhaps mean nothing, for his works indicate the only historically valid direction: a revolutionary art inspired by, and acting, in turn, as inspiration to a humanity which hopes and suffers.

"Verità e poesia:
Verga e il cinema italiano",
Cinema, 127, October 10, 1941.

Notes

1   Robert Wiene was an actor, scriptwriter, and director. It is open to question how much credit is due to him personally for *Das Kabinett des Dr Caligari* (1919) and how much to the writers (Carl Meyer and Hans Janowitz) and the art directors (Hermann Warm, Walter Reimann, and Walter Röhrig) in the light of his previous and later films, although *Genuine* (1920), *Orlacs Hände* (1924), and *Raskolnikov* (1923) share a similar expressionistic vision. At any rate, the point of the essay remains.
  Oskar Kokoschka is the Austrian playwright and painter.

2   René Clair's *Entr'acte* (1924), which was conceived as a section of Rolf de Maré's Swedish Ballet production of Picabia's *Relâche*, might be described as Dadaist as well as Surrealist, although it is perhaps a matter of the two movements merging and overlapping.

André Breton's *Manifeste du surréalisme* (1924) proposed most of the basic tenets of the movement, including automatic writing as a way of tapping Freud's idea of the unconscious.

3   Man Ray was an American as well-known for his photography and painting as for his experimental films. *L'Etoile de mer* (1928) might as easily be called Surrealist or Dadaist as Symbolist.

Gustav Machaty was a Czech director whose most famous film was *Extase* (1933); its fame was based as much on a nude Hedy Lamarr and several then-daring sex scenes as for anything else about the film.

4   E.A. Dupont's *Varieté* (1925) is as famed for its use of the moving, subjective camera, its parallel editing to shape and movement, and its telling a story without titles, as for the "literary" aspects listed in the essay.

5   While *Kameradschaft* (1931) was a sound film, *Abwege* (1928) was silent.

6   *Hallelujah!* was made in 1929, following *The crowd* (1928) and *Show people* (1928). Vidor did not shoot *Our daily bread* until 1934, having made several films in between.

7   Rouben Mamoulian's *City streets* (1931) is not without interest. At the time it was rather innovative in its use of sound. That Alicata and De Santis consider it *the* masterpiece in the gangster genre must be put into the context of what was, or what was not, in release in Italy prior to the writing of the essay.

8   Julien Duvivier's *Pépé le Moko* (1936) and *La belle équipe* (1936) are from the central and best period of the director's long career (he made over 100 films) and are examples of *"réalisme poétique"* in which social environment is carefully observed and overlaid with a veneer of romantic resignation.

9   Jules Renard (1864-1910) is most noted for his careful, almost scientific, observation of natural objects and human behaviour which he was often able to raise to cryptic poetry. His best known novel, *Poil de carotte* (1894), was twice filmed by Duvivier.

10   *La grande illusion* (1937) was based on an original script by Renoir and Charles Spaak; *La bête humaine* (1938) was adapted by Renoir from the Zola novel. The latter film was remade by Fritz Lang in 1954 as *Human desire*. A comparison of the two versions makes the point of Alicata and De Santis even stronger. Renoir's protagonist is a psychopath, albeit sympathetic, while Lang's is an innocent caught up in the intrigues of unpleasant characters.

11   Many Italian comedies had sequences set in the night clubs along the *via Nazionale* in Rome. The reference to the street in 1941 would have been as clear as a reference to the *via Veneto* in the late Fifties and early Sixties.

12   *Una romantica avventura* (1940) was directed by Mario Camerini. Mario Soldati is as well known for his novels and short stories as for his films, many of which are based on novels and short stories (although infrequently his own). He has adapted Fogazzaro (including *Piccolo mondo antico* in 1941), Moravia, Balzac, Bersezio, and others.

13   *Risotti con i tartufi* is the famous Italian dish of prepared rice with the rich, and often expensive, truffle. To attribute the pseudo-rarified atmosphere the dish suggests to the work of Fogazzaro is here polemical and not entirely fair.

14   Antonio Fogazzaro (1842-1911) is best known for his tetralogy beginning with *Piccolo mondo antico* (1895) which deals with the clash between faith and reason. His novels were denounced both by non-Catholics who found the religious content too respectful and orthodox, and by Catholics (several of his novels were placed on the Index) for being too "modernist".

15   Girolamo Rovetta (1851-1910) was a novelist and dramatist who treated all levels of society somewhat critically, using Milan, in particular, as a setting. He is noted for his observation and careful reproduction of detail (which many critics have claimed is rather overabundant) and his ability to tell a story simply. His best known novel is probably *La baraonda* (1894) which deals realistically with materialistic Milanese society. Other realists whom the authors mention in an aside are the "minor realists" Lucia D'Ambra, Flavia Steno, Nino Oxilia, and Luciana Peverelli. Whilst none of these would be absolutely unrespectable sources for realistic screen adaptation (however "dated"), Alicata and De Santis are, of course, writing a polemic,

downgrading other authors in order to stress the importance of the "main entrance" to screen-literary realism, Giovanni Verga.

16   All four titles are novels from Verga's later, more realistic (and more poetic) period. *I Malavoglia* (1881) and *Maestro Don Gesualdo* (1888) were part of a projected cycle, *I vinti*. The first was used as the basis of Visconti's *La terra trema* (1947) six years after this essay was written.

13. A Discourse on Neo-Realism
by Luigi Chiarini

Luigi Chiarini became the director of the Italian film school, the *Centro Sperimentale di cinematografia*, the founder and editor of several film magazines, most notably *Bianco e nero*, and the author of innumerable articles and books on Italian cinema. In 1942, he directed an experimental film *Via delle cinque lune*, and went on to direct two more features and to write the scenarios for a half dozen more.

Premises

Another discourse on neo-realism in the Italian cinema could easily become boring. It has been so much spoken of, and with such a tone! such hyperbolic accents! These are characteristics of film criticism, whose ancestors are publicity and propaganda, for film is both industry and commerce. A discourse could be boring if there were not some intention to say something new with the will to analyse that phenomenon which is important in the history of the cinema from more than simply a stylistic point of view. It is the expression of the ideological orientation and the state of mind of our people in recent years, the expression of a singularly happy moment when people believed that they would be able to create, without further struggles and suffering, a peaceful and better world from that which had so tragically collapsed.

Today, those hopes have been shattered; we should better say those illusions, for it was really an illusion to think that history could make such leaps, and that the tragic events of war should suddenly develop in people's minds the need for justice and liberty — which in fact requires a slow and deep process through the long and painful experience. If we do not remember this, the arc of neo-realism remains incomprehensible; I say "arc" because that trend, that aspect, of our cinema has just begun a decline through a process of involution into a mannerism without soul and therefore without bite.

Our chrysalis has not become a butterfly.

Neo-realism: an Improper Definition

There has been much talk about neo-realism, a term which originated beyond the Alps, and which is surely improper from either a critical or an aesthetic point of view. It has, however, entered common usage; thus the meaning needs to be properly defined rather than dismissed with easy arguments, especially as concerns the films attributed to neo-realism.

It is clear that the term should not be understood as an exclusively stylistic classification, because it describes films which are widely different from each other: *Roma città aperta, Caccia tragica, La terra trema, Ladri di biciclette,* to name just a few. For the same reason, we cannot speak, as some have done, of a "new Italian school", for it is not a formal orientation common to a certain number of artists among whom one might even find a leader. It is rather a spontaneous movement lacking both literary origins and an "intellectual" attitude; it does not seek to propose any solution to general problems of style as an immediate goal.

Neo-realism Is not Verism

The great equivocation has been to confuse neo-realism with verism, and to believe that the former shaped its substance from the real materials of reality, doing without actors and replacing them with people taken from life — even from the same conditions and trades corresponding to the characters of the film. That is a mistake which led subsequently to the belief that documentaries were the antecedents of neo-realism. As a consequence, a spiritual position became confused with a technical and material fact.

Roma città aperta, the first and most famous neo-realist film, availed itself of the collaboration between two excellent actors, Anna Magnani and Aldo Fabrizi, not to mention the secondary characters who were also interpreted by professional actors.

It is a technical and even stylistic fact that directors like Visconti (in *La terra trema*) have stuck to a scrupulous verism, but that is due to the particular content of a film.

The artistic fiction, or the transfiguration, was transposed by the director in elaborate, refined shots whose effects were strictly calculated. Rossellini has dealt with the fiction of his film in an almost documentary technique, while Visconti, inverting the terms, elaborated his document with the sophisticated techniques of artifice. As anyone can see, these are two different techniques and styles. In the same way, the baroque qualities of De Santis's *Caccia tragica* differ from his technique in *Riso amaro.*

Yet even in these differences there remains a shared world, a common way for identical interests, a similar attitude towards reality, which makes of neo-realism neither a school nor a stylistic tendency, but a spiritual movement, invested with a concept of art and assuming a decisively polemic position, not of a formal nature so much as of a continuum of the details of content, compared to other tendencies in the cinema. This historical dialectic is thus reflected in the artistic.

Human and Social Meaning of Neo-realism

It springs from a sincere need for truth and humanity after so much suffering, from a need for pure air painfully acquired during the war and the foreign occupation which had made the individual drama (of a psychological order) dissolve into a collective drama. It developed in us the incentive to begin a social inquiry so that we could discover the causes of so many evils and so much pain. The soul of neo-realism was the social reality, the human condition of our people during the German occupation (*Roma città aperta*), during the allied occupation (*Sciuscià*). It was that soul which led to a deeper understanding and an opportunity for it to remake itself, as in *La terra trema*, on an older, more profound basis.

That is the current of neo-realism, which has not always expressed such content in new forms; every other interpretation is arbitrary, tendentious, and provokes equivocation.

That being admitted, it is obvious that neo-realist films could not engage in polemic and retain a political tone at the same time, giving to the word "political" a larger meaning than "the programme of a political party". The position of film-makers was not preconceived

141

within ideological schematizations, and when they were introduced they ruined the expressive force of the films. Their position was determined in confrontation with the historical and social reality that they were discovering with the camera.

Facts speak through the suggestive force of neo-realism; not as brutal documentary, because absolute objectivity is impossible and is never "purified" out from the subjective element represented by the director; rather, in the sense of the historical-social meaning of facts.

Neo-realism and the Origins of Cinema

It is necessary to clarify this concept. With Italian neo-realism, film returns to its origins, but with a maturity of fifty years of existence and with a consciousness of the autonomy of its expressive means and the knowledge of its force and responsibility as mass art.

The cinema was born in 1895 as the miraculous reproduction of life in its most obvious aspect: dynamism. The small films made by the brothers Lumière are, in fact, brief and simple documentaries: workers leaving their factories, a train arriving in a station, movement through a city street.

The interest and wonder provoked is not linked to movement, but to the faithful reproduction of life in all its dynamism. Baudelaire, in *Art romantique*, had already, after all, hinted at the wonders of the Fantascopio which, through the circular rotation of twenty pictures, could show with a stupendous precision the different leaps of a dancer or the exercises of a gymnast.

If the "daguerrotype" was a success, which prompted Baudelaire to pen bitter words against "disgusting society, like a Narcissus, contemplating its vulgar image on metal" and to forecast the demise of painting due to the intrusion of industry and science in the field of art, that success renewed itself in a much more clamorous way on the evening of the 28th of December 1895 in Paris, in the cellar of the *Grand Café* on the *Boulevard des Capucines*, where the first projection of a series of films took place. *Le radical*, a newspaper of the time, said about this wonderful invention: "It is the reproduction through projection of scenes of life, photographed in a series of snapshots. Whatever the scene and however many people taken in the middle of acts of life, you can see them with their own height, colour, and perspective, with skies, houses and streets, with all the illusion of real life. For example, there is the scene of the blacksmiths: one makes the bellows work and smoke rises from the hearth; the other takes the metal, beats it on the anvil, immerses it in water, from which a large column of white steam rises. *L'Arrivé d'un train en gare (The arrival of a train at the station)* with its movements of trams and passers-by, is even more startling, but the film which created the greatest enthusiasm was *La mer (The sea)*. That sea is so true, so turbulent, those bathers running and diving are really true to life."

Documentarism and Fantasy

Then came Méliès with his short fantasy films like *Le voyage dans la lune (A trip to the Moon)*. Men started enjoying themselves with that new extraordinary toy especially suited for producing what D'Annunzio called *"truccherie"*.[1] The realism of Lumière and the fantasy of Méliès represent the two poles between which film has since oscillated.

Here, I would like to note something important: the industralization of the cinema pushed it further and further toward sham and artifice, even triviality, acting against the taste of an ever-growing public. The exceptions, the films which can be considered as authentic works of art, can be counted on the fingers of one hand.

Advice from F. De Sanctis

It has already been said that neo-realism returns film to its origins. The screen again becomes a mirror of life, caught not naturalistically in its external aspects, but in its concrete dialectic. The camera, invented fifty years ago, now discovers the reality of its historical fulfillment; it no longer isolates man in the abstract situation of an abstract character, but links him to the ideals, aspirations, and sufferings of a social structure. Far removed from hypocrisy and rhetoric, it has rediscovered the concrete values of the homeland, of liberty, work, and family.

After more than fifty years, only neo-realist cinema seems capable of hearing the message of Francesco De Sanctis, who concluded his *History of Italian literature* (1871) like this:

> Italy must seek itself with clear sight, without any veil, looking for what is effectual with the spirit of Galileo or Machiavelli.
>
> In this quest for the real elements of its existence, the Italian spirit will remake its culture; it will remotivate its moral world. It will refresh its impressions.
>
> It will find in its intimacy new sources of inspiration: woman, family, nature, love, liberty, country, science, virtue — not as brilliant ideas seen isolated in space which turns around them, but as concrete and familiar objects which become its contents.
>
> To look at ourselves, in our habits, ideas, prejudices, in our qualities good or bad; to convert the modern world in our world, studying it, transforming it; "to explore one's own heart" according to Leopardi's testamentary note.[2]

Neo-realism as Awareness of Italian Society

These words of the "Great Master" might seem a bit exaggerated when applied to the cinema. However, those who are free from academic and literary prejudice, those who understand the prophetic value and moral strength of such words, will be neither surprised nor outraged at our applying them to film. Indeed, perhaps the instinctive innocence of cinema is needed, an innocence which is not yet weighed down with academic and intellectual tradition, to express that exigency of sincerity and truth which all our people felt, after the tragedy of war and occupation destroyed so many ideological and rhetorical structures and so many illusions. Moreover, shared suffering and common danger contributed to engender a deeper consciousness of social solidarity and a perception that the fate of each person was linked with the fate of society as a whole. Despite the tragic fraternal struggle, the force of events created that collective soul which is the sign of the non-extinguished vitality of a people.

Lumière's wonderful machine was there: the picture mill, as it has been called, the maker of so many cheap dreams, but also the most powerful means with which to represent reality.

This representation was no longer that of the peaceful life of 1895, the simple reproduction of which, because of the novelty of the invention made people think it was a miracle. It was rather the representation of a world turned upside down; a representation which aroused in everyone the same ideas, the same emotions, the same reactions, and, I should add, the same conclusions.

The first neo-realist films left us with the impression that cinema had been rediscovered. The audience faced life in its tremendous truth, in a similar situation, to some extent, to that of 1895, save that now it did not reveal itself in its pleasant exterior, but in its deepest human content, in the dialectic between war and peace, civilization and barbarism, reaction and progress: the mechanical reproduction had become artistic representation.

An audience which had grown accustomed — during half a century of the development of the expressive means of the cinema — to seeing images of actors' faces, now saw on the screen the tragedy and pain of their own. No longer following a mere story, but history, the audience saw life reflected from the screen. Hence the noisy success (in Italy as well as abroad) of those first neo-realist films, and the astonishment of the men of letters, the aesthetes of cinema, who were hard put to explain the phenomenon because (it is necesary to remember) those films appear primitive and crude like the small films of the Lumière brothers. Certainly, they lacked the shrewd refinement which cinema has developed in over half a century.

Neo-realism and the Previous "Realists"

Why such great "luck"? Such success? The answer is obvious if one observes that neither realism nor the political-social film were new phenomena. We need only mention a few films: from America, Vidor's *Hallelujah!* and *Our daily bread*; from Russia, Eisenstein's *Battleship Potemkin* and Pudovkin's *The end of St. Petersburg*; from France, the realism of Renoir (*La bête humaine*) and Carné (*Quai des brumes*)[3] — all stylistically more advanced than our *Roma città aperta*, *Paisà*, or *Sciuscià*.

In fact, in the Italian cinema which precedes neo-realism there also runs a realistic vein, from *Sperduti nel buio* of Martoglio to *Ossessione* of Visconti, in which historians believe they have found famous precedents.

American Realism

In my opinion, Italian realism was, to a certain extent, different. In the best American cinema, realism is linked to the investigation and elaboration of an autonomous language of film and the effects of spectacle. We must remember that the art of cinema is relatively young. Therefore a good deal of weight has fallen on the investigation, exploration, elaboration, and conquest of the means of expression, on the technical and formalistic side. This side has been so stressed that, along with the films themselves, a poetic conception was elaborated from the technical-critical-theoretical activity; certain "laws" and formulas became fixed and developed into a grammar. Today we are faced with a grammar that is inadequate and which cannot cope with new artistic facts, with new content.

Revolutionary Russian Realism

That great event, the Russian Revolution, was reflected in the cinema through stylistic elaborations. Russian films expressed the dialectic of revolution, the class struggle, the polemical-ideological content of that revolution through a dialectical editing, which assaulted the spectator with images whose pace and proximity in time produced in the viewer strong emotions, as well as that ideological synthesis which the artists had before them as their international goal. Thus, on the one hand, we have the formal composition of each shot in the most efficient manner according to the significance it should have (hence the theory that the tyrant must be shot from below so as to be deformed and powerful, and the victim from above so as to seem miserable and dominated). On the other hand, we have the dialectical editing of those shots to make the matching of images as clear and efficient as possible. The theory of the *theme* as being the

146

ideological axis of the film is of a primarily intellectual nature.

The importance of Russian cinema in the stylistic evolution of the cinema is so well known that it will suffice simply to note again the decisive part played by the Russians in the development of cinematic theory, especially in the writings of their two greatest directors, Eisenstein and Pudovkin.

Socialist Realism

In two speeches made in Rome and Perugia, Pudovkin criticized the more formalistic aspects of this cinematic theory, particularly its schematisation of editing. Russian cinema of today has undergone a deep stylistic evolution compared with those films made twenty years ago. That evolution followed the transformation of its government through a fighting, polemical phase to the construction of a Communist society.

The basis of socialist realism — which, according to the aesthetics of Marxism, should prefigure the development of such a society — is the exaltation of men and of past and present events in relation to an optimistic vision of the future; it is didactic and edifying, not polemical and critical. In Perugia, Pudovkin said that the common trend of Russian cinema was to "show on the screen the fact of positive man as a living example to encourage imitation."

There is no relationship between that and Italian neo-realism.

Pre-War French Realism

Its literary derivation is quite obvious. The critic Pietro Paolo Trompeo, writing about Renoir's *La bête humaine,* clearly demonstrated that the third phase of French naturalism (after the narrative represented by Zola and his disciples, and the drama best represented by the names of Henri Becque and André Antoine[4] finds its expression in the cinema. French realist cinema is of the "slice of life" variety, but one which is formal and literary; which is re-elaborated through learned and technical artifice in a style which was once successful, but which has degenerated into a historical, baroque fantasy.

Realism in the Italian Cinema before the War

Even the Italian precedents of realism have either a literary origin or one derived from foreign cinematic movements, as in the case of Blasetti's *Sole* — in a line from *Sperduti nel buio* — which echoed Soviet cinema, or Visconti's *Ossessione,* which gained its impetus from the French realist film.

Only Rossellini and De Robertis, with *Uomini sul fondo* and *La nave bianca,* in some way foreshadowed neo-realism, in spite of the fundamentally artificial aspects of those "documentary" films.

Realism and Formalism

Do not misunderstand me. I have no intention of underestimating realism in the history of the cinema. On the contrary. I simply mean that, up until a certain time, which we can pinpoint as the last war, the emphasis was always placed on the formal aspects of cinema. It was not for nothing that there was so much talk about "pure cinema", of "cinematic cinema", of the aesthetic basis for editing film, of "plastic material", and so on.

The Solitary Grandeur of Chaplin

Charles Chaplin, that great and solitary artist, is the only one who is not linked to the formalistic elaboration of cinema; his reluctance to use new technical methods is famous. He always, constantly tried to elaborate social reality through the technique which could gradually, but more immediately, express it: hence, his linear style, which some critics found uncinematic because it neglected editing, which then comprised *the* aesthetic basis of film theory. Still, among all the artists of the cinema, he is certainly the least formalistic *because* he is the most artistic.

148

The Anti-Formalistic Origins of Neo-realism

Since the first neo-realistic films were made with reduced technical means, which were far from being perfectly efficient, content assumed predominance, and all at once poetics, film grammar, preoccupation with formal expression, and even orthodox techniques died out.

Film-makers, like everyone else, emerged from the war with anxious souls, to face a world in ruins. At the same time, however, they felt that, in spite of such destruction, they had gained a freedom of expression, which they had lacked for years, and which only the best among them had either desired or had achieved despite the web of censorship surrounding them. Here, then, is the example of their first true cinematic expression, warm, tearful, uneven perhaps, but trembling with sincerity and truth, and pervaded with hope and faith in a better world.

Roma città aperta

It was a revelation. It had a success without precedent. They say that, in America, producers watched the film again and again, attempting to understand just what the secret was in a film that had provoked such widespread enthusiasm. Naturally, judging it by the old standards, the secret was rather difficult to discover.

The film lacks the usual structure: sometimes it proceeds rapidly, sometimes it skips over essential points of the story to insist on aspects which might appear secondary — although, thanks to their human richness, they never are. The photography is without virtuosity, often rough, almost documentary, and the editing has a rhythm not born from the formalistic cadences of orthodox film theory. Such a difference from the technical perfection of American films!

Here, then, is the secret: Rome, Italy, during the German occupation, with its suffering and its hopes; and, for all men who have experienced it, the tragedy of war, its bestiality and wickedness.

Though one does not remember a "great shot", one will never forget the painful, proud face of Anna Magnani, her rebellion before the Nazi soldiers, her desperate shout broken by a discharge of machine-gun fire, while she runs behind the lorry which is taking her husband away. In her character, there resides the anguish and heroism of all wives and mothers, of all women, whom war so cruelly struck.

None will forget the priest (Aldo Fabrizi), generous, sympathetic to the victims, a man among men. "The roads of God are infinite," he answers the German officer who has reprimanded him for defending a Communist. He is able to reach the supreme sacrifice with simplicity.

How true and authentic Rome appears, with its wide streets, with its working-class quarters of blocks of flats of eight floors, swarming with anguish and revolt. Rome, where the SS did their worst.

During the projection of the film, the audience no longer sees the limits of the screen, does not sense a skilful artifice, and no exclamations are uttered about the virtuosity of the director and actors. The images have become reality, not seen with lucid detachment as in a mirror, but grasped in their actuality and very substance. The formal presence of the film-makers has dissolved in that reality.

Anti-Formalism Does not Imply a Lack of Style

I trust that no one will conclude that I am maintaining that the success of the film — the secret those American producers sought to uncover — is due to its rough substance, no matter how vivid and scorching, nor to a startlingly new *lack* of style.

Rather, the reality of the time determined a different attitude on the part of the film-makers, a completely new feeling which now became the content of the film, and which, in order to express itself, violated the criteria of the old poetics, and so gave life to new forms which lacked the mature refinements of those which had gone before, and which could *appear* rough and primitive.

Roma città aperta constituted a great lesson: a hearkening back to the essential values of cinema — those values of humanity which are common to all art — against all formalism and commercialism. Cinema which itself is comprised of a collective soul is the best means for the expression of the collective soul called society.

Paisà: an Improvement in Style

If *Roma città aperta* had, so to speak, a story, a plot which dealt with the people of Rome during the German occupation, *Paisà*, also by Rossellini, did away with even the last remaining vestiges of plot, to tell, in fragmented episodes, about Italy during the Allied progress from Sicily to the Po Valley.

From the first episode, in Sicily, to those in Naples, Rome, Florence, Bologna, and the epic conclusion in Camacchio, the whole of Italy is reflected in its tragedy, its sorrows, its qualities and defects, its religion and its heroism. Compared with *Roma città aperta*, the film shows a progress even in style; there is greater balance, a more secure breadth and a larger, more solemn rhythm.

Neo-realism Is not a Gratuitous Representation of Cruelty

It has often been reiterated (even satirically) and can still be heard now, that the "crude representations" of our problems in *Paisà*, particularly in the Roman "signorina" episode, constitutes a reprehensible form of sadism and defeatism. These ideas would not be worth taking into account were there not the danger that they are again becoming fashionable.

In those neo-realist films which merit being called art, this "cruelty" comprises courage and manly good sense, which only do honour to our cinema. In part, it was a reaction against all the rhetoric of the past years, a reaction to traditional hypocrisy, as well as a love of sincerity, and a desire to put men in the presence of reality-as-it-is, which motivated our film-makers. In these films there is no pleasure in scandal, nor a taste for the shocking through the repulsive and the obscene, which impelled certain writers to create a baroque literature about the human pain of the people of our wonderful city — wonderful like men and like nature. Neo-realism did (and does) not celebrate this cruelty, but rather exposed — without pleasure, without exaggeration and without an evil taste for the picturesque — the human conditions which constituted *per se* both a condemnation of certain social systems and a warning against them.

Sciuscià

And what of De Sica's *Sciuscià*, which had the bad taste to represent Italian boys as thieves and tricksters who used Negroes to polish their shoes?

Is it not really one of the most courageous and anguished defenses of childhood, and a terrible accusation against an entire "civilisation" which, every twenty years, makes ever greater wars, the burden of which innocent children must bear? It is an accusation against the inhuman systems of imprisonment which add evil to evil; an accusation coming from one who knows how to capture poetry and innocence even in their degeneration, a degeneration which is itself caused by adults.

In De Sica's film there is, perhaps, less strength than in the films of Rossellini, but there is more warm human participation, a more loving comprehension of the drama of his characters. His soul is attuned to another chord, but the spiritual attitude towards the painful reality of the post-war period is the same, and the motives which urged him to represent it are the same.

The brutal violence which for many years covered our country with blood; that violence which children had witnessed first with frightened eyes, and then with eyes that were accustomed to it as if it were a natural condition of existence; that violence is present in all its enormity at the end of the film, in which one of the protagonists kills his friend with a belt.

Even in its excitement, *Sciuscià* is not a completely balanced work; it lacks, for example, the technical sophistication of *Teresa Venerdi* (also by De Sica), but then, new bottles were needed for new wine. For this reason, it is easy to understand that the major contributions to neo-realism have come from the young. But the movement also appealed to a number of older directors, clever men of experience who, however, were not always good because they remained unmoved by individual need.

The Political Value of Neo-realism

The films made by Rossellini and De Sica cannot be called "political" or "ideological" in the ordinary dictionary sense of the terms. Their moral position developed from an attempt to represent reality itself. Perhaps to observe that reality, to be aware of it, was already to assume a political position, just as to hide from it or to transform it was also a political position, albeit a hypocritical one.

In fact, all those who chose the road toward neo-realism, if they served no party, have made valid contributions to theories of social renewal. *Il sole sorge ancora* of Vergano, *Caccia tragica* of De Santis, *Gioventù perduta* of Germi, *Anni difficili* of Zampa, even when they do not represent the people as protagonist, nonetheless maintain a critical attitude towards the corruption of bourgeois society and its flaccid composition and slow transformation.

Neo-realism and Varying Styles

Neo-realism can now be considered according to the characters and temperaments of the various directors of the movement. It can assume satirical aspects, and indeed can seek a variety of new styles in different directions depending on the character of each director.

The attempts of Blasetti and Camerini to infiltrate the movement remain sterile. Blasetti, after the cold and rhetorical *Un giorno della vita*, has returned to his former love for historical spectacles and gives us *Fabiola*, which only serves to make everyone miss Pastrone's *Cabiria* and Guazzoni's *Quo vadis?*, which were much more vivid and sincere, because they were an expression of a world in which the genuine rhetoric of the Roman spirit was its own *raison d'être*. Even Camerini was not happy with *Una lettera anonime*, a film made with some expertise, but completely lacking in any genuine feeling.

Zavattini and Realism

Undoubtedly, Zavattini is someone who should not be neglected in any study of neo-realism: his contribution to it is certainly equal to that of any of the best directors. He has deepened the vision of daily reality to make of it not merely a chronicle but a rediscovery of the importance of the moral value inherent in even the smallest acts of life, and in this way, has always and at every moment recalled man to an awareness of his human responsibilities.

Zavattini, as he himself wrote, felt the spirit of the new Italian cinema of the post-war period "which has contributed as no other has, to make explicit and definitive the moral function of that art" whose "destiny is to remain stuck to the heels of time, to tell what is happening and not what happened, because the present, the actual, is the real measure of man's dignity, in so far as it implies man's immediate responsibility." He wrote that two years ago, and added, "It is true that our most illustrious directors have dedicated themselves to fables and apologues . . . but no one should be fooled; these are brief excursions. They will be faithful to the brilliant ideas inspired in them by the war; then Italian cinema will continue to show us the real duration of man's pain." It may well be that what Zavattini took to be "excursions" were cessations caused by more complex reasons. There is some cause to believe that a year later he became aware of it, for, after all, he is the co-author of such films as *Sciuscià* and *Ladri di biciclette*.

With the latter film, De Sica achieves the perfection of his style in discovering, with Zavattini, a point of fusion which gives the film an organic coherence. It has been said that De Sica tends more to the lyric than to the epic; the reason is that he needs to follow a character, to be really near him, to gather together the impulses of his soul. He tends to individualize society (and the world) in the concrete feelings of his characters. To achieve this, he attaches importance to the small things and imparts a profound sense to the most ordinary events.

De Sica's neo-realism happens to link up happily with Zavattini's, and finds its best expression in the simple incident of a workman who, with his young son, looks for his stolen bicycle. Yet with that simple story he has been able to offer us a true representation of Rome, as well as of a social class, in its desperate and dramatic struggle for life.

La terra trema and Formal Perfection

Luchino Visconti's *La terra trema* is of a totally different nature, representing the most notable example of an effort to crystallise neo-realism in a single work which achieves formal perfection. Carried to an extreme, the realism of *La terra trema* — with its abolition of all artificiality: actors, sets, literary dialogue, music — was born of a sincere desire to understand and to depict the suffering humanity of the Sicilian fishermen.

It was not without good reason that the director wanted the dialogue to flow from the mouths of his characters naturally so as to make the words seem their own, both in terms of psychology and dialect. The director gave to the fishermen the simple content of each speech; they then expressed it in their own Sicilian tongue, according to their own individual temperament. Thus, the dialogue, invented by the fishermen in all their honesty and simplicity, is more effective and full of imagination and music than the spoken dialogue of any other Italian film.

Corresponding to the extreme realism in Visconti there exists a refined and confident taste; he reminds one of the still lifes of certain Flemish painters, so wonderful in their truthfulness and precision. Yet in my opinion, the limit of the film's value is in a fusion that is not always felicitous between form and content, a fusion which from time to time is endowed with a precious aestheticism that freezes the narrative and breaks the rhythm.

Among many beautiful episodes, such as the love between the girl and the bricklayer, the primordial joy and happiness of the fish-salting, or the nocturnal fishing-party, glittering with lights and voices on the "bitter sea", we find descriptive episodes in which the director's taste for beautiful images alone guides him to digress in refined arabesques. Of course, the film itself is the wonderful and sorrowful discovery of a new world for the director, who, in that discovery, finds everything interesting and moving, even the most minute details: a window with a flower-pot, a woman leaning against a wall, a man crouched near a boat; in stressing all of them, he occasionally forgets the essential elements.

Very rarely however has the cinema, represented the people with such nobility, with such emotion, nor has it exalted the profound dignity of humanity to so high a degree.

The Brief Vital Cycle of Neo-realism

Roma città aperta was made in 1945, *La terra trema* in 1948: two dates which mark the beginning and the end of a period in which it really seemed that the earth did tremble, and that the structure of Italian society was about to undergo radical changes. In that climate of anxiety and hope, fear and dread, Italian neo-realism courageously and sincerely created its own world which was drawn from the vivid reality which confronted the artists in all its didactic form.

The Involution of Neo-realism

After 1948, the involution began. The country slowly rearranged itself in accordance with the old structures, in the cinema as well as in all other aspects. Distributors and exhibitors — the merchants of the industry — became more important in determining the orientation of production according to non-aesthetic requirements of an audience which demanded strictly escapist entertainment.

On the other hand, the critics started a "tug-of-war" over neo-realism. Left-wing and right-wing journalists competed for the best works; they tried to woo each director with a wink. Each wanted to convert a director to his own cause.

Moreover, at certain moments, the crude and bare representation of reality became inconvenient for countless reasons; there are thousands of ways and as many possibilities to influence the course of the cinema.

Cinema as the Expression of a Social Climate

Cinema is not an individual product. One or two artists are not enough, as in the other arts, to determine an atmosphere, a stream, a school. Cinema is a collective expression. Film is always the fruit of a society and the atmosphere it creates. Even when political activity does not appear directly on the screen, it is nonetheless present in the substructure and is visible enough to those who possess an acute sense of sight.

It is obvious that just as one can speak of a Fascist cinema, one can also acknowledge an Italian cinema of liberation free from the fetters of rhetoric, conformity and opportunism; a cinema which, for a brief length of time, has been able to achieve a rare liberty.

Cinema and Liberty

More than any other art, cinema needs liberty to live and prosper. Concomitantly, with cinema it becomes especially possible to see that liberty is illusory if it has no economic base. The writer, the painter and the musician, are self-sufficient: they can create their work by themselves with a minimum of means. Strictly dependent upon industrial organisation, on the other hand, the artist working in cinema is tied directly to the economic life of his nation. He requires considerable capital in order to create. Even though the country in which he lives is governed by liberal democratic institutions, if it can not give him economic liberty he can not profit from its general policies.

The Mannerism of *Cielo sulla palude*

In failing to understand the deep needs from which neo-realism sprang, some directors have exchanged style for mannerism. They have retained only the recognition that they were confronted with a new cinematic language, a new film grammar, which they took to be seasoning for all dishes.

In 1949, the prize of the Venice Film Festival went to *Cielo sulla palude*, made one year after *La terra trema*. The form of that film is neo-realistic, in so far as such a form can be deduced from the external examination of the common denominators of films properly called neo-realist. There is that sickening verist quality in the portrayal of the atmosphere; authentic people play roles; everything is roughly and strongly represented. But all is style, everything lacks any deep justification, so that the inner balance of the film is, paradoxically, false. The centre of the film should have been derived from

157

the exaltation of the young girl who faces the supreme sacrifice in defense of her purity; instead, the desire to respect a style has led the director away from his theoretical task. To do so, he had to describe in minute detail the atmosphere of the swamp, to exploit the misery there, to insist on the character of the brute who tortures the girl, because these thematic devices, and only these, lent themselves to the development of the style he had chosen — whereas the exaltation of the girl's purity itself would have led him to a mystic ambience instead: towards that of Carl Dreyer's *The passion of Joan of Arc*, for , example. Instead, the film has become a film of the swamp; of misery, of vice, in a swamp which does not even exist any longer. It became (all unknown to the director) a film in which the brute's gestures remain both unexplained and unjustified, because they are over-emphasised; for stylistic reasons only, environmental causes are offered as the source of the brutality. Style betrayed the director and turned him away from the theme which inspired him (about which, anyway, he could obviously not have felt very deeply).

The man who is unable to feel the deep motivation which has brought about neo-realism, he who, as an artist, cannot live in its atmosphere, will fail to achieve valid creations, and will produce only premeditated exercises in mannerism. Such an "artist" will merely repeat a style and echo a polemic without experiencing its inner logic. A word of warning: the same artist can even pass, without being aware of it, from style to mannerism. Our recent cinema offers us enough examples.

Involution of Rossellini

In Rossellini's *Stromboli, terra di Dio*, even more than in *Francesco, giullare di Dio*, this path can be discerned. Having shifted the theme of his inspiration from the people of the island to the foreign woman, an unjustifiable and gratuitous character, his realism is limited to a documentary on tuna-fishing, completely external to the story the director wanted to tell. Even so, we can feel from time to time during the film what a vigorous piece of work Rossellini could have given us had he remained faithful to neo-realism, not as a form but as an inspirational motive.

The fact that the film was really shot on the island of Stromboli, that the eruption was fortunately real, that the fishing for tuna actually occurred, that the inhabitants spoke in dialect: none of this matters at all, since the emotions which move the characters are not true and the reality presented is not their profound reality but only an external aspect of it, a simple naturalism.

The Cognitive Value of Art

As I suggested at the beginning, the extraordinary strength of neo-realism consisted in its return to the common source of all art: authentic humanity and the experience of life, to faith in humanity's true emotions, to that form of knowledge "through images" which includes all of man.

However, when art, instead of finding its inspiration in the truthful reality of life, limits itself to the reproduction of abstract schemes and conventional feelings, it reduces itself to mere fiction, no matter what external verism or naturalism it employs. To this, we must add once again (for it needs to be repeated) that neo-realism, unmotivated by the programme of any particular party, took the point of view of a clear human and moral polemic. Without that polemic, one can not speak of neo-realism.

The Naturalism of Castellani

Georges Sadoul, an astute French critic, saw this clearly on the occasion of the Paris release of Castellani's *Sotto il sole di Roma*. He made a distinction between cinematic realism and descriptive naturalism:

> *Sotto il sole di Roma* is a second-rate film which commercializes the formula of neo-realism without understanding the lessons of *Paisà, Sciuscià, Il sole sorge ancora,* or *Caccia tragica.*
>
> *Sotto il sole di Roma* is reduced to a mere description of events which remain on the level of picturesque adventure.

We never see that gradual but determined arrival at awareness as in, for example, *Ladri di biciclette*.

Confronted with the stark drama of Roman youth moved by the collapse of Fascism, by the German occupation, by the madness of liberation, by the black market and felony, we cannot give credence to a picturesque, objective tone which is better suited to the activities of bees and birds.

We need human warmth; we need a critical point of view; we find neither in Castellani.

The truth is that neo-realism, reduced to empty form, degenerates into mannerism that exaggerates external aspects, as in the scene in Castellani's film which takes place, for no good reason, in a lavatory.

Neo-realism Cannot Be the Entire Cinema

At a certain point, some people came to believe that all films could and should be neo-realist, as if it were merely a question of technique or form. Such an idea is absurd because it implies that art exists as a game of empty forms outside the context of history. Neo-realism is something valid only for those who can feel the atmosphere from which it was born; only for those who, in such an atmosphere, sense its poetic appeal; only for those who are able to obey the polemic of neo-realism as the sole creative law. But neo-realism is only one aspect of the art of the film; it is not film itself. Not everyone can feel that polemic and work within its limits. Not everyone can find his inspiration in that particular world peculiar to neo-realism.

For those artists who are possessed of another temperament, of other origins, and other styles, other artistic laws apply, laws with correspond to their own vision of life, to their own interpretation of the "filmic fact", to their own way of conceiving and expressing themselves. Theirs are also proper laws, equally legitimate from the point of view of art, and censurable only in relation to the aesthetic results, major or minor, which derive from them.

The Causes, True and False, of Involution

The digression above was necessary to clarify my own thesis concerning the present crisis of involution in neo-realism. It would be interesting to analyse the causes, but it would lengthen this essay intolerably. Certainly this involution has influenced a change both in the spiritual atmosphere of these last few years and, to a certain extent, in a public, which by demanding cinema for the sake of mere entertainment, has influenced the distribution and exhibition of films, and in this way had an influence on the production of films itself.

The influences continue: censorship, the system of state prize money; political struggle becomes embittered, provoking factionalism and excess. Criticism fails to support the best works in the cinema and fails in all the other constructive ways by which it is possible to influence production. Yet production should be directed, even under a libertarian regime.

Someone has said that the fatal decadence of neo-realism set in with the disappearance of vivid subjects like the end of the war and the immediate post-war period. This observation is mistaken, as *La terra trema*, demonstrates, which is not in any way linked to such subjects.

Actually, even today, there are numerous problematic subjects to be found in various aspects of our social life which would serve as bases for films. The true Italy has to be discovered, and with it the new protagonist of its story: the people. In such a world of turmoil we must commit ourselves, to a knowledge of reality but not in a strictly political sense, — knowledge implies critical judgement.

The crisis of involution has various causes. I believe I have briefly hinted at them.

Attempts to Find Other Paths for Neo-realism

Before drawing any conclusions, and omitting, for reasons of space, a discussion, of such films as Blasetti's *Prima comunione,* (which can be judged in the terms already applied to Castellani), and Malaparte's *Cristo proibito,* (the inhuman rhetoric of which is a contradiction of neo-realism in spite of its artificial cruelties) we cannot neglect four significant and important films which perhaps offer a solution to the current crisis: Rossellini's *Francesco, giullare di Dio,*

Germi's *Il cammino della speranza*, De Sica's *Miracolo a Milano*, and Antonioni's *Cronaca di un amore*, the last of which indicates an attempt to shift the critical vision of neo-realism to the upper bourgeois world of Milan.

Francesco, giullare di Dio

Rossellini, who is demonstrably no mystic, no longer deals with social problems directly and concretely, but through several episodes of the *"fioretti"*[5] tries to express that same faith in man and human justice. The film has a human, corporeal tone which, through a mystic transfiguration of the legend, rediscovers a touching and striking reality — striking because it is liberated from rhetoric and literature — a reality which becomes terribly polemical for those who prefer, and are able to make, examinations of conscience.

The love of God of Rossellini's Francesco expresses itself, and is actualised, in a love for all creatures. The major strength of the film is in its refashioning great feelings to a human measure; to have dealt with great feelings *because* they are human is to have dealt with the *"fioretti"* as with the episodes of *Paisà*. The weakness of the film, however, is that is does not arrive at the point it wanted to reach, and which aroused so much criticism from religious and historical points of view. The false compromise of the film handicapped what is otherwise a work of undeniable quality.

Il cammino della speranza

Germi, up to a point, exhibits greater faith in the tenets of neo-realism. His odyssey of a group of unemployed Sicilian mine workers who, after the shut-down of a sulphur mine, attempt to leave their region in the secret hopes of a better life, is expressed with acute understanding. However, the psychologically false drama of love and jealousy which is gratuitously inserted into the narrative — including a somewhat "rustic" duel in the snow, and an optimistic ending with two dead people, one of whom is a terrible weight on the protagonist's conscience — shifts the emphasis from the reality of the group situation to the melodramatic and spectacular, and emasculates the film through its hybrid compromise between neo-realism and the hoariest of formulas. In this, the director did not remain faithful to the world he was representing and therefore failed to express the true content of his film clearly and decisively.

Miracolo a Milano

In De Sica's film, neo-realism takes another direction: that of fable and fantasy. Some time has passed since it was first released; therefore critical judgement can be passed, which is calmly detached from the not always disinterested, extra-artistic polemics which the film originally provoked.

Here I do not wish to remark on the irrelevant character of the content, but to confirm a concept which by now should be as commonplace as the refrain of a popular song: the content of a work of art is not immediately apparent — in a film the content is not the story, the plot, or the fable — on the contrary it is deeper, and is reached only through true form, which is the expression of content. The story, the plot, and the fable, like the acting, the photography and the editing, belong properly to technique, and should be judged as such. I mean that to deduce the meaning of *Miracolo a Milano* from an analysis of its single episodes, and of its "gags", as well as to judge it according to its shots, and its rhythm, is to lose oneself in arbitrary abstraction. To wander confusedly through an analysis of technique would allow the art to elude us, and with it a recognition of true content.

Following that false road, each person, according to his individual temperament, sympathies, and political ideology, could find in a film something or other with which to support his own arguments. Thus, *Miracolo a Milano* has been seen alternately, with either satisfaction or anger, as a Communist film (even, indeed, a film of total Soviet orthodoxy), as pervaded with the spirit of Christianity, or as an anarchic, reactionary, and ultimately bourgeois compromise.

Clearly, these are disparate, contradictory judgements, all of them outside the bounds of artistic evaluation, and all equally confirmed by unexceptional examples. It is easy enough to interpret the wealthy

Mobbi's control of the police as a condemnation of that kind of capitalism which uses the collective might of the state to oppress the poor. We can also acknowledge a Christian spirit in most of Totò's gestures, or confirm the anti-social nature of the poor people's insistence that they remain where oil has been discovered. Once starting down such a road, however, we can find in the film whatever we like, including a statement by the film-makers against the English monopoly of Iranian petrol.

Part of the problem is caused by the fact that people confuse the personality of the director with the director as film-maker, and so stress the personality of the director as it is expressed in his other films.[6] This would be proper if the development of his personality were not seen as a phenomenon of auto-generation on which historical, political, and social conditions exerted no influence, as if the manifestation of that personality in practical ways, such as the signing of petitions, were not to be considered. Pity the poor director! Between manifestos, appeals, meetings, public declarations, and the like, he leads a very hard life, for he knows that his actions will influence, in one way or another, the judgement of his next film, and the way in which critics, in all good faith, will be prompted to make erroneous classifications.

Miracolo a Milano was released at a particular moment in Italian life, and to a certain extent is the expression of it. The poetic nucleus of the film is no longer, as in *Sciuscià* or *Ladri di biciclette*, the moving discovery of the human condition. It does not spring from an illumination of the confrontation with reality, whose representation already implies a judgement and a will to modify it, but from a discouragement which, without falling into a bittersweet pessimism, grasps at the vain hope of a miracle.

Among the films of De Sica and Zavattini, this is the most melodramatic and desperate. Their faith in life here is somewhat similar to the whistling of a suicide attempting to cheer himself up. In fact, that is the poetic nucleus of the film. It expresses a state of mind, and an understandably rather diffuse bewilderment in the face of an unparalleled spiritual situation which is seemingly without hope. Ideological polemics cannot cling to that nucleus. The intellectual contradictions of the film remain abstract. To attempt to analyse its fits of anger on a rational and organic level would be an error. They represent merely a reaction, a hostile state of mind, to a society founded on base desires and egoism; a reaction which, for all its intellectual origins, expressed itself in satirical caricature which fails to achieve artistic validity.

Between the world of the poor, in which the poetic roots of the film are planted, and which is represented movingly enough in several scenes — the funeral of Lolotta; the scene in which Totò willingly gives his suitcase to the man who had just stolen it; the scenes of the poor who warm themselves with a sunbeam; the scenes of love between Totò and Edwige — and the world of the rich, there is no dialectic because there is no possibility of synthesis between the two, either on the level of reality or on the level of fable.

The limitations of the film are clear: on the one hand a sincere inspiration represents realistically (even with a few slips toward mannerism) the condition of the urban sub-proletariat, in which the follies of the poor are real and possible — a human comedy, one might say. On the other hand, it is a satiric fable, intellectual and literary, full of clever tricks and jokes (some gratuitous, some apt), of simple entertainment value which, like the statue that is transformed into a dancer, are all-too-real lapses of taste.

The valid section of the film achieves precise rhythm, balanced shots, incisive and homogenous acting, and an adequate photographic tone; the whole thing springs into a wonderful unity which allows us to enter the fantastic and true world of those wretches, and into the soul of everyone. The satiric "miraculous" section, however, even in the form it takes, sinks the film through its woeful lack of the same sparkling rhythm, acute editing, and unity of acting. In spite of the dove, the athletic angels, the spirit of Lolotta, the enchanted prison vans and the flying saucers, it never succeeds in achieving the true lightness of a genuine fable, perhaps because it is all conceptual thought, because there is no poet to make it live in images sustained by the light breath of art. What fabulous delicacy (to give only a single example) there is in the shot in which Totò, kneeling, holds the new shoe towards Edwige's little foot: a common image, an image of reality, so allusive and so full of meaning. But it is only an instant; the illusion fails immediately because there is no room in that society for pure and simple spirits, and Cinderella is, after all, only a fable. The entire film is imbued with that melancholy desire for unattainable gold, with that joylessness which is at the core of the film.

Someone, in his criticism, went back to the previous work of the two film-makers, De Sica and Zavattini, even to their declarations of purpose and intention, and ascribed decisive importance to the latter, as if dealing with the only authentic interpretation of a legal text. Doubtless, the past work of an artist may have a certain value in solving today's problems, as long as it is not granted too much importance, but it is a debatable matter for artists themselves to explain their own work. Very often they are the least qualified to talk about it. Consequently, what is important is not what they wanted to do or say, nor even what they believed they wanted to do or say, but what — perhaps without even being aware of it — they actually said and did.

It is obvious that *Miracolo a Milano* represents a noble effort to escape the involution of neo-realism, the validity of which, considering the film's limitations, it confirms. De Sica and Zavattini were mistaken in so far as they departed from reality. Even on that basis, as the film shows, they can still tell us wonderful and delicate fables full of poetry and morality, open to the hoped-for miracle that man will raise the victorious banner of justice, and welcome goodness, on earth, even as in Milan.

Cronaca di un amore

Antonioni's film suffers from the same defect of indecision. The director has not delved to the core of his task. He fails to discover the profound causes which motivate the characters, which in turn makes the film cold in feeling and passionless, just because the intention was to observe life at a certain level in the middle class coldly and pitilessly. On the other hand, it is a film without a thesis, either because the director did not know enough, or because he did not want to look deeply enough.

Conclusion

The panorama of Italian neo-realism ends here, and the conclusions to be drawn must surely have been anticipated before this. The crisis of neo-realism's temporary involution does not mean that neo-realism is finished, but simply that the spiritual conditions and atmosphere which gave it birth have changed, and no longer partake of contemporary reality. Its decline can only be temporary; it would be too serious to contemplate if it were otherwise. It would mean our cinema had renounced its involvement with the great expressive strength of the movement towards social renewal and progress. Its final involution would be a sign that historical change had ceased entirely.

> *"Discorso sul neorealismo"*, first delivered as an address
> before a conference in Bari, sponsored by *Circolo Amici della
> Cultura* and the *Cineclub*, Bari, April 11, 1950, and then
> published in *Bianco e nero*, XII, 7, July 1951.

Notes

1   Literally "tricks" or "trickery", but in general conversation, and even often enough in technical discussions, critics and other film people use "trucco" to mean "special effect"; one rarely sees "effetti speciali", although, according to the film vocabulary approved by the Western European Union (ex: Brussels Treaty Organization) and UNESCO, it is the "approved" term.

2   Francesco De Sanctis, the influential literary critic and historian of the 19th century, is something of a key figure to any discussion of the literary background of Italian neo-realism. He maintained that form and content were a unity, and also took a. major part in the bitter battles fought at the time over the definitions of the equivocal terms *verismo, realismo,* and *naturalismo.* He does not sound so very different from Chiarini in the defense of the work of Alessandro Manzoni as being founded on "positive reality . . . natural, positive, and historical truth, which today people call realism."

Conte Giacomo Leopardi (1798-1837) was noted for the deceptive simplicity of both his lyric poetry and his prose.

3   *Quai des brumes* (1938) was released in English-speaking countries as
     Port of shadows. Renoir's *La bête humaine* (1938) remained unre-
     leased for decades in Great Britain and the United States.

4   Henry Bécque (1873-1889) was a playwright best known for his vicious
     portraits of bourgeois life. Although his plays, like *The vultures* (1882)
     and *The woman of Paris* (1885) tend towards naturalism, they remain
     too close to the "well-made play" to qualify fully as "slice-of-life" dra-
     mas.
         André Antoine (1858-1943) was a theatrical manager and director.
     His *Théâtre Libre*, founded in 1887, became the world's leading thea-
     trical home of naturalistic plays and productions.

5   *"Fioretti"*: "little flowers"; that is, the collection of stories about St.
     Francis of Assisi which is usually known as *The little flowers of St.
     Francis*. Indeed, the French title of Rossellini's film is *Onze fioretti*.

6   Although not entirely to the point which Chiarini is making here, in
     the case of *Miracolo a Milano* it might be remembered that the subject
     was much more Zavattini's than De Sica's. As early as 1938, Zavattini
     had used the material for a treatment called *Diamo a tutti un cavallo a
     dondolo* (Let's give everyone a rocking horse). In 1940, another version
     of the same material became a scenario called *Totò il buono* (Totò the
     Good). Then, still unfilmed, the material became a novel by Zavattini
     (published in 1943), from which the film was taken in 1951.

14. Origins of Neo-Realism
by Franco Venturini

Today, the surest method of attempting a definition of Italian neo-realism is through a chronological inquiry beginning with its genesis in the history of the Italian cinema. Up to now, attempts at criticism have been concentrated primarily on the elaboration of a poetics of neo-realism, to the detriment not only of chronological motivations, but of historical, stylistic verification as well. In fact, critical inquiry has lacked an adequate awareness of the historical nature of the problems, which accounts for the exiguousness of the critical results obtained so far in the study of neo-realism, as well as for the scepticism of some criticism and the apologetics of others.

This study will attempt to unearth, in both the recent and past history, the roots of neo-realism, and, starting from these roots, to trace the organic growth of its historical development. I believe in a history of art; terms like "romance", "Gothic", and "baroque" are not, for me, speculative categories, but definitions of historical realities, stylistic facts, moments in the life of the mind. Even "neo-realism" is not an invention of critics, but is a real fact, within, of course, the limits of its history. In the course of my study, I shall try to indicate exact antecedents and specific influences, and we shall see that both are wide-spread and pervasive, so that the entire history of the Italian cinema is encompassed in them. Such a study implies a summary of the salient moments in the history of Italian cinema. From my point of view, these moments are: (1) the regional tradition; (2) caligraphism; (3) the influence of French realism; (4) Camerini and Blasetti; (5) Luchino Visconti; (6) the documentary tradition.

1. The Regional Tradition

Between approximately 1909 and 1915, Italian production was inspired by regional narrative, very often of a popular nature; such production was particularly abundant in Naples (it is quite proper to speak of a Neapolitan cinema) where people nourished themselves with a certain realist literature, from Bracco to Serao.[1]

Today, unfortunately, that production is almost entirely lost. Almost the only things remaining are the titles remembered by critics like Paolella. Nevertheless, a few works were rescued, among which are numbered the most significant in a movement which unquestionably produced works of a high artistic level of achievement. Among them we must remember *Sperduti nel buio* (1914), *Cavalleria rusticana* (1915), *Assunta Spina* (1915), and *Teresa Raquin* (1915).

Parallel to this production existed another which, although it dealt with broader themes, showed similar characteristics: *Histoire d'un pierrot* (1913) by Badassare Negroni and the series *Topi grigi* by Emilio Ghione.

The point common to each is a definite naturalistic note which corresponds both to the orientation of the literary texts from which the subjects were taken and to an exact realist definition of the characters and atmosphere. The memory of the older Italian cinema's naturalistic tone was then overwhelmed by historical trends. After *Cabiria* (1914), these absorbed almost all our production, so that, according to superficial historian — especially foreign historians — the archetypal image of early Italian cinema, even today, is that of the historical "formula" film. Of course, even in the Italian historical film there remain naturalistic elements, such as a predilection for external scenery, the fashion of mass-movements, and even certain details of archaeological reconstructions. Indeed, in *Cabiria* there are scenes which are clearly naturalistic (the passage of the Alps, the tavern, and so on). This realistic attitude was manifested so strongly in the regional movement that it survived the latter's demise and continued as a fermenting agent in the development of the Italian cinema.

The Italian cinema, then, has had a realistic tendency from the very beginning. We must remember that the Italian cinema had no expressionistic experience,[2] and that the *avant-garde* was limited to a

170

few futurist experiments[3] which in no way influenced Italian cinema, although to some extent they influenced the evolution of the French and German *avant-garde*. Moreover, even the regionalist trend, especially the meridional one, tends to crop up from time to time in specific works, as in *Napoli d'altri tempi* (1937) and *Cavalleria rusticana* (1939), both by Amleto Palerini. Around 1940, this tendency re-appeared, and was re-valued on another basis: "calligraphism."

2. Calligraphism

The term is one of convenience by which I mean to designate — without intending to be derogatory — the production which went on between 1940 and 1943, connected with the names of Chiarini, Castellani, Lattuada and Soldati, and which indicated a critical awakening of the Italian cinema and the burgeoning of more specific cultural intentions.

Having said this, it may be useful to include here a consideration of the functions of Italian cinema criticism between 1940 and 1943. In spite of the limitations of its inquiry, with which I shall reckon in a moment, the film criticism of the period constitutes one school of several among which it must be counted as the most coherent and concrete. It distinguished itself by its concern for the future of the Italian film industry, concern which caused questions to be asked in certain other areas of production. When the history of the last ten years of Italian cinema is written, a whole chapter will have to be devoted to criticism. Such an analysis can contribute a great deal in revealing the hidden roots and lateral movements which are of great interest in understanding the genesis of neo-realism. In fact, in terms of culture, it was this criticism which posed the problems involved in seeking an original cinematic style — a "national" style, as it was then called. Between 1940 and 1942, the debate surrounding the search acquired paroxysmal aspects, particularly due to political instigation. (This was the time when there was an insistence on art in Italy being Italian). For months, in newspapers and reviews everyone talked, about what might have been defined, in Pirandellian terms as: "the style to be formed." Critics exercised a pitiless watch, analysing scrupulously the most disparate and insignificant experiments, expecting results at any moment which could have allowed the birth of that "style to be developed".

The behaviour of Italian critics in those years was similar to that of an obstetrician called in to look after a difficult pregnancy, always ready, forceps in hand, to exchange the ordinary and organic phenomenon for hints of an exceptional delivery. Critical research, complex as it was, seems to have been dominated by a common motive: the innoculation of the native tradition from Giotto and Dante down though Verga, Fogazzaro, Manzoni, Goldoni, Caravaggio, and Masaccio[4] under the illusion that it would be possible to discover a quintessential Italian genius for use in our cinema.

That was the limitation of so much of our criticism: an archaeological prejudice, an attempt to squeeze creative originality out of books on the history of art. Those were the years in which, in all seriousness and with the conviction of fulfilling a social function, people quoted Martino or Vico[5] in order to pass judgement on films by Mastrocinque or Guazzoni.[6] Such equivocal criticism also constituted the limits of several areas of production during the war.

Calligraphism was born at the moment in cultural development (culture in the larger sense, not simply as pertaining to cinema) when there arose the aspiration to derive an ethnic originality of cinematic style from literature (from Pushkin as much as from Fogazzaro), a source of inspiration which led to results that were essentially decorative. Even the term "calligraphism" hints at a frigid taste for intellectual arabesques. Here it must be considered in terms of its value as a trend, without considering the merit of individual works, several of which were of some consequence.

Political restraints also influenced production. with the rise to power of the Fascist government, film production came under the severe control of the censor. Subject matter which dealt with concrete social problems or which took its inspiration from too "crude" a reality was not allowed.

Moreover, with the affirmation of a literary, decorative, cultural tendency in the Italian cinema, the movement of Italian intellectuals into the cinema blossomed. It had already begun in 1930 with the coming of Cecchi to the Cines.[7] It constituted a positive experience for our cinema, because it meant the end of purely regional practices.

172

The "self-made-man" was more typical of the profession). It introduced into the cinema more concrete spiritual requirements and more mature and more aesthetic consciousness. In fact, in spite of often unsatisfactory results in the so-called "calligrahic" productions, they represented a step upward in the level of our cinema.

After all, the search for an original style, even if it led in an over-intellectual direction to a ground of inspiration which was extra-cinematic, was in itself courageous; it was an indication of a rigorous, artistic conscience. Moreover, in spite of the error of method, the search eventually led to some desirably original and valid results.

Antonio Pietrangeli has already pointed out in a rather interesting study which has helped to clarify matters, that those "calligraphic" experiments successfully presented some true portraits of an original Italian landscape: "In search for a style our film-makers again began to film outside the studios, slowly rediscovered the Italian landscape, and became reacquainted with the reality of their time and the problems of their country, which they have only understood and expressed in these latter years. Even in those intellectual directors who were attracted towards aestheticism by nature, a desire arose to paint a lively, non-conventional Italy."[8]

Piccolo mondo antico (1940) and *Tragica notte* (1941) by Soldati, *Sissignora* (1940) and *Gelosia* (1942) by Poggioli, *Via della cinque lune* (1941) and *La bella addormentata* (1942) by Chiarini are all works which, while still uncertain, show some ingenuity, contain some original moments, and reveal a ferment of exploration which seems to foreshadow a national style. To a certain extent, those results attest to an internal evolution accompanied by criticism. The quest for "the style to be formed" progressively limited "clever" theorizing. No longer did people speak of Dante and Caravaggio; instead, they attempted to particularize from our artistic history those qualities which, by their very nature, are ideal to serve cinema. What was sought was definite plastic atmosphere and environment. The search was aided more by literary tradition, especially that of the Nineteenth Century, than by the figurative arts; not only because it is closer to us and offered continuity, but because the Nineteenth Century offers a repertory of more organic harmonies, more concrete atmospheres and customs, and firmer delineation in ethnic terms — in fact, more realism.

173

Thus, from that somewhat erudite inquiry, the realistic sense
which had guided the artisan tendency of regional cinema returned.
Criticism rested on a particular chapter of the Nineteenth Century:
on the narrative and theatre of the South — Verga, Capuana, Serao,
De Roberto, D'Annunzio with *Novelle della Pescara* included.[9]
That, in turn, led naturally to a general cultural revaluation of the
old regional cinema. The critics of the time associated the name of
Martoglio[10] with that of Verga, and in so doing pointed out a more
secure formula for the creation of "the style to be formed." One can
recall, in this connection, some long digressions concerning Verga in
the book reviews by the young De Santis, the critic for *Cinema* during
the period 1942-1943."[11]

Calligraphism, to a certain extent, grafted itself on the old trunk of
regional realism and, in this way, branched out onto a wider cultural
plane. In 1940, Barbaro and Chiarini, who had constituted the most
important sector of Italian criticism, collaborated as script-writers
and assistant directors for *La peccatrice* by Palermi, who could still
consider himself a representative of the regionalist faction.[12]

Still another factor was important to the evolution of the calligraphic movement: French realism.

---

3. The Influence of French Realism

By "French realism", people generally mean both that socio-
aesthetic experience introduced by *La chienne* and *Sous les toits de
Paris* — which show traces of both German *Kammerspiel*[13] and of
certain *avant-garde* documentary qualities — and certain names
(Renoir, Feyder, and Carné being among the most famous). Today
we can examine the phenomenon in its proper perspective, and can
assess its absolute value dispassionately. It can now be seen to be
rather modest, because it is basically spoiled by literary impulses. At
the time when it appeared, and even up until the first years of the Second World War, French realism was the object of over-valuation by
many European critics. In Italy especially, certain critics gave French
realism much more credit than it merited. Even in the criticism of De
Santis in *Cinema* (and, generally speaking, the journal's entire tone
from 1942 on) one always found more or less explicit judgements and

comparisons of our own cinema being made on the basis of the standards of French realism as the point of reference.

French realism exerted a great influence on the atmosphere in which our cinema, still, at this time, in the process of being established, was created. It determined an authentic spirit of emulation. The films were particularly striking in their presentation of the homogeneous French experience, which appeared as a well-defined, original tendency in neatly characterized ethnic form. Through their scheme of literary rhetoric and a seeming formlessness (often false), the films of Renoir and Carné offered a *stimmung* typically and unmistakably French. This French example of a national style acted as a catalyst on the Italian search for "the style to be formed". It also influenced, the development of our ethnic realism, which had from time to time grafted on a new node from the old regional stem.

Beside the names of Verga and Martoglio, many critics added Renoir as an example of ethnic originality. Added to its influence as a catalyst, French cinema had an even more direct influence on our films, for there were a number of attempts at direct imitation. *Piccolo hotel* (1940) by Ballerini, *La statua vivente* (1943) by Mastrocinque, and *Fari nella nebbia* (1942) by Franciolini were all inspired by models from beyond the Alps, and are the most significant examples, although it nonetheless remained a marginal experience in our cinema. Moreover, the imitation was in no way passive, but was accompanied in certain cases, such as *Fari nella nebbia*, by a search for original inspiration. Even *La peccatrice*, with all its obvious French influences, revealed original elements.

4. Camerini and Blasetti

Between 1940 and 1943, the Italian cinema underwent a complex, eclectic experience made up of many impulses and open to various simultaneous influences which are difficult to separate and classify, but which have a common denominator in their more or less consciously realistic orientation. Even Mario Camerini — with Blasetti, the most representative figure of the Italian cinema's pre-war era — is substantially oriented towards realistic atmosphere and situations (even though through humorous methods) which he derives from the observation of an intermediate social group — between the petit-bourgeoisie and the working class. Camerini's world (similar to that of René Clair) consists of lightly satiric humour shot through with pathos, and, is consequently, open here and there to dramatic inflections (*Come le foglie*). His most valuable works (*Gli uomini che mascalzoni, Darò un milione, Batticuore*) are those which succeed in achieving a balance between them. It is from such a world that Vittorio De Sica was to make his start.

Quattro passi fra le nuvole (1942), a unique work in Alessandro Blasetti's career, gets its inspiration from Camerini. Blasetti is the most eclectic among our directors, and the only one who was sensitive to the direction European cinema would take, from *Sole*, which was vaguely inspired by some Russian models, to *La corona di ferro*, which borrows motifs from early Fritz Lang. Therefore, it is difficult to place him historically and to define his position with an easy formula. For all his eclecticism, Blasetti remains something of an isolated figure in the history of Italian cinema. Even his importance in connection with the history of neo-realism seems rather modest, more modest, at any rate, than Pietrangeli's assertion suggest: "*1860* really foreshadows the Italian neo-realist school." *1860*, is, I believe, a genuine and over-flowing work which combines the effects of artifice with the rhetoric of jingoist melodrama, and shares little in common with the bare, essential humanity of Rossellini or De Sica. Even the acting of the "types" seems more modest than is usually credible. *Vecchia guardia* seems more noteworthy in terms of realism, although here too one sees some of the same limitations of *1860*. Blasetti's most valid contribution to realism remains *Quattro passi fra le nuvole*, which was inspired by Camerini. Blasetti seems unable to move on, however. When, in 1946, under the influence of Rossellini, he attempted to film in the neo-realist style with *Un giorno della vita*, he actually retreated to the mannerism of *1860*.

Therefore, it is Camerini, rather than Blasetti, who is important as a precursor — however distant and indirect — of neo-realism. When *La corona di ferro* (1942) appeared, the critic Filippo Sacchi wrote, with justice, that the merit of the film was that it had escaped the methods of that vein of verism typical of Camerini.

Apart from Camerini's work, there were several other minor projects which were substantially oriented towards realism: *L'Assedio dell'Alcazar* and *Bengasi* by Genina, and *Cavalleria* and *Don Bosco* by Alessandrini, who was assisted on both films by Aldo Vergano.

---

5. Luchino Visconti

The atmosphere of realist inspiration underwent a decisive clarification with the appearance of Luchino Visconti. In *Ossessione*, the regional tradition, the cultured-literary research, the French influence — all blended harmoniously to produce a valid and original result. *Ossessione* is part of the trend exemplified by *La peccatrice, Tragica notte, Gelosia,* and *La bella addormentata*; that strain which first discovered an original Italian landscape. The region of Ferrara with its lanes in "chiaroscuro", the sands of the Po, the country inns, the celebration of San Ciriaco in Ancona, the third class coaches, all give us the image of an Italy that is extremely vivid and real, an expression of an Italian *stimmung*.

Ossessione shoulders the ethnic task of the regional tradition, and can be seen as the culmination of the cultural quest which had begun in the art history books; in fact, the critic Umberto Barbaro linked *Ossessione* with early painting when he asked: "Does not the appearance of a small ice-cream cart in a Ferrara square have heraldic precedents which go back to Ercole De Roberti?"[14]

Luchinio Visconti had been an assistant to Renoir, and certainly *Ossessione* does not lack quotations from Renoir. Visconti's language obviously derives from French models, but his language and his style are both different and original. Pietrangeli says that *Ossessione* marks the birth of an Italian style; "the style to be formed" has finally been found. Pietrangeli also suggests that neo-realism begins with *Ossessione*.[15] That is obviously true, for in Visconti's films we already find characters whom we shall meet again in the films of later neo-realist directors. Nonetheless, as we shall see, the development of these directors was nourished from different sources, deriving more from *Uomini sul fondo* than from *Ossessione*.

While *Ossessione* marks the birth of a cinematic culture, it is also the *result* of a cinematic culture. The theorizing about the history of art has now become concrete; in terms of cinematic expression, it has reached a formal consistency. The lesson learned from the French had a determining hand in that. In the Italian tradition, cinematic culture was the conscious inheritance of expressive experiment and inquiry. The most remarkable results were obtained on the practical level of work; even Camerini remained a director "on the job" — in the most positive meaning of the phrase. There was, it is true, a documentary experience, but, as we shall see, it was too fragmentary, too isolated. The only *cultured* film-maker was Blasetti, whose eclectic attempts, as I have pointed out, lacked organic unity and constituted an unrepeatable experiment, linked only to the urgency of his tormented characters.

Until *Ossessione*, the Italian cinema, like that of pre-Grierson England,[16] remained a provincial cinema, far removed from the mainstream of European cinema as a whole. German Expressionism, the *Avant-Garde*, the Russian school, the *Kammerspiel*, had only sporadic and weak repercussions in Italy. In 1940, the Italian film-maker who wanted to look backwards would have had to return to *Cabiria* for any Italian example with international reverberations. The situation of the Italian cinema in 1940 was exactly parallel to that of our poetry prior to *L'Allegria* of Ungaretti.[17] At that time, we had no poets at all, really, to cover the epoch during which France possessed Baudelaire, Rimbaud, Mallarmé, Valéry, and Apollinaire. Montale[18] once spoke of the miserable state of his generation of poets, of having to go back to Leopardi and Foscolo[19] to renew the tradition of Italian poetry with validity. As he said, one had the impression of having to start again from the beginning. That is exactly what the Italian cinema has had to do; like lyric poetry, the Italian cinema has had to join the mainstream of European culture.

Like Ungaretti, who condensed the inner experience of fifty years of poetry, from Baudelaire to Reverdy,[20] in the prosody of *L'Allegria*, Visconti, concluding the work begun by the calligraphists, transfused twenty-five years of international cinema into our own. Grierson did so with the English cinema. With Grierson, however, the didactic attention of a theoretician and aesthete went back to the sources of the various cinematic schools of the world, and summed up their contributions in the illuminating and original manner of *Drifters*. Visconti, less systematic, relived the world's film experience almost exclusively though French realism. Certainly, the influence of *Ossessione* on the Italian cinema was not as great as that of *Drifters*

178

on the English cinema, but that was due to the differences in the respective historial moments. *Ossessione* came too late to exert much influence on "the style to be formed", for it occurred at a time when other attempts had already begun. Consequently, the search for "the style to be formed" continued after *Ossessione*. In spite of the historical concreteness of its lesson, *Ossessione* remained a marginal experience, and to a certain degree non-participatory in the dialectical development of the Italian cinema.

---

6. The Documentary Tradition

Another movement then came to maturity: the documentary. The comparative study of cinema teaches us that the documentary had an essential influence on the formation of certain national schools. One thinks immediately of the Russian school as an example. Vertov, Tissé, and Golovia were already active at the time of the 1917 Revolution. Vertov then founded the "Cinema-Eye" and Tissé and Golovia worked, respectively, with Eisenstein and Pudovkin. Even French realism owes something to the documentary experience: Cavalcanti, Vigo, Carné, and Lacombe — those who constituted the "*arrière-garde*" of the *Avant-Garde*.

In Italy, the documentary remained a more modest and isolated trend, one scarcely linked to normal production. It might well be, as Casiraghi and Viazzi maintained, that the "lack of a fervent practice in the field of documentary" helps to explain "the late formation of a unified, national style."[21] At any rate, even if small and limited, the experience of the documentarists exerted some influence on normal production, and thereby contributed to "the style to be formed". Today, we can now see that this contribution was more important than could be perceived in 1942. Moreover, the documentary provided nourishment for the formation of a climate for cinematic activity.

Intellectuals ventured into documentary — not intellectuals from other disciplines, like Soldati, but those who came from within the cinema itself, like Pasinetti — because its isolated, non-commercial character allowed for a more rigorous artistic theory than major cinematic orthodoxy would allow. Between 1938 and 1942, a group of documentarists was active, and their work constituted some of the most effective cinema of the time: Pasinetti, Paolella, Magnaghi, Emmer, Gras, Paolucci, Cerchio, Ferroni, Pozzi-Bellini, and others. Some of them (Cerchio and Paolucci, for example) moved towards an original investigation of the environment, a trend which was dominant in the best Italian cinema of the time. However, the most interesting, and historically the most fecund area of exploration, was that of the war documentary, an area which constitutes a chapter in itself. The demands of war determined the content of many documentaries, most of them of a propagandistic character. Dozens of cameramen travelled with the troops on land, in ships and planes, while many others on the home front interested themselves in situations arising from the preparations for war. The vast majority of those productions were poor, and even the best of them failed to rise much above the workmanlike level. If today we still speak of it as a vital trend, it is because De Robertis and Rossellini acquired their training at that particular time. In other words, the war documentary — like other trends of the era — never succeeded in becoming a fully coherent school, but it did provide the opportunity to gain experience with which to provide, in turn, the foundations of a true school of cinema.

De Robertis, De Sica, Rossellini

Francesco De Robertis, an effective officer of the wartime Navy, made a documentary in 1940, *Mine in vista*. If we are to believe the French critic Georges Auriol, De Robertis in 1937 had already taken the 800 typewritten pages of his first scenario, *Il nastro azzurro*, to producer Luigi Freddi, complete with all technical indications and even the designs for each shot.[22] Between 1940 and 1941, he made *Uomini sul fondo*.[23]

As De Robertis specified, *Uomini sul fondo* was born from a documentary subject. He wanted to illustrate the methods by which submarines were rescued by the Navy. The style is visibly inspired by the tone of the Italian war documentary; indeed, it is in *Uomini sul fondo* that this vein was fully developed and thus became a fixed style. Moreover, the film was made during the first months of the war, that is, at a time when the war documentary could not yet have provided an organic tradition. What the war documentary, therefore, brought to *Uomini sul fondo* was limited to "tricks of the trade" linked to a common need for expression, which De Robertis then provided. At any rate, however tenuous the contribution of the documentary, it provides the concrete link between De Robertis and the mainstream of contemporary Italian cinema. *Uomini sul fondo* remained separate from those trends which culminated in *Ossessione*, and therefore to a certain extent, constituted a new factor. In 1942, Casiraghi and Viazzi wrote:

> If within a few years people speak of an Italian school and, especially abroad, of a certain flavour; of an immediacy of execution; of a style and, perhaps, of a manner typically and purely Italian; then this will be due exclusively not only to the general climate of production in 1940-1941 but to the first work of the director Francesco De Robertis, which is elementary and Mediterranean in its exposition, but quite good nevertheless, and almost refined in its cultural preparation. The films of De Robertis are carefully made according to theoretical models and the creations of other Europeans, with superifically researched, but nonetheless obvious, prevalent influences from the Russians.[24]

Today, Italian criticism of the post-war period tends to overlook the historical influence of *Uomini sul fondo* on the genesis of neorealism, an influence recognised by the Belgian critic, Carl Vincent.[25] Perhaps political prejudices were not entirely absent from the position held by Italian critics towards De Robertis[26] — preconceptions which are partially supported by his later works, such as *Alfa tau* and the more recent *Fantasmi del mare*, which was swamped by the rhetoric of war. But the attitude of current criticism towards *Uomini sul fondo* has deeper roots which perpetuate that ambivalent archaeological approach which marks the criticism of bygone days. Apart from the review by Casiraghi and Viazzi, which, after all, came almost two years after the film's release, the whole of Italian criticism refused to understand the value of *Uomini sul fondo*, either in terms of its intrinsic merit or with reference to "the style to be formed." In fact, critics were pointing in another direction: Verga, Martoglio, Renoir. They could not admit that "the style to be formed" failed to materialise from the equations they had constructed. Moreover, *Uomini sul fondo* could not be integrated into the structure of the art history books; it had no precedents in Ercole De Roberti. Failing therefore, to understand that the former was a point of culmination while the latter was a starting point, they followed the example of *Ossessione* more than that of *Uomini sul fondo*.

Yet it would be an error to view that starting point as a phenomenon of primitivism. De Robertis is a director who was well prepared, up-to-date, and even, to a certain extent, cultured. *Uomini sul fondo* reveals a good knowledge of the poetics of the cinema and is even a cinematically orthodox work. From the point of view of film grammar and practical technique, the film is substantially a "correct" one. On the other hand, the later films of De Robertis, until *Fantasmi del mare*, reveal a certain technical ignorance. Therefore, it is not improbable that for *Uomini sul fondo*, De Robertis availed himself of the assistance of Bianchi and Perilli, men who knew their job. However, we must not conclude from this that the collaboration influenced the resulting style; that is unmistakably De Robertis at work, and is also to be found in the best moments of even his worst films.

Casiraghi and Viazzi's judgement seems exaggerated and should be revised. De Robertis's cultural preparation, unlike Visconti's, should be seen only as a correct knowledge of the cinematic means of expression, without aesthetic preconceptions, not as a pre-established adherence to a traditional cultural tendency. Consequently, it is rather difficult to identify models in assessing De Robertis's work. Casiraghi and Viazzi speak, it is true, of Russian models. Certainly, certain aspects of his work recall the Russian school: his use of dialectic cutting, his use of rhythm, of the "expressive object" according to Pudovkin's conception of the phrase. Nevertheless, we must not forget that the Russian example is a common heritage of world cinema and that its elements are to be found in the most varied areas: Ruttmann, the *Kammerspiel*, the English documentary, and so on. The analogies between De Robertis and the Russians can therefore be explained without insistence on a specific and direct influence, for they are part of the legacy and correct theoretical groundwork of every filmgoer. The reference to the Russians by Casiraghi and Viazzi becomes more valid if it is interpreted as an attempt to make a connection between creative sensibilities. De Robertis really does have certain points in common with directors like Pudovkin and Donskoi, but we do not find them specifically quoted or imitated in his films. *Uomini sul fondo*, in fact, represents something spontaneous and original. Although deliberately grounded in cinematic orthodoxy, it was, at the same time, free from overtones of past culture, from calculations based on the history of cinema. While making *Uomini sul fondo*, De Robertis probably had no suspicion that he was contributing to "the style to be formed." Yet this film opened the way to a new Italian cinema. That is why it is superior to *Ossessione*; even if, in itself, it is inferior as a film to Visconti's it is historically of more importance and fecundity. It is from *Uomini sul fondo* that the most representative figure of Italian neo-realism emerged: Roberto Rossellini.

In 1938, after making several documentaries — *L'aprés-midi d'un faune, Fantasia sottomarina, Il rescello di Ripasottile* (films seen by almost nobody, and about which we know only that the last two concerned fish) — and after collaborating on the script of *Luciano serra pilota*, Roberto Rossellini, in 1941, signed a contract to make *La nave bianca* in collaboration with De Robertis from a scenario by the latter. De Robertis has recently claimed "artistic paternity" of *La nave bianca*. Whatever the role of Rossellini in the creation of the film, it is unquestionable that its style is identical to that of *Uomini sul fondo*. De Robertis has also noted that *La nave bianca* had originally been conceived as a short documentary about the sanitary equipment of the wartime navy. The basic production, the conception and construction, of *La nave bianca* followed the lead of *Uomini sul fondo*. Even Rossellini's films *Un pilota ritorna* (1942) and *L'uomo della croce* (1943) repeat the tone, if not the style, of De Robertis. They are pale films, not entirely clean of propagandist contamination, and are rather vulgar, especially the second one. The revelation of Rossellini's personality came only with *Roma città aperta*, in 1945, in which the lessons of De Robertis, even if they remain at the basis of his filmic expression, are overwhelmed by Rossellini's personal vision.

Paisà, in 1946, marks the apex of Rossellini's evolution and remains his purest creation. After *Paisà*, Rossellini was only to make the rhetorically self-indulgent *Germania anno zero*, and attempt the insincere extemporaneous lyricism of *Amore*. At his best Rossellini — the one who made the Florence episode of *Paisà*, and the ending of

Germania anno zero — is an epic poet, who brings the daily conditions and events of humanity to a dramatic tension.

The Florence episode is worth noting in some detail. It is the drama of a wounded city, divided by its bombed bridges, with German patrols and Red Cross stretcher-bearers moving through its deserted streets; beyond the Arno are the quiet and self-controlled English (about whom Jean-Georges Auriol justly observed "they are portrayed in the manner of a novelist, not photographed as if by a reporter."[27]) who gaze at the bell towers through binoculars; at the end, there is the furious execution of the Fascist soldiers. There is a sense of the ordained, unavoidable happening. In those inspired moments (rather rare in his work), Rossellini taps a very pure and personal language. Otherwise, when he is not touched by inspiration, Rossellini's style is illegitimate, uncertain, and sometimes commonplace.

Rossellini's limitations are, above all, limitations of temperament. He is an extemporizer who, like Eisenstein, relishes filming without a script. His instinct, however, lacks enough concreteness of definition to rescue him from the stimuli of either melodrama or purely descriptive solutions. Rossellini's day may be over. Certainly, to make another good film, he will have to return to his original sense of artistic conscience. Here I shall not analyse his work in detail. What is important for our purpose is to point out that neither during his apprenticeship, when he was linked with De Robertis, nor in his original maturity, nor in his premature decline, did his career reveal any particular connection with those cultural trends of the Italian cinema from which *Ossessione* was born. Rossellini's neo-realism is a relatively new aspect of Italian cinema and must be linked through De Robertis to the documentary tradition. We cannot establish, and therefore cannot deny, the part that influences from more remote traditions had on Rossellini's development, nor, more generally, the influences of a whole climate of production. At any rate, Rossellini's neo-realism is not all of Italian neo-realism, but only one vein of it.

Neo-realism is a lively movement, in perpetual evolution, and cannot be summed up in any easy, static formula. Other attempts were made, parallel to those of Rossellini, and were nourished by different sources, particularly those of De Sica.

Vittorio De Sica had already been an actor in "variety" and the theatre, and later a stereotype protagonist in the best of Camerini's films, before he began to direct. Initially, working within the orbit of Camerini's vaporous and polite humour, De Sica immediately introduced a more overtly satirical attitude and revealed a tendency to solve narrative matters incisively by including exaggerated scenes which contain the premises of his moral judgement and social polemic. In this respect *Teresa Venerdi* was already a significant achievement. It is only necessary to recall, for example, the brief scene in which the patroness visits the school. At the same time, De Sica is sensitive to the pathos of Camerini's world, which his meridional temperament urged him to emphasize with the sensibility of a De Amicis.[28]

The original personality of De Sica was revealed almost unexpectedly with *I bambini ci guardano* which he finished in the spring of 1943 but which remained unreleased until 1944. *I bambini ci guardano*, its theme implicit in its title, developed typically familiar situations of the Italian bourgeoisie between the wars, with a critical eye and marked the first time that Italian cinema was actually involved in polemic and moral pronouncements. Polemic inspiration dominates even *Sciuscià* (1946) in which De Sica, rising to the creation of a total image of humanity, freed himself from the forced exaggeration and excessive sentimentality which had marred *I bambini ci guardano*.

In *Ladri di biciclette* (1948), his masterpiece, and the absolute masterpiece of the entire Italian cinema, De Sica's *stimmung* is even more precise: the cruel solitude to which man is doomed in his struggle for existence, the determinist vision of humanity without catharsis. The nature and range of his social and moral polemic, which is never an end in itself, but a symbol of the human condition, is a question which does not wait for an answer. The Italian cinema before De Sica had never adopted themes of such total human involvement nor achieved such results.

The startling formal evolution of De Sica corresponds to the evolution of his inner purposes. As part of Camerini's team, he was, in fact, linked to practical experience in directing, from the very beginning having "on the job training" in the basics of cinematic expression. Even *I bambini ci guardano* and *Sciuscià* were, from a formal point of view, never successful in displaying a coherent style, perhaps because the urgency of their inspiration never overcame the uncertainty of their formal structure. *Ladri di biciclette,* on the other hand, demonstrates a perfect assimilation of the means of cinematic expression. De Sica had conquered the poetics of his poetry — a late conquest, but spontaneous, without aesthetic influences, and therefore more valuable.

De Sica is the only example of an artist who developed gradually, consciously, and in absolute sincerity, even in the face of his own limitations. Thus the work of De Sica links neo-realism to Camerini, whose influence he perpetuates through his interest, even with progressively diverse sensibility, in popular and petit-bourgeois environments. Even from the standpoint of style, until *Sciuscià,* De Sica remained linked to Camerini. The influence of *Roma città aperta* encouraged De Sica with *Sciuscià* to transcend the models of Camerini. Although it is an orginal work, *Ladri di biciclette* bears precise antecedents in the history of Italian cinema, as De Sica's own experience bears something in common with that of De Robertis and Rossellini: a substantial indifference to the trends of calligraphism and French realism.

De Robertis, Rossellini, and De Sica delimited a seemingly homogenous area. They moved within realism from the basis of instinct and inspiration without cultural preconceptions. Thus an examination of their antecedents and a delineation of their place in history has only a relative value, because their work is above all the product of individual intuition. The play of influence is not a matter of mechanical determination, but of a creative dynamic which answers to personal impulses. De Robertis, with a number of vague allusions, created something new with *Uomini sul fondo.* Rossellini started from De Robertis, but added something of his own, and created something new. De Sica, incorporating Camerini influences and certain echoes of Rossellini, also achieves a completely personal result. The work of these three opened a new and original chapter of Italian cinema. Their experience constitutes the main road of neo-realism.

Neo-realism in Culture

It would be arbitrary, nevertheless, to restrict neo-realism only to the names of De Robertis, Rossellini, and De Sica. There are other facets, other names, which are part of neo-realism, and which, although influenced by the three, have different origins and varied ambitions.

Aldo Vergano was script writer and assistant on Blasetti's *Sole* and fulfilled the same functions for Alessandrini on *Don Bosco* and *Cavalleria*. He then directed several insignificant films (*Pietro Micca, Quelli della montagna*). His first and only significant work has been *Il sole sorge ancora* (1946), for which he had Giuseppe De Santis as assistant. Visibly imitating the Rossellini of *Roma città aperta*, Vergano conceived *Il sole sorge ancora* with a sensibility which shows traces of a vaguely epic inspiration.

Giuseppe De Santis attended the CSC. course in directing[29] and then became a critic for *Cinema*, after which he worked as screen-writer and assistant director for both Visconti on *Ossessione* and Vergano on *Il sole sorge ancora*. His first film *Caccia tragica* was made in 1947; the second, *Riso amaro* was first shown at the Cannes festival of 1948. De Santis, whose personality is drawn to the essentially decorative and non-naturalistic, is attracted to neo-realism by cultural suggestion. For him, neo-realism consists of incidents in a certain plastic and narrative repertory, which, in his hands, becomes rhetorical, and offers only a pretext for decorative exercises. What an abyss lies between the bicycles of De Santis and those of De Sica!

Caccia tragica and *Riso amaro*, like *Il sole sorge ancora*, are works based on cultural experiences. That is to say that De Santis and Vergano have used the examples of De Robertis, De Sica and, above all, of Rossellini, as a cultural basis, tying it all to the complex ferment of the search for "the style to be formed" in which they themselves participated: Vergano in the tracks of Alessandrini and Blasetti, De Santis following Visconti. With this very solid cinematic culture, they enlarged the area of the search for style by grafting it, especially in the case of De Santis, on to memories of the entire history of cinema within the requirements of a rigorous cinematic orthodoxy. With them, then, a second movement within Italian neo-realism begins, that of a cultural elaboration of the rough results obtained by the first-hand experience of De Robertis and Rossellini: it is a fecund and historically necessary movement because it restores and blends together that area of research which De Robertis and Rossellini ignored. The circle is perfectly closed with *La terra trema*, in which Visconti turned from *Ossessione* to the example of Rossellini.

With reference to this cultural basis, there is also the work of Pietro Germi, a young director with undoubted gifts who has also emerged from the CSC and who is looking for his own direction with absolute sincerity. Germi's beginning was typical of the new cultural movement within neo-realism. His first film, *Il testimone* (1945), followed a narrative structure near to Carné and Duvivier and was set in an original landscape. Visconti's own beginning was not very different. In *Gioventù perduta* (1947) and *In nome della legge* (1949), Germi succeeded in freeing himself from the French influence to attempt an original direction which sided with the neo-realistic tendency without indicating specific connections to it. *In nome della legge* marks a particular achievement in its use of a poetic landscape and is, perhaps, the best Italian film of the post-war period after *Ladri di biciclette* and *Paisà*.

Apart from those names already mentioned, there are others who are also active, but their activity has remained within the limitations of the movement's scheme, outlined here, without adding anything original to it. I am thinking, primarily of Luigi Zampa and Alberto Lattuada. Zampa, coming from CSC, is a skilful (and lucky) director who tends, in his work, to make the meaning of the word "chronicle" absolute within the neo-realistic framework (*Vivere in pace, L'Onorevole Angelina, Anni difficili*).

On the other hand, Lattuada, having worked as assistant to Soldati, brings to his concept of neo-realism (*Il bandito, Senza pietà*) an over-flowing sentimentality and a calligraphic method which are probably close to his real personality but which tend to weaken the effect of his neo-realistic manner. In *Il mulino del Po* (1949), Lattuada, as Giulio Cesare Castello shrewdly points out,[30] achieves something of a compromise between the two directions.

Even Augusto Genina, with *Cielo sulla palude,* performs an act of allegiance to neo-realism while remaining apart from its true and proper creative tendencies; an act in which we can see mannerism and fashion developing. All this, perhaps, is an indication of another step in the evolution of neo-realism, which, for many directors, was no more than a formative climate in which to find their own personal solutions, and which served a function similar to that served in France by the realism of Renoir, Carné, and Feyder.

The case of Renato Castellani is particularly significant here. With neo-realism he found the key to unlock the fetters of his own instinct (*Sotto il sole di Roma, E'primavera*) and thus to overcome the calligraphic stage of his early work.

The work of Vergano, De Santis, Germi and Lattuada taken together leads us to presuppose the existence of a school. The term "school", however, by which we usually mean a creative stream, which is endowed with its own coherent homogeneity, above all on the formal level, seems inappropriate when applied to neo-realism. The Russians, the German Expressionists, and the English Documentarists, for example, have properly named schools. However, while the neo-realists utilise similar methods of expression, their work, taken as a whole, lacks a common *basis* of expression and a distinct *formal* personality. Rather than a "school", neo-realism is a tendency, a trend. Moreover, its very lack of formal precision reflects the standard of expression which characterizes the current moment in cinema. The demands of narrative impose on nearly all filmmakers a more or less common film language. In the past, there existed a great chasm between the methods of expression of the various schools, as illustrated by the differences between the contemporaneous phenomena of the Russians, German Expressionism, and the French *Avant-Garde*. Today the differences between the various environments in which production takes place are minimal; schools no longer exist, and the dreariness of a uniform narrative extends throughout the larger part of the cinematic globe. Currently, the only original, historically interesting, theoretical ideas concern the first person and the depth of field, but even these are degenerating into mannerism.

At any rate, neo-realism already possesses a definite personality in terms of expression, and when considered in its historical perspective, it is an ample personality indeed. It marks, at least in its most valuable achievements, *Paisà* and *Ladri di biciclette,* a return to the analytic editing of the silent Russian school, and the atmosphere of the German *Kammerspiel.* In reacting to certain current trends, it resolves itself through plastic cinematic expression. Even in the use of sound, neo-realism explicitly renews the lesson of "asyncronism", denying the pan-verbalism of literary and theatrical derivation. In that sense, *Ladri di biciclette* is a stupendous achievement. In the dynamic of world cinema, Italian neo-realism constitutes a recall to the purer, more genuine and classical foundations of cinematic expression.

The Function of Tradition

My analysis clarifies the profound connection between the development of neo-realism and the earlier history of Italian cinema. I have examined the roles played by regionalism, literary origins, and the classic French cinema. I have noted the documentary origins of De Robertis and Rossellini, and how they constituted a new opening for the Italian cinema. Then we have seen De Sica, beginning under the influence of Camerini and benefitting from Rossellini's experience, to evolve into his proper artistic personality. We have also seen Vergano, De Santis, and Germi intellectually welcoming Rossellini's example and linking it to the ambitions of the cultured literary and French styles. That, then, is the development cycle of the neo-realist phenomenon.

Multiple factors intervene and integrate themselves with one another, in the origins of neo-realism, making it difficult to establish a hierarchy among all those relationships. We have, perhaps, granted a greater credit to the documentary vein, but this does not mean neo-realism does not owe a great debt to other influences. Even among all the various streams, documentary is the least defined stylistically. In the genesis of neo-realism, a decisive and unilateral contribution does not exist; it did not rise from a single factor, but from a sum of factors which influenced the movement in a complex way.

To understand this I must refer to the provincial condition of the Italian cinema prior to neo-realism, whose various channels remained in a fluid state, not quite materializing into a solidified, concrete tradition. Neo-realism is similar to soil whose fecundity is fruitless without proper implantation. Neo-realism draws nourishment from these modest but substantial country essences, which are unburdened by a codified tradition. Due to their very state of fluidity and lack of tradition, there was never a question of a limitation of growth. The substance of neo-realism and its rapid development are linked to the provincial condition of Italian cinema. Perhaps

Uomini sul fondo would not have had the influence it did, if it had appeared in a more cinematically mature culture. From that point of view, the origins of neo-realism bear a certain resemblance to the birth of the English documentary, although the latter originated in a specific cultural situation.

Certainly I do not believe that neo-realism differs from realism. There is, indeed, a current joke to the effect that "neo-realism = realism plus neo". Neo-realism is merely a convenient term, like most such terms. Still, whatever we call it, it remains a fact which corresponds to something real. From *Uomini sul fondo* to *Ladri di biciclette* something original occurred in the Italian cinema which made up a new chapter in the national cinema. With neo-realism, the rare realistic attempts of the Italian cinema became concrete and identifiable by a definite style; something was created which was new, and, above all, the movement found adequate cinematic expression. Even *Don Bosco,* for example, was undoubtedly a realistic film, but one in which the realistic purpose was preconditioned (and nourished) by a pursuit of what was essentially pictorial, a pursuit which betrayed cinematic inspiration at its source, and which was common to all Italian cinema at the time. Only with neo-realism does Italian cinema, even in its minor directors, orient itself towards a freedom of experimentation, unprejudiced, yet planned in terms of its independent expression.

From its provincial origins, neo-realism borrowed certain elements of primitivism: the use of non-professional actors, the lack of declamatory narrative, a certain ingenuousness in the scenarios, and, generally speaking, a total lack of practical experience at the technical level. These are the basic characteristics, of course, of a cinematic civilization still in formation, as can be seen, for example, in the young Mexican cinema. Moreover, in neo-realism certain limitations of national temperament, a certain rhetorical and typically Italianate excessive sentimentality are perpetuated — the Romagna episode of the convent in *Paisà,* for example.

In spite of its heritage, neo-realism marks the transcendence of the condition of provincialism which had confined Italian cinema since *Cabiria.* Neo-realism represents the climactic moment in the search for the "style to be formed", an original Italian style, the real beginning of an Italian film culture. With neo-realism, Italian cinema brought itself to the attention of the entire world. It has stood at the centre of international criticism for four years now. René Clair, Abel Gance, Orson Welles, Marcel L'Herbier, G.W. Pabst, all now work in Italy. Pabst, indeed, has asserted explicitly that what appeals to him about Italy is the vitality of the new Italian cinema. Undoubtedly, Italian neo-realism constitutes the most concrete and interesting aspect of an otherwise dreary post-war period of international cinema.

"Origini del neorealismo",
Bianco e nero, XI, 2, February 1950

Notes

1   Zola was reputed to have remarked to Verga: *"Le vérisme italien, oui, oui, je comprends: c'est mon naturalisme."* Although many Italian critics and historians of the period would have agreed, just as many would have not. The differences between "naturalism" and "realism" can be made clear enough — although they obviously slide into one another — the differences between "realism" and "verism" are not clear, save perhaps to a specialist in 19th century Italian literature. Verism is usually applied to the literary output of those Italian writers of the late 19th century who described life, characters, and social situations realistically. A good deal, if not all, such material took the South as subject and setting. Although Verga is the most famous of these, Matilde Serao (1856-1927) is not without interest. She was a journalist as well as a prolific writer of stories and novels, and, with her husband, founded four newspapers: *Corriere di Roma, Corriere di Napoli, Il mattino,* and *Il giorno.* Her most famous and popular novel, *Il paese di Cuccagna* (1890) concerns the madness of the lottery as it permeates every level of life in Naples, which was also the setting for the best of her work.

2   The reference to the "expressionistic experience" is to the artistic and literary movement in Germany, which in film took place roughly

between 1913 and 1933, with most activity occurring in the Twenties. An extended definitive history of this movement in relation to film is Lotte H. Eisner's *The haunted screen*. A more brief and more general history (with few references to cinema) is R.S. Furness's *Expressionism*.

3   The Futurist movement was founded by Filippo Marinetti (1876-1944), whose *Futurist manifesto* (1909) contained most of the basic ideas of the aesthetic: the rejection of all formal rules in literature, the search for new sources of inspiration and modes of expression in science and technology, the use of the "unconscious" mind of the artist freed from logic, and the isolation of art from history and tradition.

4   Fogazzaro: see note 16 following *Truth and Poetry* by Alicata and De Santis.

Alessandro Manzoni (1785-1873) is Italy's greatest novelist, known for his exact observation and description of detail and for his analysis of social class, particularly in his best-known work *I promessi sposi* (1840-42).

Carlo Goldoni (1707-1793) was the comic playwright whose work marked the beginnings of pre-written dialogue (as opposed to improvisation by the actors of the *Commedia dell'arte*) in the Italian theatre. He had only limited success in his lifetime, and now is as well known for his memoirs (1787) as for his most popular comedy *La locandiera* (1753).

Michelangelo Amerighi Caravaggio (1565-1609) was the founder of the "naturalist" Roman school of painting who moved away from the idealisation of his models to more realistic portrayals, even in his religious paintings.

Masaccio (Tommaso Guidi) (1401-1428?) was a Florentine painter whose naturalistic treatment of landscape and figures, as well as his use of perspective, influenced Michelangelo and Raphael.

5   Simone Martino (sometimes Martini, 1283-1344) was one of the central figures of the "delicate line" of painting in Siena.

Giambattista Vico (1668-1744) deliberately turned his back on Descartes, looking back on man's history in an attempt to understand what "man has made". His *Scienza nuova* (1725) is the history of mankind seen through a series of rises and falls.

6   Two minor directors of almost totally standard commercial films. Camillo Mastrocinque is perhaps of slightly more interest as he

directed a new version of *Sperduti nel buio* (1947) and because he appeared as an actor in *Roma città aperta* and *In nome della legge*.

7   Emilio Cecchi (1884-1966) was a critic, essayist, and scriptwriter who became the Head of Production at the Cines company. There is a slight discrepancy in the date he took charge of production there. The standard sources list 1932, although some agree with Venturini's 1930. He was also the father of Cecchi d'Amico who collaborated on the scripts of a good many neo-realist films.

8   Venturini's note: "Antonio Pietrangeli, *'Panoramique sur le cinéma italien', Revue du cinéma*, 13, May 1948."

9   Luigi Capuana (1839-1915), a realist novelist and critic. He introduced the ideas of the French naturalists into Italy, and is generaly credited with helping to "convert" Verga to regional realism. His ideas on what the realist novel should be (observation in semi-scientific fashion, less emphasis on story) have certain similarities to those of Cesare Zavattini on film.

    Federico De Roberto (1866-1927) brought to his fiction a blending of Verga-like regional realism and a coldly scientific psychological attitude to character.

    Gabriele D'Annunzio (1863-1938) wrote several collections of short stories early in his career under the influence of the regional realist tales of Verga. *Nouvelle della Pescara* (1884-1886) was one of three such collections.

10   Nino Martoglio directed the original version of *Sperduti nel buio* (1914).

11   Giuseppe De Santis was a critic for *Cinema* during the war, collaborated on scripts for several directors, and then turned director himself. It was not only in "book reviews" that De Santis championed Verga as a source of cinematic inspiration: see his and Mario Alicata's essay on the subject here.

12   Umberto Barbaro (1902-1959) lectured on film, translated theoretical and critical works on the cinema into Italian, and collaborated on the screenplay of *Caccia tragica*, as well as co-directing two films with Roberto Longhi, *Carpaccio* (1947) and *Caravaggio* (1948).

12   Luigi Chiarini (1900-1975) was one of the founders of the *Centro Speri-*

mentale di Cinematografia in 1933, and remained its director until 1950. In 1937, he was one of the founders, as well, of *Biano e nero*, of which he was editor until 1951. In 1952 he edited *Revista del cinema Italiano*, and was the director of the Venice Film Festival from 1962 to 1968. In addition, he lectured on cinema at the University of Urbino, and wrote several books and many articles on the cinema, even while collaborating on a number of screenplays and directing a half-dozen films himself.

13   An authoritative, succinct definition of *Kammerspiel* as it relates to film: "the psychological film *par excellence*: it was to comprise a limited number of characters living in an everyday ambience": Lotte H. Eisner, *The haunted screen.*

14   Venturini's note: "Umberto Barbaro, '*Neorealismo*', *Film*, 1943."

15   Venturini's note: "Pietrangeli, *op. cit.*"

16   John Grierson was a co-founder of the Empire Marketing Board Film Unit (1930) for which he made *Drifters* (1929), a study of herring fishermen. It was both much admired and much despised. It was, nonetheless, heavily influenced by the "Russian school of montage". Grierson transferred with the EMB Film Unit in 1933 to the GPO, and later (1939-1945) became a director of the Canadian Film Board. Deeply committed to didactic, non-fiction film, Grierson set the tone for British film production and criticism for some years. The merit, or lack of merit, of his influence is still being debated.

17   Giuseppe Ungaretti (1888-   ) is an Italian poet and translator whose work was much influenced by Mallarmé and Valéry. *L'Allegria* (1919) is a series of war poems, each with a precise setting and time.

18   Eugenio Montale (1896-   ) is a poet, translator, and critic. He has been the literary editor of the influential *Corriere della sera* since 1947, and has translated T.S. Eliot into Italian, who seems to have influenced his own work, although Ungaretti was perhaps the even greater influence.

19   Giacomo Leopardi (1798-1837) was primarily a lyrical poet who, in spite of a very small number of poems, is considered by many to be the greatest lyric poet of 19th century Italy.
    Ugo Foscolo (1778-1827) was a poet, novelist, and translator. He is

best known for his patriotic poems.

20   Pierre Reverdy (1889-1960) wrote both poetry and prose, passing in
      1910 along the edges of the *Avant-Garde* and Surrealist movements,
      through Cubism in the early Twenties. In 1926, he moved to Solesmes
      where he continued to produce work concerned with isolation and reli-
      gious feeling.

21   Venturini's note: "Ugo Casiraghi and Glauco Viazzi, '*Presentazione
      posthuma d'un classico*', *Bianco e nero*, April 1942".

22   Venturini's note: "Jean-Georges Auriol, '*Entretien romaine sur la
      situation et la disposition de cinéma italien*', *Revue du cinéma*, 13,
      May 1948".

23   Venturini's note: "De Robertis's films provide curious problems
      (which might perhaps be described as 'philological'), some of which
      have recently been exhumed by journalistic polemic. It has been sug-
      gested that *Uomini sul fondo* was the fruit of Giorgio Branchi's artis-
      tic direction. In a letter to *Cinema* ('*Libertas, unitas, caritas*', *Cinema*,
      7, January 30, 1949), De Robertis claimed full credit for the film —
      including subject, staging, direction, editing, mixing, and collabora-
      tion on the musical score — and further charged that Giorgio Branchi
      was only an assistant director of the interior scenes shot in Trieste.
          Some of those scenes were filmed entirely by Branchi in the absence
      of De Robertis, who later approved and accepted them. Exterior shots
      were done in La Spezia with the assistance of Ivo Perilli. Décor by
      Bonetti, and the camera operated by Caracciolo (later De Sica's camera-
      man). Bureaucratically speaking, De Robertis was merely the Head of
      the Naval Cinema Service.
          Roberto Rossellini was the director of *La nave bianca*, yet in his let-
      ter, De Robertis seems to claim responsibility for that film as well,
      although he appears in the credits only as scriptwriter."

24   Venturini's note: "*Casiraghi and Viazzi, op. cit.*"

25   Venturini's note: "Carl Vincent, '*Lettre de Rome*', *Cinéma* (Brussels),
      April 1942.

26   Although one must always be careful in assigning political align-
      ments to film people during the Fascist period, there is no ambiguity
      in the case of De Robertis. Venturini is here making reference to the

196

hostility felt by many critics towards De Robertis because of his total commitment to Fascism. He was Director of Cinema Services of the Naval Ministry during the war, but more to the point, he followed Mussolini in 1943 to Lake Garda to undertake the reorganization of the government's cinema industry for the Salò Republic.

27   Venturini's note: "Jean-Georges Auriol, '*Faire des films? pour qui?*', *Revue du cinéma*, 4, January 1947."

28   Edmondo De Amicus (1846-1908). Although he wrote many other things, Venturini obviously has in mind here the sensibility of *Cuore*, a collection of stories published in 1886 dealing with boyhood.

29   CSC.: the Italian film school, *Centro Sperimentale di Cinematografia*.

30   Venturini's note: "*Il mulino del Po*', *Bianco e nero*, 9, September 1949."

15. Neo-Realism: Yesterday
by Giuseppe Ferrara

Giuseppe Ferrara's book *Francesco Rosi,* published in 1965, was the first to attempt to set the work of a post-World War Two Italian director in the context of Neo-Realism, as well as the first full length study of one of the central figures of contemporary Italian film.

It is by now a commonplace to assert that the Italian cinema of the immediate post-war period came out of the cultural, moral and political climate provoked by the resistance to Fascism; that the camera went into the streets, after so many years of lies, to look for the truth, however rotten and degrading; that people sought a sense of history in a direct participation in current events. People say that all of that is past, and suspect it is all rhetoric anyway; certainly, in the light of current production, it is inconvenient to remember such things. There are those who also assert that "neo-realism" — that term which sums up the impetus to possess the real, through cinema, at a moment of effective participation in events — is only a label. There are even those who, from another point of view, and in all good faith, seek to discover, in those first rough chapters of anti-decadent and anti-romantic expression, such as *Roma città aperta* (1945), *Paisà* (1946), *Sciuscià* (1946), *Ladri di biciclette* (1948), and *La terra trema* (1948), the ideological vices and cultural shortcomings which might serve as the obvious premises, the clearest explanations, of the successive declines, of the evasions — whether opportunistic or hedonistic — that the "Masters" of the first period (the Rossellinis, Viscontis, De Sicas) went through in their later works. Why does neo-realism, at a certain point in its history, "fall into the mud of compromise"? Because it already contained within itself the seed of that compromise, because it possessed nothing, or almost nothing, "clear and valid from the ideological point of view."[1]

Ironically, in a society which wrongly proclaimed itself as having been born from a revolution of resistance; which did not admit to having compressed, deformed and blunted, the authentic revolutionary spring of the partisan formations; which prepared the compromises (certainly not foreseen by those who had fought in the resistance) of restored Fascist codes and laws; which, because it bred all the equivocations and errors which had brought the anti-Fascist forces of the proletarian left to the tragic defeat of the Spanish Civil War, lacked in its progressive leanings that clear-sightedness necessary and proper to political and ideological grounds; in that society a small group of film-makers, instinctively and ingenuously, utilising the revolutionary ferment, put forward an art form that, at a precise historical moment, was much more ideologically advanced than it was possible to realise. Today the art form is judged according to its obvious weaknesses, which are then presented as the reasons for its serious decline.

It is too easy to accept this thesis and so to invalidate the great neo-realist lessons of *Roma città aperta*: to ascribe its vague pacifist hints as the origins of the offensive mystification about the resistance contained in *Era notte a Roma* and *Il Generale Della Rovere*. To follow Croce's theory of the monolithic development of artists, leads, in the history of cinema above all, to false perspectives.[2] For many years now, perhaps since *Amore* (1949), Rossellini has been a different artist, not because he turned his back on himself, but because he did not want to deepen some of the great insights of his famous trilogy,[3] and instead developed the Catholic decadence which, during the immediate post-war period seemed to flatten itself; everyday events no doubt, needed to emerge in spiritual forms but, because of their very substance and urgency received a certain cold level of emphasis; the aggressiveness of the content was expressed in a form which even now appears to be historical.

Thus the validity or failure for today, of that first period of neo-realism will have to be looked at, not through its dregs, but from its greatest achivements. We must not lose ourselves in an easy revisionism, but simply remember that if, in its central period, neo-realism was an *avant-garde* movement, on its periphery, both before and after, it always retained vestiges of the older culture. Of course, these traces never seemed old at all, for the entire movement was one of renewal, and even the remaining aspects of the old culture were renewed and were able, in this way, to exert an attraction of undeniable charm.

We cannot deny in *Francesco, giullare di Dio* (1948) a certain amount of refreshing non-conformity, although it essentially reflects a glib and romantic subjectivism that exalts the faith of others only when the faith is shown to be of transcendental origin; that is to say that once agan, Rossellini's non-conformity is exasperatingly ego-centric and abstract in its underestimation of the deep connections existing between the "I" and the development of actual society, between the "I" and historical time, between the "I" and human knowledge of things. Neo-realism, in its best work, and at its best moments put forward precisely the opposite view. It answered, with all the means at its disposal, a desperate call best summed up by Vittorini in *Il politecnico*, in which he expressed the moral essence of, and the desire for, a renewal of Italian culture in the immediate post-war period. Vittorini asked if, in the last conflict in which people had not hesitated to tread on "all the forms which had passed as the civil progress of man", the only great one which remained was culture, whose influence on men, alas, was shown to have been almost nought, since it had always generated and regenerated itself without identifying with society as a whole: "Won't we ever have a culture able to protect man from suffering instead of merely soothing him? Will the voice of the artist, of the scientist, of the philosopher be able to live with society itself as society itself lives?"[4]

That question is stimulating for several reasons because if, on the one hand, it neatly rejects the idealist concept of culture, (which in Italy, through the presence of the ideas of Croce, maintained that all could enter the aristocratic garden of thought without fear, once the moral illness of Fascism had been eliminated), on the other hand, the question invites a revision of the Marxist concept of art, plainly understood as superstructure and therefore easily reduceable to an opaque instrumentalism. Neo-realism answered the call and attempted a rediscovery of the human dimension, a revolution in which the transformation of taste and content did not happen in the *internal* expression of culture; on the contrary, with an overbearing manner, it formulated that regeneration properly "within the possibilities of creation" within the society from which it was born. Neo-realism answered "yes": that art indeed possessed infinite possibilities of intervention. Conserving its own autonomy, it could dirty its hands with social reality, even with politics, taking sides in a situation where facts were conflicting, for to remove oneself to an ivory tower would have meant an evasion of responsibilities and a renunciation of the dialectic of history. The core of the neo-realist lesson lay, in that point: to have put art directly in the struggle, rejecting positions that were either external or peripheral. The problem is not merely one of content but of a choice of a new artistic language. Neo-realism, in fact inspired by events, seeks to represent the true rhythm of conflict, taking care neither to alter nor to exaggerate that rhythm but to convey it with the full knowledge of its entire social ramifications. Neo-realism, in short, gives birth to a language of struggle which grasps not only momentous historical connections but simultaneously the minutes lived by men within the historical perspective. The elements in the death of Pina;[5] her running briefly behind the German trucks as they take her husband away, her shout of rebellion immediately followed by a charge of machine-gun fire, her body on the bloody pavement, explain in precise detail both an individual and a collective tragedy; not only does it represent the tragedy of the entire Italian people, but it constitutes, in the history of cinema and human culture, one of the first expressions of *historical man* through the language of conflict. But of what does the anti-decadent nature of that language consist?

Neo-realism was the first attempt of our culture to attain a "national-popular" expression in the sense meant by Gramsci. It has rejected the detachment of the traditional intellectuals who neither know nor feel the "needs, the aspirations, the diffuse feelings" of the people, which form "something detached, in the air, a cast and not an articulation with organic functions of the people itself."[6] Instead, it has often represented (even if non-organically) profoundly democratic demands with sympathy for, and a sense of participation with, the masses. In doing so, it has expressed a firm will towards change, if necessary through open rebellion or subversion of the established order.

Moreover, neo-realism refused to consider that man is alone in the universe with his problems and anxieties, that he can only attempt to shelter himself in a desperate subjectivity. This sets neo-realism apart in several ways. Decadent artists, even those most hostile to bourgeois society, moved towards an un-historic lyricism, a neo-romanticism; neo-realism rejects such deep irrationality. It also rejects the traditional relationship between film and audience. No longer will this relationship consist of the magic of illusionistic "demoniac persuasion" in which the author tends to confound himself with the character and to insist that the spectator identify with character through a "non-cathartic contemplation". The spectator will no longer escape into a timeless limbo between past and present, nor be directed towards an equivocal individualism which puts poetry forward as the "absolute organ of knowledge."[7] Neo-realism proposes "anti-pathos"; it excludes any form of illusion to reach a relationship of an aesthetic-moral nature between author and spectator. "The subjective spectator will no longer be a body enhaloed by an aura of irrationality, but a man from whom one wants to tear the veil obscuring his true condition, and to place it in direct relation to past history and the present potentialities of the development of societal man."[8] The author will no longer be "one" with his character, but will propose a new dialectic between reason and feeling. He will reveal an "ethical intention to break with the contemplative or emotive criteria of art."[9] "When the critical separation between author and character occurs, the author requires explicit means with which to demonstrate to the spectator the different levels of relationship between necessity, existence, and possibility: things as they are, what separates 'me' from 'them', and what I assert *should* be, in such a way that my assertion would be neither a thesis nor an apology for an as yet non-existent future, but an expansion of my ethical intentions. That is to say, the author must seek the revelation of the negative elements of character (not to destroy him, but to collaborate with the audience), either focusing in this way on the insoluble contradictions in character and the world, or moving to irony and anti-pathos."[10]

So, a language of struggle develops which draws the spectator in and forces him to participate, almost as if he were one of the elements of the struggle itself. However, we should note that even Eisenstein's language, like that of Chaplin, was of a dialectical and historical nature. A work like *Potemkin* (1925) realises stupendously the conflict between oppressed and oppressors through the contrapuntal play of opposing images: the Odessa Steps sequence, for example, in which Eisenstein placed on one side the crowd of workers escaping in confusion and leaving the dead scattered on the ground, and on the other the orderly rows of soldiers who proceed mechanically like a machine of death shooting at the defenseless, every five steps.

In Chaplin's films the conflict was between the optimistic tramp and the negative world, permeated with pessimism, which surrounds him. If the little man, so small and defenseless, succeeds in conquering Goliath (the society in which he is compelled to live), the spectator laughs, because the victory appears completely absurd. If he loses, the spectator is moved, because precise moral values have been defeated, because something deeply human has been humiliated.

Both Eisenstein and Chaplin arrived at a figurative expression for symbolic conflict. The one exaggerated the conflict between a blocked society and a society on its way to coming into being; the other exalted the individual and, hence, anarchic struggle. Like Eisenstein in *Potemkin,* and Chaplin in *Modern times,* many artists find their inspiration in the conflicts of history, but the works of many of them form a rather fantastic curve. Starting from reality, they eventually represent it by abstract characteristics, expressing themselves by reducing the real to its absolute essence.

Neo-realism goes much further forward, even if it also begins in history and reaches an emblematic significance — as in the final episode of *Paisà* — for it remains forever attached to the object, refusing to transfigure it or give it a rhythm other than its own. The "musicality" of the Odessa sequence is the author's superimposition on the facts, according to a concept of beauty that he possesses in the abstract before even knowing the fact itself. For neo-realism, such a process is impossible because "beauty" *is* the historical truth itself, as it is comprehended through an elaboration of the facts and things themselves, by the untiring labour of eliciting from history its own true nature.

Artistic research of an abstract aesthetic order allows for the organic increment of rational life to pass in order to point to "absolute truth." This cultural position was developed between 1945 and 1948. Even if it advanced, albeit unwillingly and perhaps unknowingly, in the footsteps of Brecht, it could not carry filmic expression beyond a dryly historical illumination; the substance of *La terra trema,* for example, is elaborated in terms of social class. It would be too much to call it Marxist art in a society still in its confused formative stages; a society still entangled in neo-Fascist and Stalinist webs.

Even the contrary has been true, that the neo-realist perspective, as it was formulated, represented a position almost impossible to sustain because it was too progressive within an atmosphere which renewed itself only on the surface, leaving the ideological substructure unaltered. For the artists to have grasped the core of neo-realism and to have developed that, would have meant putting themselves on a revolutionary platform, both within and without the labour movement. It is interesting to observe how almost all the directors of the Italian film, young and old, have developed *after* the first rebellious wave of the neo-realist movement. In the last days of neo-realism, there are few directors who have remained faithful to the original core of the aesthetic; among these is Francesco Rosi.

Notes

1   Ferrara's note: "Pio Baldelli, '*Il "mito degli inizi" e la parabola di Roberto Rossellini*', *Il contemporaneo*, 68, January 1964."

2   Benedetto Croce (1866-1952) was a philosopher, historian, critic, and political theorist. His work and throught had an overwhelming influence in every sector of Italian cultural and political life. His artistic theory, which is relevant here, can be summed up in a series of main points:

   ● A work of art must be considered in terms of the "interior significance of its conception" in the mind of the artist, not in terms of the final material result.
   ● Everything external to the work itself is not to be considered in attempting to assess it; this includes all details of the time, place, and life of the artist.
   ● Although art can include the functions of pedagogy and propaganda, criticism is concerned only with the aesthetic fact itself.
   ● A work of art is an "individual movement in the life of the spirit" and a "form of intuition" which must be studied in itself without considering any connections it may appear to have with works of similar form. Genre and form do not exist outside of individual works. Only lyric feeling matters.
   ● Art is a synthesis of many things and constitutes a new thing. It is

fruitless to consider the components of that synthesis which includes influences, sources, etc.
● Each work of art is unique. Therefore works with similar themes are not to be studied in conjunction with one another.
● While the study of poetics itself is interesting, it is external to the work of any artist and therefore is not to be a part of the consideration of any single work.
● Each artist has his own language and expressive style which are to be studied by themselves for themselves.

3   Rossellini's "most famous trilogy" comprises the three films dealing with the war and post-war period: *Roma città aperta, Paisà,* and *Germania anno zero.*

4   Ferrara's note: "Elio Vittorini, *'Una nuova cultura'*, *Il politecnico,* I, September 29, 1945."

5   The scene described here is from Rossellini's *Roma città aperta.* Pina was played by Anna Magnani.

6   Ferrara's note: "Antonio Gramsci, *Litteratura e vita nazionale* (Einaudi, 1953)."

7   Ferrara's note: "Roberto Raschella, *'Sei paragrafi sull'alienazione'*, *Cinema nuovo,* XIII, 169, May-June, 1964."

8   Ferrara's notes: "Raschella, *op. cit.*"

16. Neo-Realism Betrayed
by Luigi Chiarini

The Congress of Parma[1] took place just a little more than a year ago. Proud and unanimous in their devotion to neo-realism, many voices were raised in defense of what *was* (today, alas, we must use that tense) the vital stream of Italian cinema.

Six months have now passed since yet another Congress (or counter-Congress) at Verese was called to celebrate the death and the resurrection (in a new body, of course) of neo-realism.

To the blast from the right there is an answering blast from the left. Among the buglers there is *Cinema nuovo* and my dear friend Aristarco[2] who plays his cavatina to the stentorian "do" of our friend Salinari. And what did the Catholic trumpet play? Neo-realism is dead; or, better, it has evolved, enriching itself with spiritual values (human and religious). *La strada* by Fellini, for example, was awarded the UCIC prize at the Venice Film Festival.[3]

Neo-realism is dead; or, better, it has evolved into realism, passing from daily reality and events to the story. Yet Visconti's *Senso* was boycotted by government authorities, by the censors, by the jury at Venice, and "forbidden to all" by the watchdogs of the Catholic Centre of Cinematography.

The battle still continues, although the war is being fought on a different front; and where is it all leading? Let us at least allow those who do not believe in these evolutions and metamorphoses, which have brought cinema into the welcoming embrace of literature (in its most traditional forms), to weep for the dead and pay tribute to it in a few words before friends, for there will be no heirs.

A New Dimension

Neo-realism might not have been the proper term. Nonetheless, what was meant by it was a cinema made up of films like *Roma città aperta, Paisà, Sciuscià, Ladri di biciclette, La terra trema,* and *Umberto D,* to list just the most important. With differing limitations, defects, and attitudes, such films possessed in common a new spirit, born from the Resistance, and revealed the fruit of a deepening (almost a conquest) of cinematic expression in the illumination of a new form. Hence their success throughout the world, which recovered with them (as with the great Russian films after the October Revolution) the expressive values of cinema in a new dimension of time and space: (1) men derived from the audiences' own reality replaced the pre-conceived characters in conventional narratives of the past; (2) the chronicle (if we can call it that), events and facts culled from the daily existence of men, replaced the prefabricated adventures of novels and comedies; (3) the throbbing photographic document replaced pictorial and figurative virtuosity; (4) the cities and countryside, with people effectively living there, replaced the *papier-maché* scenery of the past.

That is Italy, people said, with its miseries, its injustices, its greatness. Those films tried to give a portrait as faithful and true to life as possible, a reality, without artificiality or apparent intrusions. The directors were simply curious. They wanted to know, so they could make others know.

Spectacle and Film

From a curiosity so fraught with love and emotion, from the effort to be as objective as possible, was born the new style of Italian cinema in which idea and reality were synthesised. Films spoke with an untranslatable language and with a specific realistic force different from painting and the printed word.

Was it not just that vehemence of a realistic will which proclaimed the autonomy of the means of cinematic expression, not really the "conquest of a new point of view from which to look at the world" (to use Salinari's words), which made everyone throw away the rule-books, the beautiful stars, and the white telephones? Is it not from the *form* of the films, a form which carried ideas, that one can judge them?

It was called "naturalism", but that was inaccurate, at least for those films which are truly neo-realist, in so far as representation was not an end in itself, nor their stories only the cold registration of facts. Neo-realism sprang from the inner need to express ideas and feelings which are neither abstract nor schematized, but those suggested by reality itself. The danger of neo-realism falling into mannered naturalism is real; it is still necessary to recognize insincerity, imitativeness, false art, not merely the absence of an idea. After all, it is true enough that *Cielo sulla palude*, externally neo-realistic, is based on a precise spiritual idea, but it remains an artistic failure.

If the choice of subject, as Goethe said, is already poetry, it is because, that choice in the method of presentation is already present. It is not by chance that the subjects of neo-realist films have a social background, far from any psychological analysis; more or less dramatic, in so far as they tend to express with all the elasticity and resources of filmic language the relationship of man with nature, his immediate environment, and society — relationships which have been brought to the foreground by the great historical vicissitudes of the last forty years. The artist is expressed in the form; that is, his way of feeling, way of thinking, way of judging the content (subject, if you will) which he chooses for his work.

Now let us come to *Senso*, the object of current critical polemic. I have asserted that it is not possible to call that film neo-realist, not because it would mark a "step forward to realism", as my critical opponents maintain, but because, on the contrary, by returning to the traditional point of view of literary and theatrical spectacle, the film represents an overt contradiction of neo-realism. It is a negation rather than a development and deepening. It is a direction which cannot lead to the achievement of greater realism. The equivocations into which so many fall are characteristic of an abstract "content-ism", which is indifferent to form and judges a film from subject alone; evaluation is made through literary forms (character, hero, etc.) thus allowing the true content to elude them. True content is necessarily linked to the means of expression.

Senso is, above all, a spectacle on a high level, but still a spectacle! I shall try to explain what this means.

The cinematic spectacle tends to achieve its effects through the externalization of a text, focusing on one or two of the elements which compose it. This focus can be on the subject itself (the "originality" of the plot), the exceptional psychology of the characters, the "literary" value (theatrical or novelistic), the force of suggestive atmosphere, the beauty and richness of the images, the force of the attraction of the actors, or finally the use of expressive cinematic techniques to bombard the audience with superficial emotions. The effects towards which the spectacle leans can be coarse and commonplace or refined and intelligent, but they are always effects determined to enhance the mode of representation rather than the substance of the thing represented.

The effects of *Senso* are certainly rather refined and even enoble the usual mediocrity of cinematic spectacle, but the very refinement overwhelms the characters and events with the visual splendour of its realization. In this film, one might suggest that the setting came first and the story followed. Did not something similar happen with Castellani's *Romeo and Juliet?*[4]

In fact, because of the cinema's great possibilities at the level of spectacle, an aspect of Visconti's artistic personality appears clearly with *Senso*: his great visual taste, which had already revealed itself in his truly wonderful staging of *The three sisters* in the theatre. The poetry of Chekhov seems to have given him the proper measure.[5]

Visconti's Personality

Take note! This is not intended to be negative criticism, but only an examination of Visconti's artistic personality and an effort to see clearly the limitations of his films. They garner much praise and evoke so many reservations. The simple spectator usually says first "beautiful, but . . . ." Then come the reservations about content, emotional force, and clarity of meaning.

It is not that Visconti lacks a precise ideological vision, for that can be found in *Senso* as well as in his other films. Vision, theme, and thesis are not to be sought here and there in polemical or political hints, but in his visually refined language which, if it restrains and freezes feelings and ideas in the composition of each frame, is neither totally empty nor made up only of abstract arabesques. The end of the film — Mahler's execution — is born from a precise moral condemnation of a cynical protagonist who symbolizes a world bound for decay, a world in which he has had his day of glory, but which will fall into darkness. But the clever effects of lighting, the dark areas, the white costumes, and the harmonious and geometrical distribution of the characters acquire such a pictorial importance, composed in such a beautiful space, that there is an appeasement, a conciliation through admiration, and the deep significance from which they were born is lost.

What a difference from the shooting of the priest in *Roma città aperta*!

Thus, even though *Senso* is a very valuable and important film, which demonstrates that even on the level of spectacle a talented director who has something to say can do first class work, those who consider the film as a revolutionary bridge between neo-realism and realism are wrong. Salinari compared it to *Metello*,[6] but apart from the fact that the problems of literature are not those of the cinema, it would seem that Pratolini's wonderful novel shows the influences of cinematic neo-realism, especially when it draws near to social reality in its depiction of the love and simplicity of unexceptional men far removed from any overly complex psychological implications.

Let such works as *Senso* appear then! To a blast from the right, we refuse to answer with a blast from the left. Of the realism saddled with adjectives — Catholic-, Socialist-, Historical-, or the like — we still prefer neo-. The fact is that reality is not frightening. There is only one lesson to be learnt by those who are faithful to it — the lesson already demonstrated by the films of the immediate post-war period.

"Tradisce il neorealismo",
Cinema nuovo, 55, March 25, 1955.

Notes

1   The Congress on Neo-Realist Cinema at Parma was held on the 3rd, 4th, and 5th of December 1953. Sponsored by some twenty organizations, ranging from professional groups to cinema clubs, the Congress was intended as a demonstration of solidarity in the face of governmental repression of neo-realism (which had begun officially in 1949 with the passage of the "Andreotti Law", had reached something of a climax in the government's campaign against *Umberto D* in 1951, and was still very much in evidence in 1953). A good many critics, directors, screenwriters, and theorists spoke on a wide variety of subjects related to neo-realism. The Congress at Parma was one of many held over the years in all parts of Italy; the results were similar to those of other such Congresses: extremely interesting speeches and essays, but very few practical plans or actions.

2   Guido Aristarco, founder and editor of *Cinema nuovo,* is a Marxist film critic and one of the major figures in Italian film criticism and history. The first volume of what is to be a full history of contemporary Italian cinema is his *Neo-realism and national environment.* Bazin's defense of Rossellini has been translated by Hugh Gray in *What is cinema?,* II.

3   Ufficio Cattolico Internazionale Cinematografico.

4   Renato Castellani's *Romeo and Juliet* (1954) was a British production filmed in Italy with Laurence Harvey and Susan Shentall playing the doomed lovers. Its main virtues were its sumptuousness of setting, its costumes, and its luminous photography; it was not noticeable as an original interpretation of the play or for its performances which were less-than-adequate. Franco Zeffirelli's film of the same play (1966) followed this example.

5   Although several of his productions are internationally known, outside of Italy it is sometimes forgotten that Visconti had a solid reputation as a stage and opera director, and that his work in the theatre and in film often nourished one another.

6   *Metello* (1957) is a novel from Pratolini's "second" period, in which he

212

broadened his perspective from detailed pictures of family life (*Cronaca familiare*, 1947) to include the whole of Italian history, of which *Metello* is the first in a series. In his belief that the smallest details of daily life have a wider significance on the social level, in his political sympathies with the oppressed lower classes, and in his attempt to link the past with present reality, he might be seen as a neo-realist novelist. As he has been active since about 1939, however, it is difficult to assess direct influences from or on the neo-realistic cinema. It may well be that Pratolini, like Pavese and Vittorini, is the product of the same causes that produced neo-realism in the cinema.

17. In Defense of the Italian Cinema
by Pietro Germi (I), Giuseppe De Santis (II)
Luchino Visconti (III)

The occasion for a series of "testimonials" and reactions "in defense" of the Italian cinema, the "Andreotti Law", has been already mentioned in the introduction and elsewhere. Each of the individual defenses (of which ten were originally published) takes on the colouration of the personality of each author, as well as being in part based on the function of each man within the industry. The original ten were directors (Lattuada, Germi, Zampa, De Santis, Blasetti, Visconti, and De Sica), writers (Sergio Amidei and Piero Tellini), and an actor (Gino Cervi). Some are merely statements of solidarity, while others are repetitions of what others have said. Therefore, I have chosen only three of the ten to reprint here: Germi, De Santis, and Visconti.

I

What I have to say is, I think, useful. It is at least something I want to communicate to others.

I lived for a long time near the *Tritone*[1] where I had my own business, although my greatest wish even then was to work in the cinema. I must confess something which strikes me as extraordinary: the only time I really "saw" the *Largo Tritone* was in *Ladri di biciclette*. I "saw" it for the first time in those pictures, because the cinema helps men to see and to know themselves. It is in this way that cinema is necessary to Italians for, if they suffer from any chronic malady, it is that they have never learned to look at themselves nor known how to judge themselves.

Italian directors possess the capability to contribute, more than all other artists put together, to the important and decisive work of moral auto-criticism, to that examination of conscience which will be decisive in delivering us from that childish psychological immaturity which makes us lose the precise shape of problems by giving up the knowledge of truth and struggle. That is why, previously, reality did not provide us with inspiration, not even in the cinema.

I, for example, made efforts in my own *Testimone* to suppress every characteristic of the Roman landscape. It was my first film, and it is only now that I realize that I felt compelled to do it through fear! Our cinema has, now, begun to understand the value of the real, its importance and its concrete character, and is moving away from momentary opinion and inspiration. Rome has become Rome in our cinema, with its streets, beautiful and ugly, with its sun and its rain, just as in other films we have learned to know London, Dublin, New York, or Paris. Even better: today, if an Italian wants to make a thriller, he does not think in terms of the stupid thrillers made by English or American "specialists", but of our own police as they exist, who arrest criminals here, and have their own uniforms and their own faces. He thinks of an *Italian* thriller. If he wants to tell the story of a cuckold, he does not have to merely rework some old French stories. If he wants to have true moral commitment, both new and Italian he will have to think again of De Sica and *I bambini ci guardano*.

The protests which are raised are perhaps those of Mr. X who has not understood that we want to help him solve most of his problems, although some of them might be of greater importance than those we have so far chosen for our films. Sometimes, of course, there will be exaggerations, or emphasis on aspects from which we are unable to draw any positive conclusions. But these excesses and indulgence can be forgiven. It is, after all, the first time that Italian art, thanks to the cinema, has broken the barrier of an academic conformity that separated it from truth. Every such effort carries with it its own harshness and commits its own errors.

At any rate, whatever it is that helps that Italian people to overcome its inferiority complex is, I believe, sacred. Besides, the latest neo-realist films have shown that we have gained a mode of expression which permits us greater balance. The "froth", a certain verist rhetoric, is disappearing bit by bit; or, better, it is becoming more elaborate. The whole of Italy, from Puglia to Liguria, is now the field of cinematic expression. All its hidden problems of life, painful and vital, are at the forefront of the attention of Italian directors. Every form of Italian life, from the city to the life of the most secluded regions, attracts our lens. That is why I believe in the cinema, above all in the Italian cinema.

I want to conclude these few lines (a bit disorganized, perhaps, but sincere) with an assertion which many will find paradoxical. One of the most tragic aspects of the current crisis in Italian cinema is not that it might suddenly make thousands of workers jobless. It is that it could deprive the Italian people of the instrument it has itself struggled for and won: cinema. It is now indispensible to a people in order for them to know themselves, to criticize the negative aspects of their lives, and to educate themselves toward a higher concept of liberty.

II

Italian distributors proffer two arguments in their attempt to diminish the artistic importance of our cinema. First: that so-called neo-realism is now exhausted; that it is old-fashioned, for it is no longer possible to reproduce situations of the immediate post-war period from which it gained its original vitality. Second: the audience does not now want, and has never wanted, to see on the screen the misfortunes which oppress their own daily lives. We are told that, anyway, these conditions are merely "contingent", that the misery, rags, and pain will be overcome by the benefits of "reconstruction plans" (Marshall and otherwise), and that we should show them overcome. It is obvious that there is something of a contradiction in the admission that millions of Italians are still oppressed by these "contingent" conditions. The truth is that although it looks as though aesthetic judgements are being made contradictions are being affirmed from political motives.

In fact, who are these "distributors"? They are wealthy speculators, the élite, Christian Democrats; in other words, the members of a few powerful, conservative families and their minions. Who supports them? It has been demonstrated in the legislature and the country that they are supported by the current upper-class government. Who spreads their slogans and propaganda in an attempt to make them popular among the people? The political journalists and chroniclers of the government press.

On the other hand, what is neo-realism in its human and social substance? It is the existence of a popular art in Italian culture. "Popular" does not mean "that which has adopted a compromised and vernacular language". It means an art based on events told of and lived by the people themselves, a people with hopes, sufferings, joys, struggles, and — why not? — its contradictions. The very people which the Italian government, while defending the interests of producers, distributors, and American capitalists, tries to suppress, moved forward with relentless strength as the mass protagonists of an art, or a story which represents the second *Risorgimento*[2] in Italy, the story of a people struggling to become a modern nation. It is particularly significant that those who relate this tale, who talk of the steps along the way, are not only the directors who side with the people's struggle, but are also often notoriously apolitical figures, men like Rossellini, De Sica, Blasetti, Zampa . . . They are sincere and genuine artists. Their instincts lead them forward in the only vital ferment which man's life offers today.

Neo-realism is not a fashion or a craze. It does not spring from casual or "contingent" sources. If it is so for some, such people will be left behind, and will finish by betraying art. Others have achieved their ambition after years of toil. They will not move backwards; they must move forward. The truth is also this: that perhaps realism has not yet been born. The films made until now, drenched as they are with romantic motifs and eager to expose many things, have been created during a period of transition. The current Italian cinema is taking part in a long and difficult struggle for a new, civil, and modern Italy. Its works represent the "lists of grievances" of a period. *Sciuscià* is the "list" of the street boys of the post-war period; *La terra trema* and *In nomme della legge* are the "lists" of Sicily; *Ladri di biciclette* is the "list" of the unemployed; *Caccia tragica* is that of the peasants of Romagna, and so on. Even *Fabiola*, which tells a tale of the long ago and far away, contains a warning which solemnly arises from the people.

When Italy had a government which needed to repress any attempt to move in an honest direction, most work in the cinema resulted in the exploration of private emotions, or in national epics. Then it all exploded with *Roma città aperta*. From that moment, the cinema was able to move forward on a path which has, perhaps, been completely opened, but which has only now become clear. The Italian cinema has discovered a new language, an inexhaustible source of inspiration. But it is a discovery which has just begun and whose development cannot be planned or imagined. To smother that ferment would be a crime not simply against Italian, but against world culture. This is the ultimate reason for the struggle which has brought a unity to workers and producers alike in defense of the Italian cinema.

III

In my opinion the situation can be summed up in the following three points:

1. *Eighty days of compulsory programming*:[3] They can be used as a temporary stimulus, as an encouragement while waiting for the normalization of national production. However, if to "normalize" or to "stimulate" production means to encourage the sorts of films which constitute nine-tenths of the current production, then I am against the eighty days. I am for *quality*, and the eighty days might well encourage poor productions that will only further displease audiences and drive them further away.

2. *Taxation on dubbing*:[4] I agree with it, on the understanding that it will not restrict the liberty of importation, as the government maintains, but will only affect the plethora of bad films. The limitation would serve as an automatic control, and would allow distributors and exhibitors to support the best national production, which would in turn be encouraged to better its selection (as far as quality is concerned) in order to remain at an international level as well as to win audiences at home.

3. *Who will choose these films?*: Those, of course, who work in the cinema; not people from the ministries, nor representatives of groups who have nothing to do with the cinema. Neither the usual distributors nor the producers. No group should be privileged!

In conclusion, I declare useless any measure which intends to protect production without protecting quality. The Italian market must take care of itself; that is, it must be conquered by itself, and the world market can be seen to later. If measures are needed, they should tend to make business easier, without being protectionist. They must be such measures as those which increase production credit and agreements with foreign nations.

"In difesa del cinema italiano",
Rinascita, VI, March 3, 1949.

Notes

1   *Tritone*: the neighbourhood around the *via Tritone* in Rome, which runs from "The Column" to *Piazza Barberini*, is intersected about midpoint by the *"Largo Tritone"*, and is in the vicinity of the Trevi Fountain and the *Quirinale*.

2   The "first" *Risorgimento* was the period roughly between 1815 and 1870 during which Italy became a united nation. In its confusions, factionalism, opposing allies and accommodating enemies, secret pacts, foreign and domestic occupations, De Santis's use of it as a parallel to the immediate post-war period in Italy is not so far-fetched.

3   The "80 days compulsory programming" was part of the government's plan of quota screenings to force Italian products into Italian cinemas.

4   Such a tax on dubbing takes on more significance if it is remembered that in Italy virtually every foreign film is dubbed into Italian. Even in the major cities it is all but impossible to find a film in its original language with Italian subtitles; even cinema clubs (and several minor festivals) often show dubbed versions. A dubbing tax, therefore, in practice would become an added tax on virtually every foreign film imported into Italy.

---

18. Neo-Realism: Today
by Giuseppe Ferrara

Twenty years after its best period, Italian cinema still occupies an honoured position in the framework of international entertainment, but it is no longer a corrosive and burning cinema; or, if it is, it is so only in exceptional cases. It has lost its first perceptive fury, and has abandoned the attempt to transform itself into a national art of the people; it has, instead, become bourgeois. Slowly, it has withdrawn its cry of "No!" against the old culture, against "crepuscularism",[1] against D'Annunzianism,[2] against the prosaic in art, against the position of irrational individualism; everything, even what is most trite, has been put back into the game. What has happened to the cinema is exactly what has happened to the entire nation of Italy: the scum of our civil life that rose to the top during the Fascist period, and which seemed swept away forever after the war, has returned in full force and has demanded (not without a certain arrogance), and obtained, legitimacy.

Everything has returned to a "normal" state, even in the cinema. The pioneers — De Sica, Zavattini, Rossellini, and, to a certain extent, even Visconti — have all yielded to the pressures of this "restoration". For the team of De Sica/Zavattini, the year of complete compromise was 1953. With *Stazione termini* the wheel took an unexpected and sudden turn, and the result was a hybrid pastiche somewhere between neo-realism and the ordinary movie "made in the USA"[3] This decline was all the more precipitous for having occurred immediately after the production of one of the masterpieces of neo-realism, *Umberto D* (1952), perhaps the most advanced work of so fortunate a pair. *Stazione termini* marks the surrender of neo-realism — which had already refused to adapt its contents to the dictates of actors, using "the man in the street" to supply what the actors lacked — to the star-system, which then took firm root in Italy. With the advent of the star, and the subsequent slavery of both story and characters to the star personality, De Sica and Zavattini accepted the commercialisation of neo-realism, putting their talents at the service of a

221

limited actress like Sophia Loren; understandably, Blasetti had had a tremendous box-office success with the *diva* in *Peccato che sia una canaglia* (1954) by confecting a product which seems to have anticipated the way De Sica would go.[4] It is not by mere chance that the old Blasetti — in difficulty during the post-war period — felt secure again, just at that moment. The "limit of balance, objectivity and proportion", that "at least minimal commitment to a sane and constructive optimism" which the Honourable Andreotti had demanded, is included in this commercial compromise. And no wonder: if the rules as laid down by the film industry are even passively accepted, only a certain clever intelligence and the ability to be expedient will be left alive, and the entire system will then be quite peacefully accepted. Nor, once compromise is accepted, is there any return. Witness the pathetic attempts to escape the system; like *Il tetto* (1956), they are mere nostalgic echoes of the past, but echoes which no longer even scratch the surface of reality. The road to becoming the most well-bred director and the most entertaining screenwriter of Italian neo-capitalism has opened for De Sica and Zavattini; the way is irreversible.

Yet the team remains faithful, in the worst sense, to its naturalistic bent, though it is ever becoming more adulterated. Relevant themes are still dealt with, but their sharrrppppness is blunted, they are turned inside out for the joys of entertainment. Thus, De Sica and Zavattini have fallen in line behind the makers of those products released in 1946-1948 which were on the periphery of neo-realism: *Vivere in pace* (1946) and *L'Onorevole Angelina* (1947) by Zampa, or even *Sotto il sole di Roma* by Castellani; the line continued, after an apparent intermission with the fresh and vivid *Due soldi di speranza* (1951) by the same Castellani, with the great commercial success of Comencini (*Pane, amore e fantasia*, 1952) and, above all, of Dino Risi who, from *Poveri ma belli* (1956) to his most recent films with Sordi and Gassman[5], won commercial supremacy, but is now, once more, seriously rivalled by that old but prestigious couple, De Sica and Zavattini. Unfortunately, they are works which *seem* to have a certain weight, but it is really more a weight of contemporary habit than of cinematic history in the making.

The young Nanni Loy and Ermanno Olmi carry on De Sica's line. Both have learned their lessons, and have channelled their creative energies into "good rules", Loy in celebrating a jingoist Resistance, and Olmi in exalting good feelings with a somewhat Catholic "crepuscularism". These directors represent what De Sica and Zavattini would have done had they remained faithful to the cultural basis of their earlier work. They would have saved what could be saved, focusing, as Loy has done, on themes with epic overtones, using massive choral movements and all-consuming emotions (the starving mother of *Le 4 giornate di Napoli,* for example who gives up eating for her son), yet taking care to avoid exciting those uncomfortable feelings which the Resistance can still engender. Or, like Olmi, they would have pushed the camera to explore the more intimate zones of the petit-bourgeois consciousness, recording with courtesy the spiritual aridity emanating from a mechanized society, but still accepting that system in the sure belief that a soul well-disposed to love and the Christian family virtues would doubtless triumph over the negative aspects of such a life. A drop of Chekhov, a dollop of De Amicus, a pinch of the Catholic catechism, all mixed together with a bit of internal suffering, and presto!, life can proceed, illuminated by goodness and the love of one's fellow creatures. These are themes of a Catholic taste which were evident even in the Zavattini films; in the midst of the "restoration" it is logical that Olmi should use them fully.

On the other hand, Rossellini's path leads to even more dramatic bifurcation. First of all, the director after *Germania anno zero* (1947), accomplished a *volte-face* of a "Catholic-D'Annunzian" nature. In *Amore* (1949), he rejected the historical spirituality of his war-trilogy and took up stories which, for the first time in his career, avoided the basis of daily reality and events, seeking to explore instead the abstract mystery of the soul, the contact between man and God outside real time and real space. In *Amore,* as in *Stromboli* (1949), the narrative now and again suddenly dissolves for brief moments. Under the crystalline varnish of the images and their apparent modernity, artificial, stereotyped characters can be glimpsed constructed on themselves alone and lacking the profound contact with others that characters possessed in his earlier films: the priest in *Roma città aperta,* the partisans in *Paisà,* Edmund in *Germania anno zero.* In comparison with them, Karin of *Stromboli* is an overly simplified figure, poetic only by intention, deprived of any connection with reality. It is not convincing that she succeeds in resolving her own hysteria with an invocation to God (apparently answered); it is merely another form of artifice, another sign of the director's uncertainty. Everything becomes simply a pretext. The war which sent Karin to the island is only a distant, mechanical cause which has not scarred her with precise, interior wounds. The South, the conditions of poverty of the island's inhabitants, constitute no more than a plainly given atmosphere; it could as well be Africa or Australia, for the setting is merely a generic stimulus to the religious resignation of the woman. Rossellini's abstract research into the mystery of the soul reduces reality to formalism.

Francesco, giullare di Dio (1950) achieves a great internal balance, an efficient figurative atmosphere, and perhaps represents the best that Catholic culture can offer in Italy. The film is non-conformist in its interpretation, far removed from any hagiographical commonplace, of the figure of the saint. But its non-conformity is only superficial, because it never hints at historical fact; we are not in the Fourteenth Century, not in Umbria, but in a world deprived of specific time and in a landscape made virginally lyrical to the point of boredom. Avoiding the polemic position Francis took in his own age, Rossellini exalts a special religious madness, regressing through poetry to the D'Annunzian mysticism of *Amore*.

In fact, these attempts of Rossellini would seem to favour a clear return to the limitations of decadence in the Italian cinema. Without taking all of this into account, Fellini cannot be explained. Further obvious derivations can also be found in the works of Pier Paolo Pasolini, blended either with a certain Viscontian aestheticism (above all of *Beauty*) or with other, more personal components, with which we will not concern ourselves here. Attempts of the same sort are to be found in the imitative Brunello Rondi, who carries them to their inevitable conclusion in the more directly D'Annunzian regurgitation of *La figlia di Jorio*. In that sense, Rondi's *Il demonio* is almost ultimate proof: did he not reach similar, if rougher, conclusions to those of the second-rate literary author Curzio Malaparte, who descended from the branches of the D'Annunzio tree to have one unique try at the cinema with *Cristo proibito* (1951)?

Fellini's position is much more complex, and represents, with Antonioni's, the most outstanding results of "neo-neo-realism". Critic Renzo Renzi was correct to include Pascoli and Campana[6] as part of Fellini's cultural background, and to define him as "a tormented subject of the Papal Romagna, whose moods, acrobatics, and infixions he reflects faithfully. He is like a pot full of pagan, Islamic, anarchist, and heretical motives, which continuously seems about to explode but which never does.[7] Fellini senses the imprisonment of the morality learned at school and dreams of escape, laughs at his useless efforts, and contradicting himself, proposes tentative solutions. "How does he do it? In *Otto e mezzo*, through acceptance, or at least passive resistance, as well as the farcical and grotesque spinning about, the product of a frightening scepticism and yet the expression of the need for self-insertion into a collectivity which is harmonious and amiable."[8] He struggles, but he asks to be forgiven by what he fights against; he sins but wants to confess. Well, it is hardly a new position in Italian culture. Indeed, Fellini's position can be oddly but easily linked with that of the Nineteenth Century author Nicolo Tommaseo, also born on the Adriatic coast.[9] *Fede a belleza*, a lyrical novel of Tommaseo, in which the contradictions between the disquiet of the senses, human limitations, and the aspirations to a spiritual puity, never reach a proper synthesis, would seem to have comprised Fellini's bedside reading.

With roots in Catholic romanticism, the director from Rimini first passed through the experience of committed neo-realism (he was an assistant on *Paisà*) and then moved with Rossellini through the *volte-face* after *Germania anno zero* (he collaborated on *Amore* and *Francesco, giullare di Dio*), becoming what might roughly be called a Catholic neo-existentialist. From neo-realism, he developed, through the use of extraordinarily rich expressive means, his spiritual aspects, always taking care not to place his characters in a social or emotional desert. He descends into the intimacy of the subconscious through pseudo-history. He seems very attentive to the links of character to society and real time by using several phenomena associated with the masses (cults and movie star worship, mysticism, public hysteria, even prostitution), and it is only when these connections are made that all this noisy apparatus serves to confirm the existential anxiety, the solitude of the soul face-to-face with itself and its multitudinous contradictions, with the deep mystery of life, in which perhaps only "Grace" can represent some salvation.

Antonioni's road is different, but it developed strangely. Although absolutely secular, it is nourished by the same decadent components which fed Fellini. Starting from a position rather close to Visconti's in *Ossessione*, and largely influenced by that work — it is not by chance one finds Viscontian echoes in *Cronaca di un amore*, 1950, and even more in *Il grido*, 1952, in which the Giovanna Bragana of 1942 lives again and waits for the tramp, rejected from the street and its incurable moral desperation[10] — Antonioni follows, in his last period, the formal neo-realist lesson at its driest; touching without, perhaps, wanting to, similar themes as those of Rossellini's *Viaggio in Italia* (1953). Comparing it with *La notte* (1961), we realise that Rossellini's couple, Katherine and Alexander Joyce, suffer a matrimonial crisis similar to that of Antonioni's. The connection between the two films becomes firmer if a comparison is made between the analogous ways of "seeing" the urban landscape as a function of the character's state of mind: more controlled in *La notte*, more casual and impressionistic in Rossellini. Yet in both cases, the directors want to reach "a mental landscape, objective as pure photography and subjective as pure conciousness."[11] Antonioni reaches the Rossellinian re-valuation of things and objects which operated, above all, in *Paisà*. Attempting to capture their purity with cold lucidity, he separates them from their historical context (in which he has no interest) and projects them into an extremely coherent and consequential individualism, repudiating even the Catholic consolation of "Grace" or any other veil of traditional hypocrisy. Whether or not this is a mystical solution, we are certainly at the door of the irrational.

Antonioni proposes again the decadent conception of "poetry" as an absolute organ of conscience, and transfers the central knot of modern tragedy to the interior plane of man through the refusal to view historical necessity as independent of individual will. In this way, the atmosphere of true alienation is created. The more all contact with history is declined, the more this alienated state is fortified. In a bourgeois artist like Antonioni, the relation of past to present, which might mean the achievement of a new historical vision, solves itself in the contemplation and supremacy of the elements of natural alienation. In *La notte* as in *L'Eclisse*, the values of the bourgeoisie are repudiated, but nothing better is proposed as a substitute, save for an ambiguous and doubtful sublimation of love as the *raison d'être* for existence.

It has been said that few artists have represented the historical moment better than Fellini and Antonioni. Without any doubt, they constitute the highest cultural product of industrialized bourgeois cinema. If one is at times too cold and aristocratic, this is compensated for by the other's bloody confidences. Perhaps the aesthetics of pimpdom is the truest vantage point from which to view Italy.

Nonetheless, our cinema is still nourished by the ferment of stifled rebellion of the masses and the urgency of their needs, which have been largely ignored. This cannot help but weigh heavily on the consciences of the most sensitive intellectuals, as evidenced in the work of Francesco Rosi, the only director among the older directors who has demonstrated, albeit in a descending spiral, the coherent forces of a style. Rosi demonstrates that democratic expression is still possible, and that the central nucleus of the neo-realist culture is still valid, still a firm point impossible to deviate from if one wishes to commit oneself to transforming society, if one wants to fight the system with an effective weapon. Above all others, *Salvatore Giuliano*, and, in part, *Le mani sulla città*, by pitilessly delving into our public conscience and encouraging us to think, follow the original path of *Paisà* and *La terra trema*.

Yet they are not isolated works. They are not born of heroic, solitary, or ingenuous rebellious positions. Younger directors also are attuned to the still-operative lessons of neo-realism. They will continue to develop the movement. Giuseppe Fina, with *Pelle viva* (1963), or the Taviani brothers and Orsini, with *Un uomo da bruciare* (1962), spring from an intolerence which answers the demands of a culture which refuses to link itself with current systems, of a nonconformist culture.

Even for Rosi it is not a question of masterpieces, but of a film's absolute validity. His films remain important and revealing in so far as they reveal the integration of the *avant-garde* intellectual within the limitations of a neo-capitalistic society. To follow Rosi is not only to encourage the evolution of the last vestiges of neo-realism, but also to allow the possibility of a culture of progressive opposition to the *status quo*.

"*Il Neorealismo: oggi*"
in *Francesco Rosi* (Rome, 1965).

Notes

1   *Crepuscolarismo* is, literally, "twilightism", but refers to a specific
    school of poetry and prose centred about Sergio Corazzini (1885-1907),
    Guido Gozzano (1883-1916), and Mario Moretti (1885-   ). Opposed
    to the grand poetic gestures of D'Annunzio, and influenced by French
    poets like Verlaine and Laforgue, the school was given to isolated, inti-
    mate psychological reverberations. Although the poetry and prose are
    full of ordinary detail, they were put to far more individual uses than
    to the somewhat social uses of which the neo-realists would have
    approved.

2   Gabriele D'Annunzio (1863-1938) was disapproved of by leftist critics
    and filmmakers on several counts: his flirting with the philosophy of
    Nietzsche, his romanticism, his glorification of sensuality and
    instinct, and his political and military actions which led to his becom-
    ing a darling of the Fascists. In recent years, however, D'Annunzio is
    undergoing a process of "rediscovery" and "re-evaluation".

3   See note following *A Thesis on Neorealism* by Cesare Zavattini.

4   Although Ferrara seems here to be blaming Blasetti somewhat for the
    career of Sophia Loren, it must be remembered that she made her début
    in 1949 in the American *Quo vadis?*, and that neither De Sica nor Bla-
    setti was the first to use her in a film. 1954, the date assigned to the
    Blasetti film in the essay, would seem to be off by one year. The film
    was released in Italy in 1955, one year *after* De Sica had already directed
    Loren with great commercial success in *L'Oro di Napoli* — At any
    rate, Loren's greatest international box-office successes were directed
    by De Sica, often with scripts by Zavattini, including the multiple-
    prize-winning and huge financial success, *La ciociara* (*Two women*)
    in 1960. It, perhaps, represents the lowest point for neo-realism in its
    use of the movement's style to decorate what is essentially a star vehi-
    cle. Ironically, two years after the publication of Ferrara's book on
    Francesco Rosi, Rosi, himself, made an uncharacteristic film, *C'era
    una volta* (1967), with Loren.

5   Risi made a series of comedies with both Alberto Sordi and Vittorio
    Gassman, the most popular of which were probably *I mostri* (1963)
    and *Profumo di donna* (1974).

6   Giovanni Pascoli (1885-1912) is less well known for his scholarship in philology and literature than for his rather old-fashioned lyrics about the closed world of children, flowers, and animals.

    Dino Campana (1885-1932) was a Rimbaud-like figure; his single volume of verse is filled with feverish symbolism for his tortured experiences.

7   Ferrara's note: "Renzo Renzi, '*Gli antenati di Federico Fellini*'", *Cinema nuovo*, XIII, 169, May-June, 1964.

8   Ferrara's note: "*op. cit.*"

9   Tommaseo (1802-1874) was known during his lifetime for his work in lexicography, but was also a novelist and poet. He was born in Sibenik, Yugoslavia; Fellini was born in Rimini (Forli).

10   Giovanna Bragana was the heroine of *Ossessione* (1942).

11   Although Ferrara quotes the Italian version (André Bazin, "*Difesa di Rossellini*", *Cinema nuovo*, IV, 65, August 1955), there is also an English translation from the original French of Bazin's important essay: "In defense of Rossellini", *What is cinema?*, II, trans: Hugh Gray. The words of Bazin refer only to the Rossellini film, as Ferrara points out in his original note.

List of English Titles
of Italian Films cited

The following list is composed of titles of Italian films cited in the text. The name of the director and the date of release in Italy are given below. The English titles are those given the films upon their first release in the UK and the USA; when a film has had no such release, a literal translation of the title appears in Roman letters. When a film is known by more than one title in English, the alternatives are given.

Acciaio..Steel
    Ruttmann, 1933
Achtung, banditi!..........................*Achtung, banditi!*
    Lizzani, 1951
Addio giovinezza..........................Goodbye youth
    Poggioli, 1940
Alfa-tau...Alfa-tau
    De Robertis, 1942
Amore..*Love/The miracle*
    Rossellini, 1947
Amore in città..............................*Love in the city/Love in the town*
    Risi, Antonioni,
    Fellini, Zavattini-Maseli
    Lattuada, Lizzani, 1953
Anna...*Anna*
    Lattuada, 1951
Anni difficili................................*Difficult years/The little man*
    Zampa, 1948
L'Après-midi d'un faune..............Afternoon of a faun
    Rossellini, 1937
L'Assedio dell'Alcazar.................*The siege of Alcazar*
    Genina, 1939
Assunta Spina..............................Assumption day
    Mattoli, 1947

Cristo proibito .... *The forbidden Christ*
    Malaparte, 1950
Cronaca di un amore .... Chronicle of poor lovers
    Antonioni, 1950
Cronache di poveri amanti .... Chronicle of a love
    Lizzani, 1954
Darò un milione .... I'd give a million
    Camerini, 1935
Il demonio .... Little devil
    Rondi, 1967
Domenica d'agosto .... *Sunday in August*
    Emmer, 1949
Don Bosco .... Don Bosco
    Alessandrini, 1935
Due soldi di speranza .... *Two pennysworth of hope*
    Castellani, 1951
L'Eclisse .... *Eclipse*
    Antonioni, 1961
1860 1860
    Blasetti, 1933
E'primavera .... *Springtime in Italy*
    Castellani, 1949
Era notte a Roma .... It was night in Rome
    Rossellini, 1969
Europa '51 .... *Europa '51 / The greatest love*
    Rossellini, 1952
Fabiola .... *Fabiola*
    Blasetti, 1948
Fantasia sottomarina .... Undersea fantasy
    Rossellini, 1939
Fantasmi del mare .... Phantoms of the sea
    De Robertis, 1948
Fari nella nebbia .... Lights in the fog
    Franciolini, 1942
I fidanzati .... *The fiancés*
    Olmi, 1962
Francesco, giullare di Dio .... *The flowers of St. Francis*
    Rossellini, 1949

I fuorilegge .... The outlaw
   Vergano, 1950
Gelosia .... Jealousy
   Poggioli, 1942
Il Generale Della Rovere .... *General Della Rovere*
   Rossellini, 1959
Gente del Po .... People of the Po
   Antonioni, 1943-1947
Germania anno zero .... *Germany, year zero*
   Rossellini, 1947
Una giornata particolare .... *A special day*
   Scola, 1977
Un giorno nella vita .... A day in the life
   Blasetti, 1946
Gioventù perduta .... Lost youth
   Germi, 1947
Il grido .... *The outcry*
   Antonioni, 1957
Histoire d'un pierrot .... A story of pierrot
   1913
In nomme della legge .... *In the name of the law*
   Germi, 1948
Ladri di biciclette .... *Bicycle thieves / The bicycle thief*
   De Sica, 1948
Lucky Luciano .... *Lucky Luciano*
   Rosi, 1974
La macchina ammazzacattivi .... *The camera that kills the wicked*
   Rossellini, 1948
Le mani sulla città .... *Hands over the city*
   Rosi, 1963
Mine in vista .... *Mines in sight*
   De Robertis, 1940
Miracolo a Milano .... *Miracle in Milan*
   De Sica, 1950
Il mulino del Po .... *Mill on the river*
   Lattuada, 1948   *Mill on the Po*
La nave bianca .... The white ship
   Rossellini, 1941

La notte ....*La notte/The night*
   Antonioni, 1961
L'Onorevole Angelina   *Angelina/Angelina, M.P.*
   Zampa, 1947
Ossessione ....Obsession
   Visconti, 1942
Otto e mezzo *8½*
   Fellini, 1963
Paisà ....*Paisà*
   Rossellini, 1946
Pane, amore, e fantasia ....*Bread, love and dreams*
   Comencini, 1953
La peccatrice ....The sinner
   Palermi, 1940
Piccolo hotel ....Little hotel
   Ballerina, 1940
Piccolo mondo antico ....*Little old-fashioned world*
   Soldati, 1940
Pietro Micca ....Pietro Micca
   Vergano, 1938
Un pilote ritorna ....A pilot returns
   Rossellini, 1942
La porta del cielo ....The door of heaven
   De Sica, 1944
Il posto ....*Il posto/The job*
   Olmi, 1961
Poveri ma belli ....*Poor but beautiful*
   Risi, 1956
Prima comunione ....First communion
   Blasetti, 1950
Le quattro giornate di Napoli ..... *The four days of Naples/*
   Loy, 1962   *The battle of Naples*
Quattro passi fra le nuvole ....*Four steps in the clouds*
   Blasetti, 1942
Quelli della montagne ....Those of the mountains
   Vergano, 1943
Quo vadis? ....*Quo vadis?*
   Guazzoni, 1912

Riso amaro..............................*Bitter rice*
   De Santis, 1948
Rocco e i suoi fratelli ....*Rocco and his brothers*
   Visconti, 1960
Roma città aperta ....*Rome: open city/Open city*
   Rossellini, 1945
Roma ore undici..........................*Rome eleven o'clock*
   De Santis, 1952
Una romantica avventura...........A romantic adventure
   Camerini, 1940
Rotaie......................................Rails
   Camerini, 1929
Il ruscello de Ripasottile ....The stream of Ripasottile
   Rossellini, 1941
Salvatore Giuliano......................*Salvatore Giuliano*
   Rosi, 1962
Sciuscià....................................*Shoe shine*
   De Sica, 1946
Senso ....*Senso/The wanton countess*
   Visconti, 1954
Senza pietà ....Without pity
   Lattuada, 1948
Sissignora................................Yes, ma'am
   Poggioli, 1942
Sole..Sun
   Blasetti, 1928
Il sole sorge ancora......................The sun rises again
   Vergano, 1946
Sotto il sole di Roma...................Under the Roman sun
   Castellani, 1947
Sperduti nel buio.........................Lost in the dark
   Martoglio, 1914
   Mastrocinque, 1947
La statua vivente.........................The living statue
   Mastrocinque, 1943
Stazione termini..........................*Terminal station/Indiscretion
   De Sica, 1952   of an American wife*

La strada .... *La strada / The road*
    Fellini, 1954

Stromboli, terra di Dio .... Stromboli
    Rossellini, 1959

Teresa Venerdi .... Teresa Friday
    De Sica, 1941

La terra trema .... *La terra trema / The earth trem-*
    Visconti, 1947   *bles*

Il testimone .... The witness
    Germi, 1945

Il tetto .... *The roof*
    De Sica, 1956

Tragica notte .... Tragic night
    Soldati, 1941

Umberto D .... *Umberto D*
    De Sica, 1951

Gli uomini che mascalzoni .... *Men are such rascals*
    Camerini, 1932

Uomini contri .... Men against
    Rosi, 1970

Uomini sul fondo .... S.O.S. submarine
    De Robertis, 1941

Un uomo da bruciare .... Man on fire
    Orsini, Taviani brothers, 1962

L'uomo della croce .... The man of the cross
    Rossellini, 1942

Vecchia guardia .... Old guard
    Blasetti, 1934

Via delle cinque lune .... Five moon street
    Chiarini, 1942

Viaggio in Italia .... *Voyage to Italy / Journey to Italy /*
    Rossellini, 1953   *Vacation in Italy / The lonely*
                                 woman

I vinti .... The vanquished
    Antonioni, 1953

Vivere in pace .... *To live in peace*
    Zampa, 1946

Bibliography

The most comprehensive bibliography for neo-realism (containing listings for Italy, England, France, Poland, Germany, Japan, Brazil, the United States, and Switzerland) is that compiled by the *Mostra Internazionale del Nuovo Cinema, Il neorealismo e la critica: materiali per una bibliografia, Quaderno informativo 57* (Pesaro, 1974). The following list does not pretend to be as comprehensive, although it contains most of the important essays and books on the subject in English and a selection of those in French and Italian. Listed as well are those items which were consulted in the compilation of this collection even when their connection with neo-realism seems less direct.

Antonioni, Michelangelo. *Screenplays (Il grido, L'Avventura, La notte, L'Eclisse).* The Orion Press. New York, 1963.

Aristarco, Guido. *Neo-realism and national environment.* Grimaldi, Rimini, 1976.

Armes, Roy. *Patterns of realism: A study of Italian neo-realist cinema.* Tantivy Press. London, 1971.

Bazin, André. *What is cinema?*, Vol. II (trans: Hugh Gray). University of California Press. Berkeley, 1971.

Borde, Raymond, and André Bouissy. *Le néoréalisme italien: une experience de cinéma social.* Cinematheque Suisse, Lausanne, 1960.

Le nouveau cinéma italien. Premier Plan. Paris, 1963.

Buache, Freddy. *Le cinéma italien: d'Antonioni a Rosi, au tournant des années 60.* La Thiele. Yverdon, Switzerland, 1969.

Cameron, Ian, and Robin Wood. *Antonioni.* Studio Vista. London, 1968.

Carsaniga, C.M., "Realism in Italy", *Age of realism,* edited by F.W.J. Hemmings. Penguin. Baltimore, Md., 1974.

Ciment, Michel. *Le Dossier Rosi: Cinéma et politique.* Stock. Paris, 1976.

Davidson, Alastair. *Antonio Gramsci: The man, his ideas*. Australian Left Review. Sydney, 1968.

De Sica, Vittorio, and Cesare Zavattini. *Bicycle thieves*. Lorrimer. London, 1968.

Miracle in Milan. The Orion Press. New York, 1968.

Eisner, Lotte H., "A contribution to the definition of the expressionist film", in *Expressionism as an international literary phenomenon*. Akadéiar Kaidó. Budapest, 1973.

"Notes on some recent Italian films", *Sequence*, 8, Summer, 1949.

The haunted screen: expressionism in the German cinema and the influence of Max Reinhardt. Thames and Hudson. London, 1969.

Etudes cinématographiques. "*Le néoréalisme italien: bilan de la critique*", 32-35, Summer, 1964.

"*Visconti: histoire et esthétique*", 26-27, 1963.

Furness, R.S., *Expressionism*. Methuen. London, 1973.

Gough-Yates, Kevin. "The destruction of neo-realism", *Films and filming*, September, 1970.

Gramsci, Antonio. *The modern Prince and other writings* (trans: Louis Marks). Lawrence and Wishart. London, 1957.

Grant, Jacques. "*Roberto Rossellini: 'Je profite des choses'*", *Cinéma 76*, 206, February, 1976.

Guarner, José Luis. *Roberto Rossellini* (trans: Elisabeth Cameron). Praeger. London, 1970.

Harcourt-Smith, Simon. "The stature of Rossellini", *Sight and sound*, April, 1950.

Hoveyda, Fereydoun, and Eric Rohmer. "*Nouvel entretien avec Roberto Rossellini*", *Cahiers du cinéma*, 145, July, 1963.

Huaco, George A. *The sociology of film art*. Basic Books. New York, 1965.

Hughes, John. "Recent Rossellini", *Film comment*, X, 4. July/August, 1974.

Isaksson, Folke, and Leif Furhammer. *Politics and film* (trans: Kersti French). Studio Vista. London, 1971.

Jacobs, Lewis, ed. *The documentary tradition: from Nanook to Woodstock*. Hopkinson and Blake. New York, 1971.

Jarrat, Vernon. "The Italians: I and II", *Sight and sound*, Spring, 1948.

"The Italians: III", Sight and sound, Summer, 1948.

Kyrou, Ado. *"Néoréalisme"*, *Les lettres nouvelles*, 33, December, 1955.

Lambert, Gavin. "Notes on a renaissance", *Sight and sound*, February, 1951.

"Further notes on a renaissance", *Sight and sound*, October-November, 1952.

"The signs of predicament", *Sight and sound*, January-March, 1955.

Lane, John Francis. "De Santis and Italian neo-realism", *Sight and sound*, August, 1950.

Leprohon, Pierre. *The Italian cinema*. Secker and Warburg. London, 1972.

MacCann, Richard Dyer, ed. *Cinema: A montage of theories*. Dutton. New York, 1966.

Maddison, John. "The case of De Sica", *Sight and sound*. June, 1951.

Mostra Internazionale del Nuovo Cinema. Politica e cultura nel dopoguerra: con una cronologia 1929-1964 e una antologia. Quaderno informativo 56. Pesaro, 1974.

Sul neorealismo: testi e documenti 1939-1955. Quaderno informativo 59. Pesaro, 1974.

Nowell-Smith, Geoffrey. *Luchino Visconti*. Secker and Warburg. London, 1967.

Overbey, David L., "Rosi in context", *Sight and sound*, Summer, 1976.

Pozzolini, Alberto. *Antonio Gramsci: An introduction to his thought*. Pluto Press. London, 1970.

Orocacci, Giuliano. *History of the Italian people*. Penguin. Harmondsworth, 1970.

Quaglietti, Lorenzo. *Il cinema italiano del dopoguerra: Leggi produzione distribuzione esercizio. Mostra Internazionale del Nuovo Cinema*. Pesaro, 1974.

Rhode, Eric. "Why neo-realism failed", *Sight and sound*, Winter, 1960-61.

A history of the cinema: from its origins to 1970. Allen Lane. London, 1976.

Rondi, Gian-Luigi. *Italian cinema today*. Dennis Dobson. London, 1966.

Rondolino, Gianni. *Dizionario del cinema italiano, 1945-1969*. Giuilo Einauldi. Torino, 1969.

Rossellini, Roberto. *The war trilogy*. The Orion Press. New York, 1973.

Schérer, Maurice, and François Truffaut. *"Entretien avec Roberto Rossellini"*, *Cahiers du cinéma*, 37, July 1954.

Smith, Denis Mack. *The making of Italy, 1796-1870*. London, 1968.

Tudor, Andrew. *Theories of film*. Viking Press. New York, 1974.

Tyler, Parker. *The shadow of an airplane climbs the Empire State Building: A world theory of film*. Doubleday. New York. 1972.

Verdone, Mario. *Roberto Rossellini*. *Cinema d'aujourd'hui*, 15, Seghers, 1963.

Villair, Luigi. *The liberation of Italy*. University of Wisconsin Press. Appleton, 1959.

Visconti, Luchino. *Two screen plays (La terra trema, Senso)*. The Orion Press. New York, 1970.

Three screen plays (Notti bianche, Rocco), The Orion Press. New York, 1970.

Wood, Robin. "Roberto Rossellini's films with Ingrid Bergman", *Film comment*, X, 4, July-August, 1974.

"Ingrid Bergman on Rossellini", *Film comment*, X, 4, July-August, 1974.